A Wanderer in the Spirit Lands
By Franchezzo

Preface by the Transcriber.

The following narrative was written more than a year ago, and in giving it to the public I do not claim to be its author, since I have only acted the part of an amanuensis and endeavored to write down as truthfully and as carefully as I could, the words given to me by the Spirit Author himself, who is one of several spirits who have desired me to write down for them their experiences in the spirit world.

I have had to write the words as fast as my pen could travel over the paper, and many of the experiences described and opinions advanced are quite contrary to what I myself believed to be in accordance with the conditions of life in the world of spirits.

The Spirit Author Franchezzo I have frequently seen materialized, and he has been recognized on these occasions by friends who knew him in earth life.

Having given the narrative to the public as I received it from the Spirit Author, I must leave with him all responsibility for the opinions expressed and the scenes described.

A. FARNESE.

London, 1896

To those who toil still in the mists and darkness of uncertainty which veil the future of their earthly lives, I dedicate this record of the Wanderings of one who has passed from earth life into the hidden mysteries of the Life Beyond, in the hope that through my experiences now given to the world, some may be induced to pause in their downward career and think ere they pass from the mortal life, as I did, with all their unrepented sins thick upon them.

It is to those of my brethren who are treading fast upon the downward path, that I would fain hope to speak, with the power which Truth ever has over those who do not blindly seek to shut it out; for if the after consequences of a life spent in dissipation and selfishness are often terrible even during the earth-life, they are doubly so in the Spirit World, where all disguise is stripped from the soul, and it stands forth in all the naked hideousness of its sins, with the scars of the spiritual disease contracted in its earthly life stamped upon its spirit form--never to be effaced but by the healing powers of sincere repentance and the cleansing waters of its own sorrowful tears.

I now ask these dwellers upon earth to believe that if these weary travelers of the other life can return to warn their brothers yet on earth, they are eager to do so. I would have them to understand that spirits who materialize have a higher mission to perform than even the solacing of those who mourn in deep affliction for the beloved they have lost. I would have them to look and see that now even at the eleventh hour of man's pride and sin, these spirit wanderers *are* permitted by the Great Supreme to go back and tell them the fate of all who outrage the laws of God and man. I would have even the idle and frivolous to pause and think whether Spiritualism be not something higher, holier, nobler, than the passing of an idle hour in speculations as to whether there are occult forces which can move a table or rap out the Alphabet, and whether it is not possible that these feeble raps and apparently unmeaning tips and tilts of a table are but the opening doors through which a flood of light is being let in upon the dark places of earth and of the Nether World--faint signs that those who have gone before do now return to earth to warn their brethren.

As a warrior who has fought and conquered I look back upon the scenes of those battles and the toils through which I have passed, and I feel that all has been cheaply won--all has been gained for which I hoped and strove, and I seek now but to point out the Better Way to others who are yet in the storm and stress of battle, that they may use the invaluable time given to them upon earth to enter upon and follow with unfaltering step the Shining Path which shall lead them home to Rest and Peace at last.

FRANCHEZZO.

PART I.
Days of Darkness.

I have been a Wanderer through a far country, in those lands that have no name--no place--for you of earth, and I would set down as briefly as I can my wanderings, that those whose feet are pointed to that bourn may know what may in their turn await them.

On earth and in my life of earth I lived as those do who seek only how the highest point of self gratification can be reached. If I was not unkind to some--if I was indulgent to those I loved--yet it was ever with the feeling that they in return must minister to my gratification--that from them I might purchase by my gifts and my affection the love and homage which was as my life to me.

I was talented, highly gifted both in mind and person, and from my earliest years the praise of others was ever given to me, and was ever my sweetest incense. No thought ever came to me of that all self-sacrificing love which can sink itself so completely in the love for others that there is no thought, no hope of happiness, but in securing the happiness of the beloved ones. In all my life, and amongst those women whom I loved (as men of earth too often miscall that which is but a passion too low and base to be dignified by the name of love), amongst all those women who from time to time captivated my fancy, there was not one who ever appealed to my higher nature sufficiently to make me feel this was true love, this the ideal for which in secret I sighed. In everyone I found something to disappoint me. They loved me as I loved them--no more, no less. The passion I gave won but its counterpart from them, and thus I passed on unsatisfied, longing for I knew not what.

Mistakes I made--ah! how many. Sins I committed--not a few; yet the world was often at my feet to praise me and call me good, and noble, and gifted. I was feted--caressed--the spoilt darling of the dames of fashion. I had but to woo to win, and when I won all turned to bitter ashes in my teeth. And then there came a time upon which I shall not dwell, when I made the most fatal mistake of all and spoilt two lives where I had wrecked but one before. It was not a golden flowery wreath of roses that I wore, but a bitter chain--fetters as of iron that galled and bruised me till at last I snapped them asunder and walked forth free. Free?--ah, me! Never again should I be free, for never for one moment can our past errors and mistakes cease to dog our footsteps and clog our wings while we live--aye, and after the life of the body is ended--till one by one we have atoned for them, and thus blotted them from our past.

And then it was--when I deemed myself secure from all love--when I thought I had learned all that love could teach--knew all that woman had to give--that I met one woman. Ah! what shall I call her? She was more than mortal woman in my eyes, and I called her "The Good Angel of My Life," and from the first moment that I knew her I bowed down at her feet and gave her all the love of my soul--of my higher self--a love that was poor and selfish when compared to what it should have been, but it was all I had to give, and I gave it all. For the first time in my life I thought of another more than of myself, and though I could not rise to the pure thoughts, the bright fancies that filled her soul, I thank God I never yielded to the temptation to drag her down to me.

As so time went on--I sunned myself in her sweet presence--I grew in holy thoughts that I deemed had left me for ever--I dreamed sweet dreams in which I was freed from those chains to my past that held me so cruelly, so hardly, now when I sought for better things. And from my dreams I ever woke to the fear that another might win her from me--and to the knowledge that I, alas! had not the right to say one word to hold her back. Ah, me! The bitterness and the suffering of those days! I knew it was myself alone who had built that wall between us. I felt that I was not fit to touch her, soiled as I was in the world's ways. How could I dare to take that innocent, pure life and link it to my own? At times hope would whisper it might be so, but reason said ever, "No!" And though she was so kind, so tender to me that I read the innocent secret of her love, I knew--I felt--that on earth she never would be mine. Her purity and her truth raised between us a barrier I could never pass. I tried to leave her. In vain! As a magnet is drawn to the pole, so was I ever drawn back to her, till at last I struggled no more. I strove only to enjoy the happiness that her presence gave--happy that at least the pleasure and the sunshine of her presence was not denied me.

And then! Ah! then there came for me an awful, and unexpected day, when with no warning, no sign to awaken me to my position, I was suddenly snatched from life and plunged into that gulf, that death of the body which awaits us all.

And I knew not that I had died. I passed from some hours of suffering and agony into sleep--deep, dreamless sleep--and when I awoke it was to find myself alone and in total darkness. I could rise; I could move; surely I was better. But where was I? Why this darkness? Why was no light left with me? I arose and groped as one does in a dark room, but I could find no light, hear no sound. There was nothing but the stillness, the darkness of death around me.

Then I thought I would walk forward and find the door. I could move, though slowly and feebly, and I groped on--for how long I know not. It seemed hours, for in my growing horror and dismay I felt I must find some one--some way out of this place; and to my despair I seemed never to find any door, any wall, anything. All seemed space and darkness round me.

Overcome at last, I called out aloud! I shrieked, and no voice answered me. Then again and again I called, and still the silence; still no echo, even from my own voice, came back to cheer me. I bethought me of her I loved, but something made me shrink from uttering her name there. Then I thought of all the friends I had known, and I called on them, but none answered me. Was I in prison? No. A prison has walls and this place had none. Was I mad? Delirious? What? I could feel myself, my body. It was the same. Surely the same? No. There was some change in me. I could not tell what, but I felt as though I was shrunken and deformed? My features, when I passed my hand over them, seemed larger, coarser, distorted surely? Oh, for a light! Oh, for anything to tell me even the worst that could be told! Would no one come? Was I quite alone? And she, my angel of light, oh! where was she? Before my sleep she had been with me--where was she now? Something seemed to snap in my brain and in my throat and I called wildly to her by name, to come to me, if but for once more. I felt a terrible sense as if I had lost her, and I called and called to her wildly; and for the first time my voice had a sound and rang back to me through that awful darkness.

Before me, far, far away, came a tiny speck of light like a star that grew and grew and came nearer and nearer till at last it appeared before me as a large ball of light, in shape like a star, and in the star I saw my beloved. Her eyes were closed as of one in sleep, but her arms were held out to me and her gentle voice said in those tones I knew so well, "Oh! my love, my love, where are you now; I cannot see you, I only hear your voice; I only hear you call to me, and my soul answers to yours."

I tried to rush to her, but I could not. Some invisible force held me back, and around her seemed a ring I could not pass through. In an agony I sank to the ground, calling upon her to leave me no more. Then she seemed to grow unconscious; her head sank upon her breast, and I saw her float away from me as though some strong arms had borne her. I sought to rise and follow her, but could not. It was as if a great chain held me fast, and after some fruitless struggles I sank upon the ground in unconsciousness.

CHAPTER II.--Despair.

"Dead! Dead!" I wildly cried. "Oh, no, surely no! For the dead feel nothing more; they turn to dust; they moulder to decay, and all is gone, all is lost to them; they have no more consciousness of anything, unless, indeed, my boasted philosophy of life has been all wrong, all false, and the soul of the dead still lives even though the body decays."

The priests of my own church had taught me so, but I had scorned them as fools, blind and knavish, who for their own ends taught that men lived again and could only get to heaven through a gate, of which they held the keys, keys that turned only for gold and at the bidding of those who were paid to say masses for the departed soul--priests who made dupes of silly frightened women and weak-minded men, who, yielding to the terror inspired by their awful tales of hell and purgatory, gave themselves, bodies and souls, to purchase the illusive privilege they promised. I would have none of them. My knowledge of these priests and the inner hidden lives of many of them had been too great for me to listen to their idle tales, their empty promises of a pardon they could not give, and I had said I would face death when it came, with the courage of those who know only that for them it must mean total extinction; for if these priests were wrong, who was right? Who could tell us anything of the future, or if there were any God at all? Not the living, for they but theorize and guess, and not the dead, for none came back from them to tell; and now I stood beside this grave--my own grave-- and heard my beloved call me dead and strew flowers upon it.

As I looked the solid mound grew transparent before my eyes, and I saw down to the coffin with my own name and the date of my death upon it; and through the coffin I saw the white still form I knew as myself lying within. I saw to my horror that this body had already begun to decay and become a loathsome thing to look upon. Its beauty was gone, its features none would recognize; and I stood there, conscious, looking down upon it and then at myself. I felt each limb, traced out with my hands each familiar feature of my face, and knew I was dead, and yet I lived. If this were death, then those priests must have been right after all. The dead lived--but where? In what state? Was this darkness hell? For me they would have found no other place. I was so lost, so beyond the pale of their church that for me they would not have found a place even in purgatory.

I had cast off all ties to their church. I had so scorned it, deeming that a church which knew of, and yet tolerated, the shameful and ambitious lives of many of its most honored dignitaries had no claim to call itself a spiritual guide for anyone. There were good men in the church; true, but there was also this mass of shameless evil ones whose lives were common talk, common matter of ridicule; yet the church that claimed to be the example to all men and to hold all truth, did not cast out these men of disgraceful lives. No, she advanced them to yet higher posts of honor. None who have lived in my native land and seen the terrible abuses of power in her church will wonder that a nation should rise and seek to cast off such a yoke. Those who can recall the social and political condition of Italy in the earlier half of this century, and the part the church of Rome played in helping the oppressor to rivet the fetters with which she was bound, and who know how her domestic life was honeycombed with spies--priests as well as laymen--till a man feared to whisper his true sentiments to his nearest and dearest lest she should betray him to the priest and he again to the government--how the dungeons were crowded with unhappy men, yea, even with mere lads guilty of no crime save love of their native land and hatred of its oppressors--those, I say, who know all this will not wonder at the fierce indignation and burning passion which smouldered in the breast of Italia's sons, and burst at last into a conflagration which consumed man's faith in God and in his so-called Vicar upon earth, and like a mountain torrent that has burst its bounds, swept away men's hopes of immortality, if only through submission to the decrees of the church it was to be obtained. Such, then, had been my attitude of revolt and scorn towards the church in which I had been baptized, and that church could have no place within her pale for me. If her anathemas could send a soul to hell surely I must be there.

And yet as I thought thus I looked again upon my beloved, and I thought she could never have come to hell even to look for me. She seemed mortal enough, and if she knelt by my grave surely I must be still upon earth. Did the dead then never leave the earth at all, but hover near the scenes of their earthly lives? With such and many similar thoughts crowding through my brain I strove to get nearer to her I so loved, but found I could not. An invisible barrier seemed to surround her and keep me back. I could move on either side of her as I pleased--nearer or farther--but her I could not touch. Vain were all my efforts. Then I spoke; I called to her by name. I told her that I was there; that I was still conscious, still the same, though I was dead; and she never seemed to hear--she never saw me. She still wept sadly and silently; still tenderly touched the flowers, murmuring to herself that I had so loved flowers, surely I would know that she had put them there for me. Again and again I spoke to her as loudly as I could, but she heard me not. She was deaf to my voice. She only moved uneasily and passed her hand over her head as one in a dream, and then slowly and sadly she went away.

I strove with all my might to follow her. In vain, I could go but a few yards from the grave and my earthly body, and then I saw why. A chain as of dark silk thread--it seemed no thicker than a spider's web--held me to my body; no power of mine could break it; as I moved it stretched like elastic, but always drew me back again. Worst of all I began now to be conscious of feeling the corruption of that decaying body affecting my spirit, as a limb that has become poisoned affects with suffering the whole body on earth, and a fresh horror filled my soul.

Then a voice as of some majestic being spoke to me in the darkness, and said: "You loved that body more than your soul. Watch it now as it turns to dust and know what it was that you worshipped, and ministered and clung to. Know how perishable it was, how vile it has become, and look upon your spirit body and see how you have starved and cramped and neglected it for the sake of the enjoyments of the earthly body. Behold how poor and repulsive and deformed your earthly life has made your soul, which is immortal and divine and to endure forever."

And I looked and beheld myself. As in a mirror held up before me, I saw myself. Oh, horror! It was beyond doubt myself, but, oh! so awfully changed, so vile, so full of baseness did I appear; so repulsive in every feature--even my figure was deformed--I shrank back in horror at my appearance, and prayed that the earth might open before my feet and hide me from all eyes for evermore. Ah! never again would I call upon my love, never more desire that she should see me. Better, far better, that she should think of me as dead and gone from her forever; better that she should have only the memory of me as I had been in earthly life than ever know how awful was the change, how horrible a thing was my real self.

Alas! Alas! My despair, my anguish was extreme, and I called out wildly and struck myself and tore my hair in wild and passionate horror of myself, and then my passion exhausted me and I sank senseless and unconscious of all once more.

Again I waked, and again it was the presence of my love that awaked me. She had brought more flowers, and she murmured more soft tender thoughts of me as she laid them on my grave. But I did not seek now to make her see me. No, I shrank back and sought to hide myself, and my heart grew hard even to her, and I said: "Rather let her weep for the one who has gone than know that he still lives," so I let her go. And as soon as she was gone, I called frantically to her to come back, to come back in any way, to any knowledge of my awful position, rather than leave me in that place to see her no more. She did not hear, but she felt my call, and afar off I saw her stop and half turn round as though to return, then she passed on again and left me. Twice, three times she came again, and each time when she came I felt the same shrinking from approaching her, and each time when she left I felt the same wild longing to bring her back and keep her near me. But I called to her no more for I knew the dead call in vain, the living hear them not. And to all the world I was dead, and only to myself and to my awful fate was I alive. Ah! now I knew death was no endless sleep, no calm oblivion. Better, far better had it been so, and in my despair I prayed that this total oblivion might be granted to me, and as I prayed I knew it never could, for man is an immortal soul, and for good or evil, weal or woe, lives on eternally. His earthly form decays and turns to dust, but the spirit, which is the true man, knows no decay, no

11

oblivion.

Each day--for I felt that days were passing over me--my mind awoke more and more, and I saw clearer and clearer the events of my life pass in a long procession before me--dim at first, then by degrees growing stronger and clearer, and I bowed my head in anguish, helpless, hopeless anguish, for I felt it must be too late now to undo one single act.

I know not how long this lasted; it seemed a long, long time to me. I was sitting wrapped still in my despair when I heard a voice gentle and soft calling to me--the voice of my beloved--and I felt compelled to rise and follow that voice till it should lead me to her; and as I rose to go the thread which had so bound me seemed to stretch and stretch till I scarce felt its pressure, and I was drawn on and on till at last I found myself in a room which, I could dimly see, even in the darkness that always surrounded me, was familiar to my eyes. It was the home of my beloved one, and in that room I had passed, ah! how many peaceful happy hours in that time which seemed now separated from me by so wide and awful a gulf. She sat at a little table with a sheet of paper before her and a pencil in her hand. She kept repeating my name and saying: "Dearest of friends, if the dead ever return, come back to me, and try if you can make me write a few words from you, even 'yes' or 'no' in answer to my questions."

For the first time since I had died I saw her with a faint smile upon her lips and a look of hope and expectation in those dear eyes that were so heavy with weeping for me. The dear face looked so pale and sad with her grief and I felt--ah! how I felt--the sweetness of the love she had given me, and which now less than ever dare I hope to claim.

Then I saw three other forms beside her, but they I knew were spirits, yet how unlike myself. These spirits were bright, radiant, so that I could not bear to look at them; the sight seemed to scorch my eyes as with a fire. One was a man, tall, calm, dignified-looking, who bent over her to protect her as her guardian angel might. Beside him stood two fair young men whom I knew at once to be those brothers whom she had so often spoken of to me. They had died when youth with all its pleasures was before them, and their memories were shrined in her heart as those who were now angels. I shrank back, for I felt they saw me, and I sought to cover my disfigured face and form with the dark mantle which I wore. Then my pride awoke, and I said: "Has not she herself called me? I have come, and shall not she be the arbiter of my destiny? Is it so irrevocable that nothing I can do, no sorrow, no repentance however deep, no deeds however great, no work however hard, can reverse it? Is there indeed no hope beyond the grave?"

And a voice, the voice I had heard before at my own grave, answered me: "Son of grief, is there no hope on earth for those who sin? Does not even man forgive the sinner who has wronged him if the sin be repented of and pardon sought? And shall God be less merciful, less just? Hast thou repentance even now? Search thine own heart and see whether it is for thyself or for those thou hast wronged that thou art sorry?"

And I knew as he spoke that I did not truly repent. I only suffered. I only loved and longed. then again my beloved spoke and asked me, if I were there and could hear her, to try and write one word through her hand that she might know I still lived, still thought of her.

My heart seemed to rise into my throat and choke me, and I drew near to try if I could move her hand, could touch it even. But the tall spirit came between us, and I was forced to draw back. Then he spoke and said: "Give your words to me and I will cause her hand to write them down for you. I will do this for her sake, and because of the love she has for you."

A great wave of joy swept over me at his words, and I would have taken his hand and kissed it but could not. My hand seemed scorched by his brightness ere I could touch him, and I bowed myself before him for I thought he must be one of the angels.

My beloved spoke once more and said: "Are you here, dearest friend?"

I answered, "Yes," and then I saw the spirit put his hand on her, and when he did so her hand wrote the word "yes." Slowly and unsteadily it moved, like a child's learning to write. Ah! how she smiled, and again she asked me a question, and as before her own hand traced out my answer. She asked me if there were anything she could do for me, any wish of mine that she could help me to carry out? I said: "No! not now. I would go away now and torment her no more with my presence. I would let her forget me now."

My heart was so sore as I spoke, so bitter; and ah! how sweet to me was her reply, how it touched my soul to hear her say: "Do not say that to me, for I would ever be your truest, dearest friend, as I was in the past, and since you died my one thought has been to find you and to speak with you again."

And I answered, I called out to her, "It has been my only wish also."

She then asked if I would come again, and I said "Yes!" For where would I not have gone for her? What would I not have done? Then the bright spirit said she must write no more that night. He made her hand write that also and said she should go to rest.

I felt myself now drawn away once more back to my grave and to my earthly body in that dark churchyard; but not to the same hopeless sense of misery. In spite of everything a spark of hope had risen in my heart, and I knew I should see and speak with her again.

But now I found I was not alone there. Those two spirits who were her brothers had followed me, and now spoke. I shall not state all they said. Suffice it to say they pointed out to me how wide was now the gulf between their sister and myself, and asked me if I desired to shadow all her young life with my dark presence. If I left her now, she would, in time, forget me, except as one who had been a dear friend to her. She could always think tenderly of my memory, and surely if I loved her truly I would not wish to make all her young life lonely and desolate for my sake.

I replied that I loved her, and could never bear to leave her, never bear to think of any other, loving her as I had done.

Then they spoke of myself and my past, and asked if I dared to think of linking myself with her pure life, even in the misty fashion in which I still hoped to do? How could I hope that when she died I should meet her? She belonged to a bright sphere to which I could not hope for a long time to rise, and would it not be better for her, and nobler, more truly loving of me, to leave her to forget me and to find what happiness in life could yet be given to her, rather than seek to keep alive a love that could only bring her sorrow?

I said faintly I thought she loved me. They said: "Yes, she loves you as she herself has idealized your image in her mind, and as she in her innocence has painted your picture. Do you think if she knew all your story she would love you? Would she not shrink back in horror from you? Tell her the truth, give her the choice of freedom from your presence, and you will have acted a nobler part and shown a truer love than in deceiving her and seeking to tie her to a being like yourself. If you truly love her, think of her and her happiness, and what will bring it--not of yourself alone."

Then the hope within me died out, and I bowed my head to the dust in shame and agony, for I knew that I was vile and in no way fit for her, and I saw as in a glass what her life might still be freed from mine. She might know happiness yet with another more worthy than I had been, while with my love I would only drag her down into sadness with me. For the first time in my life I put the happiness of another before my own, and because I so loved her and would have had her happy, I said to them: "Let it be so, then. Tell her the truth, and let her say but one kind word to me in farewell, and I will go from her and darken her life with the shadow of mine no more."

So we went back to her, and I saw her as she slept exhausted with her sorrow for me. I pleaded that they would let me give her one kiss, the first and last that I would ever give. But they said no, that was impossible, for my touch would snap forever the thread that held her still to life.

Then they awoke her and made her write down their words, while I stood by and heard each word fall as a nail in the coffin where they were burying my last hope forever. She, as one in a dream, wrote on, till at last the whole shameful story of my life was told, and I had but to tell her myself that all was forever at an end between us, and she was free from my sinful presence and my selfish love. I said adieu to her. As drops of blood wrung from my heart were those words, and as ice they fell upon her heart and crushed it. Then I turned and left her--how, I know not--but as I went I felt the cord that had tied me to my grave and my earthly body snap, and I was free--free to wander where I would--alone in my desolation!

And then? Ah, me! While I write the words the tears of thankfulness are in my eyes again, and I almost break down in trying to write them; then she whom we had deemed so weak and gentle that we had but to decide for her, she called me back with all the force of a love none dare oppose--called me back to her. She said she could never give me up so long as I had love for her. "Let your past be what it might; let you be sunk now even to the lowest depths of hell itself, I will still love you, still seek to follow you and claim my right--the right of my love--to help and comfort and cherish you till God in his mercy shall have pardoned your past and you shall be raised up again." And then it was that I broke down and wept as only a strong proud man can weep, whose heart has been wrung and bruised and hardened, and then touched by the soft tender touch of a loving hand till the tears must come to his relief.

I went back to my love and knelt down beside her, and though they would not let me touch her, that calm beautiful spirit who was her guardian whispered to her that her prayer was answered, and that she should indeed lead me back to the light. And so I left my darling, and as I passed away I saw a white angel's form hover over her to give her strength and comfort, who was herself my angel of light. I left her thus with those spirits, and went forth to wander till her voice should call me to her side again.

After the short troubled sleep into which those bright spirits had put her, my darling awoke the next day, and went to visit a kind good man whom she had discovered in her efforts to find some way by which she might reach me even beyond the grave.

If it might be that what she had been told about those people who were called Spiritualists was really true, she hoped through their aid to speak again with me, and prompted by those who were watching over her, she had searched out this man who was known as a healing medium, and by him she had been told that if she herself tried, she could write messages from the so-called dead.

This I did not learn till later. At the time I only felt myself summoned by the voice of her whose power over me was so great, and in obedience to it I found myself standing in what I could dimly distinguish to be a small room. I say dimly, because all was still dark to me save only where the light around my darling shone as a star and showed faintly what was near.

16

It was to this good man of whom I speak that she had gone, and it was her voice speaking to him that had drawn me. She was telling him what had passed the night before, and how much she loved me, and how she would gladly give all her life if by so doing she could comfort and help me. And that man spoke such kind words to her-- from my heart I thanked and still thank him for them. He gave me so much hope. He pointed out to my dear love that the ties of the earth body are broken at its death, and I was free to love her and she was free to return that love--that she herself better than any other could in truth help to raise me, for her love would give me comfort and hope as nothing else would do, and would cheer my path of repentant effort. And she had now the best of rights to give it, my love for her had been so pure and true a passion, while hers for me was stronger than death itself, since it had overcome the barrier of death. He was so kind, this man--he helped me to speak to her, and to explain many things as I could not have done the night before when my heart was so sore and full of pride. He helped me to tell what of excuse there had been for me in the past, though I owned that nothing can truly excuse our sins. He let me tell her that in spite of all the wrong of my past she had been to me as one sacred--loved with a love I had given to none but herself. He soothed and strengthened her with a kindness for which I blessed him even more than for his help to myself, and when she left him at last I, too, went with her to her home, the light of hope in both our hearts.

And when we got there I found that a fresh barrier was raised up by those two spirit brothers and others to whom she was dear; an invisible wall surrounded her through which I could not pass, and though I might follow her about I could not get very near. Then I said to myself that I would go back to the kind man and see if he would help me.

My wish seemed to carry me back, for I soon found myself there again. He was at once conscious of my presence, and strange as it may seem, I found that he could understand much, although not all, that I said to him. He gathered the sense of what I wanted to say, and told me many things I shall not set down here since they concerned only myself. He assured me that if I were only patient all would be well in time, and though the relations might build their spiritual wall around my love, her will would at all times draw me through it to her, and nothing could shut out her love from me; no walls could keep that back. If I would seek now to learn the things of the spirit, and work to advance myself, the gulf between us would disappear. Comforted I left him and wandered away again, I knew not where.

I was now beginning to be dimly conscious that there were other beings like myself flitting about near me in the darkness, though I could scarce see them. I was so lost and lonely that I thought of going back to my grave again, as it was the spot most familiar to me, and my thought seemed to take me back, for soon I was there once more.

17

The flowers that my love had brought me were faded now. She had not been there for two days; since speaking to me she seemed to forget the body that was laid away in the earth, and this to me was well, and I would have had it so. It was well for her to forget the dead body and think only of the living spirit.

Even these withered flowers spoke of her love, and I tried to pick up one, a white rose, to carry away with me. I found I could not lift it, could not move it in the least. My hand passed through it as though it was but the reflection of a rose.

I moved round to where there was a white marble cross at the head of the grave, and I saw there the names of my beloved one's two brothers. Then I knew what she had done in her love for me; she had laid my body to rest beside those she had loved best of all. My heart was so touched that again I wept, and my tears fell like dew upon my heart and melted away its bitterness.

I was so lonely that at last I rose and wandered away again amongst other dark wandering shapes, few of whom even turned to look at me; perhaps like myself they scarcely saw. Presently, however, three dark forms which seemed like two women and a man passed near me, and then turned and followed. The man touched my arm and said: "Where are you bound for? Surely you are newly come over to this side, or you would not hurry on so; none hurry here because we all know we have eternity to wander in." Then he laughed a laugh so cold and harsh in tone it made me shudder. One of the women took my arm on one side and one on the other, saying: "Come away with us and we will show you how you may enjoy life even though you are dead! If we have not got bodies to enjoy ourselves through we will borrow them from some mortals for a little. Come with us and we will show you that all pleasure is not ended yet."

In my loneliness I was glad to have some being to speak to, that although they were all three most repulsive looking--the women to my mind even more so than the man--I felt inclined to let them lead me away and see what would happen, and I had even turned to accompany them when afar off in the dim distance, like a picture traced in light on a black sky, I saw the spirit form of my pure sweet love. Her eyes were closed as I had seen her in my first vision, but as before her hands were stretched out to me and her voice fell like a voice from heaven on my ears, saying: "Oh! take care! take care! go not with them; they are not good, and their road leads only to destruction." Then the vision was gone, and as one waking from a dream I shook those three persons from me and hurried away again in the darkness. How long and how far I wandered I know not. I kept hurrying on to get away from the memories that haunted me and I seemed to have all space to wander in.

At last I sat down on the ground to rest--for there seemed to be ground solid enough to rest upon--and while I sat there I saw glimmering through the darkness a light. As I drew near it I saw a great haze of light radiating from a room which I could see, but it was so bright it hurt my eyes to look upon it as would looking at the noon-day sun on earth have done. I could not bear it and would have turned away, when a voice said: "Stay, weary wanderer! Here are only kind hearts and helping hands for you. And if you would see your love, come in, for she is here and you may speak with her." Then I felt a hand--for I could see no one--draw my mantle over my head to shut out the brightness of the light, and then lead me into the room and seat me in a large chair. I was so weary, so weary, and so glad to rest. And in this room there was such peace, it seemed to me that I had found my way to heaven.

After a little I looked up and saw two gentle, kindly women who were like angels to my eyes, and I said to myself, "I have come near to heaven surely?" Again I looked, and by this time my eyes seemed strengthened, for beyond those two fair good women--and at first I could scarce believe it, so great was my joy--I saw my beloved herself smiling sadly but tenderly at where I sat. She smiled, but I knew she did not really see me; one of the ladies did though, and she was describing me to my darling in a low quiet voice. My darling seemed so pleased, for it confirmed to her what the man had told her. She had been telling these ladies what a remarkable experience she had had, and how it seemed to her like a strange dream. I could have cried out to her then that I was truly there, that I still lived, still loved her, and was trusting in her love for me, but I could not move, some spell was over me, some power I could dimly feel was holding me back.

And then those two kind ladies spoke and I knew they were not angels yet, for they were still in their earthly bodies and she could see and speak to them. They said much of what the kind good man had done, as to the hope there was for sinners like me.

The same voice which had bidden me to enter, now asked would I like one of the ladies to write a message for me. I said, "Yes! a thousand times yes!"

Then I spoke my words and the spirit caused the lady to write them down. I said to my beloved that I still lived, still loved her. I bid her never to forget me, never to cease to think of me, for I required all her love and help to sustain me--I was ever the same to her though now I was weak and helpless and could not make her see me. And she, ah! she gave me such sweet words in return I cannot write them down; they are too sacred to me, and still rest in my heart for evermore.

The period that followed this interview was one of deep sleep for me. I was so exhausted that when I left that room I wandered on a little way and then sank down upon the ground in deep dreamless unconsciousness. What did it matter where I rested when all was as night around me?

How long my sleep lasted I know not. At that period I had no means of counting time save by the amount of suffering and misery through which I passed. From my slumbers I awoke refreshed in a measure, and with all my senses stronger in me than before. I could move more rapidly; my limbs felt stronger and freer, and I was now conscious of a desire to eat I had not felt before. My longing grew so great that I went in search of food, and for a long time could find none anywhere. At last I found what looked like hard dry bread--a few crusts only, but I was glad to eat them, whereupon I felt more satisfied. Here I may say that spirits do eat the spiritual counterpart of your food, do feel both hunger and thirst, as keen to them as your apetites are to you on earth, although neither our food nor our drink would be any more visible to your material sight than our spiritual bodies are, and yet for us they possess objective reality. Had I been a drunkard or a lover of the pleasures of the table in my earthly body I should much sooner have felt the cravings of appetite. As it was, nature with me had ever been easily satisfied, and though at first I turned from those dry crusts in disgust a little reflection told me that I had now no way of procuring anything, I was like a beggar and had better content myself with a beggar's fare.

My thoughts had now turned to my beloved again, and the thoughts carried my spirit with them, so that I found myself entering once more the room where I had last seen her and the two ladies. This time I seemed to pass in at once, and was received by two spirit men whom I could but very faintly see. A veil seemed to hang between us, through which I saw those two spirit men, the ladies and my beloved. I was told that I might again give a message to her through the lady who had written my words before. I was so anxious to try if I could not make my darling write down my words herself as I had seen her guardian spirit do, that I was allowed to try. To my disappointment I found I could not do it; she was deaf to all I said, and I had to give up that idea and let the lady write for me as before. After I had given my message I rested for a short time and watched my beloved one's sweet face, as I had been wont to do in other happier days. My musings were interrupted by one of those spirit men--a grave, handsome young man he seemed to be so far as I could see him. He spoke to me in a quiet kindly voice, and said that if I truly desired to write my own words through my darling herself, it would be well for me to join a brotherhood of penitents who like myself desired to follow out the better way, and with them I should learn many things of which I was yet ignorant, and which would help me to fit myself to control her mind as well as give me the privilege I sought of being with her at times while she dwelt on earth. This way of repentance was hard, he said--very hard--the steps many, the toil and suffering great, but it led to a fair and happy land at last where I should rest in happiness such as I could not dream of now. He assured me (even as the kind earthly man had done) that my deformed body, which I was still so anxious to hide from my beloved one's eyes, would change as my spirit changed, till I should be once more fair to look upon, such as she would no longer grieve to see. Were I to remain upon the earth plane as I now was, I should most likely be drawn back into my former haunts of so-called pleasure, and in that atmosphere of spiritual degradation I should soon lose the power to be near my darling at all. For her own sake those who guarded her would be obliged to exclude me. On the other hand, were I to join this brotherhood (which was one of hope and endeavor), I should be so helped, so strengthened, and so taught, that when in due course my time came to return to the earth plane, I should have acquired a strength and an armor that could resist its temptations.

I listened to the words of this grave, courteous spirit with wonder and a growing desire to know more of this brotherhood of whom he spoke, and begged he would take me to them. This he assured me he would do, and he also explained that I should be there of my own free will and choice only. Did I desire at any time to leave I could at once do so. "All are free in the Spirit world," he said. "All must follow only where their own wishes and desires lead them. If you study to cultivate the higher desires, means will be given you to attain them, and you will be strengthened with such help and strength as you may need. You are one who has never learned the power of prayer. You will learn it now, for all things come by earnest prayer, whether you are conscious that you pray or not. For good or for evil your desires are as prayers and call around you good or evil powers to answer them for you."

As I was again growing weary and exhausted, he suggested that I should bid adieu to my darling for a time. He explained that I should gain more strength as well as permit her to do so if I left her for the time I was to remain in this place of which he spoke. It would also be well that she should not try to write for three months, as her mediumistic powers had been greatly tried, and if she did not rest them she would be much impaired, while I would require all that time to learn even the simple lessons needful before I could control her.

Ah! me, how hard it seemed to us both to make this promise, but she set me the example, and I could but follow it. If she would try to be strong and patient so should I, and I registered a vow that if the God I had so long forgotten would remember and pardon me now, I would give all my life and all my powers to undo the wrongs that I had done; and so it was that I left for a time the troubled earth plane of the spirit world of which I had as yet seen so little, but in which I was yet to see and suffer so much. As I left the room to go with my new guide I turned to my love and waved my hand in farewell, and asked that the good angels and the God I dare not pray to for myself might bless her and keep her safe for evermore, and the last thing I saw was her tender eyes following me with that look of love and hope which was to sustain me through many a weary, painful hour.

CHAPTER IV.--The Brotherhood of Hope.

In the spirit world there are many strange places, many wondrous sights, and many organizations for helping repentant souls, but I have never seen anything more strange in its way than this Home of Help, conducted by the Brotherhood of Hope, to which I was now conducted. In the then feeble condition of all my spiritual faculties I was not able to see what the place was like. I was almost like one who is deaf, dumb and blind. When I was with others I could scarcely see or hear them, or make them hear me, and although I could see a little, it was more as though I was in a perfectly dark room with only one small feeble glimmer of light to show me where I went. On the earth plane I had not felt this so much, for though all was darkness I could both see and hear enough to be conscious of those near me. It was in ascending even to the little distance at which this place was above the earth that I felt the absence of all but the most material developments of my spirit.

That time of darkness was so awful to me that even now I scarce like to recall it, I had so loved the sunshine and the light. I came from a land where all is sunshine and brightness, where the colors are so rich, the sky so clear, the flowers and the scenery so beautiful, and I so loved light and warmth and melody; and here as elsewhere since my death I had found only darkness and coldness and gloom; an apalling, enshrouding gloom, that wrapped me round like a mantle of night from which I could in no way free myself; and this awful gloom crushed my spirit as nothing else could have done. I had been proud and haughty on earth. I came of a race that knew not what it was to bow before anyone. In my veins ran the blood of its haughty nobles. Through my mother I was allied to the great ones of earth whose ambitions had moved kingdoms to their will; and now the lowest, humblest, poorest beggar of my native streets was greater, happier than I, for he at least had the sunshine and the free air, and I was as the lowest, most degraded prisoner in the dungeon cell.

Had it not been for my one star of hope, my angel of light, and the hopes she had given me through her love, I must have sunk into the apathy of despair. But when I thought of her waiting, as she had vowed she would do all her life for me, when I recalled her sweet and tender smile and the loving words she had spoken to me, my heart and my courage revived again, and I strove to endure, to be patient, to be strong. And I had need of all to help me, for from now began a period of suffering and conflict I shall in vain seek to make anyone fully realize.

This place where I was now I could barely see in all its details. It was like a huge prison--dim and misty in its outlines. Later on I saw it was a great building of dark grey stone (as solid to my eyes as earthly stone) with many long passages, some long large halls or rooms, but mostly composed of innumerable little cells with scarcely any light and only the barest of furniture. Each spirit had only what he had earned by his earthly life, and some had nothing but the little couch whereon they lay and suffered. For all suffered there. It was the House of Sorrow, yet it was also a House of Hope, for all there were striving upwards to the light, and for each had begun the time of hope. Each had his foot planted upon the lowest rung of the ladder of hope by which he should in time mount even to heaven itself.

In my own little cell there was but my bed, a table and a chair--nothing more. I spent my time in resting or meditating in my cell, and going with those who, like myself, soon grew strong enough to hear the lectures which were delivered to us in the great hall. Very impressive those lectures were; told in the form of a story, but always so as to bring home to the mind of each of us those things wherein we had done wrong. Great pains were taken to make us understand, from the point of view of an impartial spectator, the full consequences to ourselves and others of each of our actions, and where we had for our own selfish gratifications wronged or dragged down another soul. So many things which we had done because all men did them, or because we thought that we as men had a right to do them, were now shown to us from the other side of the picture, from those who had in a measure been our victims, or where we personally were not directly responsible for their fall, the victims of a social system invented and upheld to gratify us and our selfish passions. I cannot more fully describe these lectures, but those amongst you who know what are the corruptions of the great cities of earth will easily supply for yourselves the subjects. From such lectures, such pictures of ourselves as we were, stripped of all the social disguises of earth life, we could but return in shame and sorrow of heart to our cells to reflect over our past and to strive to atone for it in our future.

And in this there was great help given to us, for with the error and its consequences we were always shown the way to correct and overcome the evil desire in ourselves, and how we might atone for our own sins by timely efforts to save another from the evil into which we had fallen, all these lessons being intended to fit us for the next stage of our progression, in which we would be sent back to earth to help, unseen and unknown, mortals who were struggling with earth's temptations.

When we were not attending the lectures we were free to go where we might wish; that is, such of us as were strong enough to move about freely. Some who had left dear friends on earth would go to visit them, that, unseen themselves, they might yet see those they loved. We were always warned, however, not to linger in the temptations of the earth plane, since many of us would find it difficult to resist them.

Those who were strongest amongst us and who possessed the needful qualities and the desire to use them, were employed in magnetising those who were weakest, and who, by reason of the excessive dissipations of their earthly lives, were in such terrible condition of exhaustion and suffering that the only thing which could be done with them was to allow them to lie helpless in their cells while others gave them a little relief by magnetising them; and here I must describe to you a very wonderful system of healing those poor spirits which was practiced in this House of Hope. Some advanced spirits, whose natural desires and tastes made them doctors and healers, with the help of other spirits of different degrees of advancement under them, would attend upon these poorest and most suffering ones--where indeed all were sufferers--and by means of magnetism and the use of others' powers which they could control, they would put these poor spirits into temporary forgetfulness of their pain; and though they awoke again to a renewal of their sufferings, yet in these intervals their spirits gained strength and insensibly grew more able to endure, till at last their sufferings were mitigated with time and the growing development of the spirit body, and they in turn would, when fit to do so, be employed to magnetise others who were still suffering.

It is impossible for me to give you a very clear picture of this place and those in it, for although the resemblance to an earthly hospital was very great, there were many little points in which it resembled nothing which you have yet on earth, though as knowledge on earth advances the resemblance will become closer. All was so dark in this place, because the unfortunate spirits who dwelt there had none of the brightness of happy spirits to give into the atmosphere, and it is the state of the spirit itself in the spiritual world that makes the lightness or darkness of its surroundings. The sense of darkness was also due to the almost total blindness of these poor spirits, whose spiritual senses never having been developed on earth made them alike insensible to all around them, just as those born on earth in a state of blindness, deafness and dumbness would be unconscious of the things which were apparent to those fully endowed with senses. In visiting the atmosphere of the earthly plane, which was a degree more suited to their state of development, these poor spirits would still be in darkness, though it would not be so complete, and they would possess the power of seeing those beings like themselves with whom they could come into direct contact, and also such mortals as were in a sufficiently low spiritual degree of development. The higher and more spiritualized mortals, and still more the disembodied spirits in advance of them would be only very dimly discernible, or even totally invisible.

The "working" Brothers of Hope, as they were called, were each provided with a tiny little light like a star, whose rays illuminated the darkness of the cells they visited and carried the light of hope wherever the brothers went. I myself at first was so great a sufferer that I used simply to lie in my cell in a state of almost apathetic misery, watching for this spark to come glimmering down the long corridor to my door, and wondering how long it would be in earth time ere it would come again. But it was not long that I lay thus utterly prostrate. Unlike many of the poor spirits who had added a love of drink to their other vices, my mind was too clear and my desire to improve too strong to leave me long inactive, and as soon as I found myself able to move again I petitioned to be allowed to do something, however humble, which might be of use. I was therefore, as being myself possessed of strong magnetic powers, set to help an unfortunate young man who was utterly unable to move, and who used to lie moaning and sighing all the time. Poor fellow, he was only thirty years old when he left the earth body, but in his short life he had contrived to plunge into such dissipations that he had prematurely killed himself, and was now suffering such agonies from the reaction upon the spirit of those powers he had abused, that it was often more than I could bear to witness them. My task was to make soothing passes over him, by which means he would obtain a little relief, till at stated times a more advanced spirit than myself would come and put him into a state of unconsciousness. And all this time I was myself suffering keenly both in mind and in my spirit body, for in the lower spheres the spirit is conscious of bodily sufferings. As it grows more advanced the suffering becomes more purely mental--the less material envelope of the higher spirits making them at last insensible to anything like material pain.

As my strength grew so did my desires revive and cause me so much torment that I was often tempted to do what many poor spirits did--go back to earth in search of the means to satisfy them through the material bodies of those yet on earth. My bodily sufferings grew very great, for the strength I had been so proud of and had used to so bad a purpose made me suffer more than one who had been weak. As the muscles of an athlete who has used them to excess begin after a time to contract and cause him excruciating pain, so those powers and that strength which I had abused in my earthly life now began, through its inevitable reaction on my spirit body, to cause me the most intense suffering. And then as I grew stronger and stronger and able to enjoy what had seemed enjoyment in my earth life, the desire for those pleasures grew and grew till I could scarce refrain from returning to the earth plane there to enjoy, through the organism of those yet in the flesh, whose sordid lives and low desires placed them on a level with the spirits of the earth plane, those pleasures of the senses which had still so great a temptation for us. Many and many of those who were in the House of Hope with me would yield to the temptation and go back for a time to haunt the earth, whence they would return after a longer or shorter period, exhausted and degraded even below their former state. All were free to go or to stay as they desired. All could return when they wished, for the doors of Hope's castle were never shut upon anyone, however unthankful or unworthy they might be, and I have often wondered at the infinite patience and tenderness which were ever shown for our weaknesses and our sins. It was indeed only possible to pity these poor unfortunates, who had made such utter slaves of themselves to their base desires that they could not resist them and were drawn back time after time till at last, satiated and exhausted, they could move no more and were like the unfortunate young man whom I tended.

25

For myself, I might also have yielded to the temptation had it not been for the thoughts of my pure love, and the hopes she had given me, the purer desires she had inspired, and I at least could not condemn these poor erring souls who had no such blessings granted them. I went to earth very often, but it was to where my beloved one dwelt, and her love drew me ever to her side, away from all temptations, into the pure atmosphere of her home, and though I could never approach near enough to touch her, by reason of this icy invisible wall which I have described, I used to stand outside of it, looking at her as she sat and worked or read or slept. When I was there she would always be in a dim way conscious of my presence, and would whisper my name or turn to where I was with one of her sad sweet smiles that I would carry away the recollection of and comfort myself with in my lonely hours. She looked so sad, so very sad, my poor love, and so pale and delicate, it made my heart ache even while it comforted me to see her. I could tell that in spite of all her efforts to be brave and patient, and to hope, the strain was almost too great for her, and each day she grew more delicate looking. She had many other things to try her at this time; there were family troubles and the doubts and fears suggested by the strangeness of her intercourse with the world of spirits. At times she would wonder if it were not all a wild delusion, a dream from which she would awake to find there was after all no communication between the dead and the living, no means by which she could reach me again, and then a dull despair would seize upon her and upon me also as I stood beside her and read her feeling, helpless and powerless to make her realize my actual presence beside her, and I would pray to be allowed in some way to make her know that I was there.

One night when I had watched her sink into sleep after a weary time of weeping, I, who could have wept, too, in my grief for us both, was suddenly touched upon the shoulder, and looking up beheld her guardian spirit who had first helped me speak with her. He asked me if I would be very quiet and self-restrained if he allowed me to kiss her as she slept, and I, wild with this new joy, most eagerly promised. Taking my hand in his we passed together through the transparent icy wall that was to me so impervious. Bending over her the guide made some strange motions with his hand, and then taking one of my hands in his for a few moments he bade me touch her very gently. She was lying quietly asleep, with the tears still on her eyelashes and her sweet lips slightly parted as though she was speaking in her dreams. One hand rested against her cheek and I took it in mine, so gently, so tenderly--not to awaken her. Her hand closed half consciously upon mine and a look of such joy came into her face that I feared she would awake. But no! The bright spirit smiled at us both and said, "Kiss her now." And I--ah! I stooped over her and touched her at last and gave her the first kiss I had ever given. I kissed her not once but half a dozen times, so passionately that she awoke and the bright spirit drew me away in haste. She looked round and asked softly: "Do I dream, or was that indeed my beloved one?" I answered, "Yes," and she seemed to hear, for she smiled so sweet a smile--ah! so sweet! and again and again she repeated my name softly to herself.

Not for long after that would they allow me to touch her again, but I was often near, and the joy of that one meeting dwelt in our hearts for many an hour. I could see how real had been my kiss to her, and for me it was as an anchor of hope encouraging me to believe that in time I should indeed be able to make her feel my touch and hold communication with her.

The time came at last for me to leave the House of Hope and go forth, strong in the lessons I had learned there, to work out my atonement on the earth plane and in those lower spheres to which my earthly life had sunk me

Eight or nine months had elapsed since I had died, and I had grown strong and vigorous once more. I could move freely over the great sphere of the earth plane. My sight and my other senses were so far developed that I could see and hear and speak clearly. The light around me now was that of a faint twilight or when the night first begins to dawn into the day. To my eyes so long accustomed to the darkness, this dull light was very welcome, though after a time I grew so to long for the true day to dawn that this dull twilight was most monotonous and oppressive. Those countries which are situated in this, the third circle of the earth plane or first sphere, are called "The Twilight Lands," and it is thither that those spirits pass whose lives have been too selfish and material to allow their souls to reach any higher state of development. Even these Twilight Lands, however, are a degree above those "Haunting" spirits of the earth plane who are literally earthbound to their former habitations.

My work was to be begun upon the earth itself, and in those haunts which men of the world call the haunts of pleasure, though no pleasure is so fleeting, no degradation so sure, as that which they produce even during the earthly life. And now I found the value of the teachings and the experience I had gained during my stay in the House of Hope. Temptations that might once have seemed such to me were such no longer. I knew the satisfaction such pleasures give, and the cost at which alone they can be bought, and thus in controlling a mortal, as I often had to do, I was proof against the temptation such control offered of using his body for my own gratification.

Few people yet in their earthly envelopes understand that spirits can, and very often do, take such complete possession of the bodies of mortal men and women that, for the time, it is as though that earth body belonged to the disembodied and not the embodied spirit. Many cases of so-called temporary madness are due to the controlling power of very low spirits of evil desires or frivolous minds, who are, through the weakness of will or other causes, put into complete rapport with the embodied spirit whose body they seek to use. Amongst many ancient races this fact was acknowledged and studied as well as many branches of the occult sciences which we of the nineteenth century have grown too wise, forsooth, to look into, even to discover, if we can, those germs of truth with which all ages have been blessed and which are worth disinterring from the mass of rubbish in which succeeding generations of men have buried them.

The work upon which I was now engaged will seem no less strange to you than it did at first to me. The great Brotherhood of Hope was only one of a countless variety of societies which exist in the spirit world for the purpose of giving help to all who are in need. Their operations are carried on everywhere and in all spheres, and their members are to be found from the very lowest and darkest spheres to the very highest which surround the earth, and even extend into the spheres of the solar systems. They are like immense chains of spirits, the lowest and humblest being always helped and protected by those above.

A message would be sent to the Brotherhood that help was required to assist some struggling mortal or unhappy spirit, and such one of the brothers as was thought to be most fit would be sent to help. Such a one of us would be sent as had in his own earth life yielded to a similar temptation, and had suffered all the bitter consequences and remorse for his sin. Often the man or woman to be helped had unconsciously sent out an aspiration for help and strength to resist temptation, and that of itself was a prayer, which would be heard in the spirit world as a cry from earth's children that appealed to all in the spirit world who had been themselves earth's sons and daughters; or it might be that some spirit to whom the struggling one was very dear would seek for help on their behalf and would thus appeal to us to come to their aid. Our task would be to follow and control the one we desired to help till the temptation had been overcome. We would identify ourselves so closely with the mortal that for a time we actually shared his life, his thoughts, everything, and during this dual state of existence we ourselves often suffered most keenly both from our anxiety for the man whose thoughts became almost as our own, and from the fact that his anxieties were as ours, while in thus going over again a chapter in our past lives we endured all the sorrow, remorse and bitterness of the past time. He on his side felt, though not in so keen a degree, the sorrowful state of our mind, and where the control was very complete and the mortal highly sensitive, he would often fancy that things which we had done must have been done by himself, either in some former forgotten stage of existence, or else seen in some vivid dream they could scarcely recall.

This controlling or overshadowing of a mortal by an immortal is used in many ways, and those who foolishly make themselves liable to it either by a careless evil life, or by seeking in a frivolous spirit of mere curiosity to search out mysteries too deep for their shallow minds to fathom, often find to their cost that the low spirits who haunt the earth plane, and even those from much lower spheres, can often obtain so great a hold over a mortal that at last he becomes a mere puppet in their hands, whose body they can use at will. Many a weak-willed man and woman who in pure surroundings would lead only good and pure lives, are drawn by evil surroundings into sins for which they are but partly responsible--sins for which indeed those controlling spirits who have thus made use of these weak mortals, will be held responsible as well as the mortal sinner himself. For thus tempting and using another's organism those evil spirits will have to render a terrible account, since they have been doubly guilty. In sinning, themselves, and in dragging down another soul with them, they sink themselves to a depth from which many years, and in come instances many centuries of suffering cannot free them.

In my work I have had to act the part of controlling spirit many times, but I was sent to do so only in order that I might impress the mortal with a sense of the terrible consequences of yielding to sin, and also that I might, when not actually controlling the mortal myself, act as guard and watchman to protect him from the control of the wandering tempting spirits of the earth plane. My work was to raise the barrier of my strong will-force against theirs, and keep them back so that they could not come sufficiently en rapport with my charge to control him.

If, however, he had allowed himself to be already controlled by these lower spirits, they would still be able to project their thoughts and suggestions to him, though they did so with difficulty.

Although I did not know it at the time, and believed that upon myself would rest the responsibility of keeping safe those I was sent to guard, I was only the last link in a long chain of spirits who were all helping at the same time. Each spirit was a step in advance of the one below him, and each had to strengthen and help the one below him should he faint or fail in his task. My part was also intended to be a lesson to myself in self-denial and the sacrifice of my own comfort that I might help another. My condition as a spirit on the earth plane made me of use, seeing that I could oppose a material force of will against those tempting spirits in an atmosphere where a more refined spirit would have been unable to penetrate, and I as one of the earth-bound myself could come en rapport with the mortal more closely than a more advanced spirit would have been able to do. I had, by means of dreams when he slept and constant haunting thoughts while he waked, to impress upon the mind of the man I controlled what my experience had been, to make him feel all the terrible sufferings of remorse and fear, all the loathing of himself through which I had passed, and through which I passed again in bitter agony of soul while thus recalling them. All my feelings were transferred to his mind till he might truly have said he was haunted by all the terrible possibilities of his meditated sins.

Over this particular phase of my experiences I shall not dwell longer now, since it is one familiar to many on this side of life. I will but say that I returned from my mission with a consciousness that I had saved many others from the pitfalls into which I had fallen, and thereby had atoned in part for my own sins. Several times was I sent upon such missions and each time returned successful; and here I must pause to say that if my progress in the spirit world has been so rapid as to surprise most who knew of my first condition on entering it, and if I again and again resisted all the temptations that befell me, the credit is not so much due to myself as to the wonderful help and comfort that was given to me by the constant and unvarying love of her who was indeed my good angel, and whose image ever came between me and all harm. When all others might have pleaded to me in vain, I ever hearkened to her voice and turned aside.

When I was not helping someone yet in the earth body, I was sent to work amongst the unhappy spirits of the earth plane who were still wandering in its darkness even as I had at first done. And to them I went as one of the great Brotherhood of Hope, bearing in my hand the tiny starlike light which is the symbol of that order. Its rays would dispel the darkness around me, and I would see poor unhappy spirits crouching on the ground two or three together, or sunk in helpless misery in some corner by themselves, too hopeless, too unhappy to heed anything.

To them it was my work to point out how they could either be taken to such a House of Hope as the one in which I had been, or in other cases how they might, by trying to help others around them, help themselves and earn the gratitude of those who were even more hopeless than themselves. To each poor suffering soul a different balm of healing would be given, for each had known a different experience and each had had a different cause for his sins.

When my period of work in any place was finished, I used to return to the Twilight Land to rest in another large building which belonged to our brotherhood. It was somewhat like the other place in appearance only not quite so dark, nor so dismal, nor so bare, and in the little room which belonged to each there were such things as we had earned as the rewards of our labors. For instance, in my room, which was still somewhat bare-looking, I had one great treasure. This was a picture of my love. It seemed more like a reflection of her in a mirror than a mere painted image, for when I looked intently at her she would smile back at me in answer, as though her spirit was conscious of my gaze, and when I wished very much to know what she was doing, my picture would change and show me. This was regarded by all my companions as a great and wonderful privilege, and I was told it was as much the result of her love and constant thought for me as of my own efforts to improve. Since then I have been shown how this living image was thrown upon the light of the astral plane and then projected into its frame in my room, but I cannot explain it more fully in this book. Another gift from my darling was a white rose-bud, which I had in a small vase and which never seemed to fade or wither, but remained fresh and fragrant and ever an emblem of her love, so that I called her my white rose.

I had so longed for a flower. I had so loved flowers on earth and I had seen none since I saw those my darling put upon my grave. In this land there were no flowers, not even a leaf or blade of grass, not a tree or a shrub however stunted--for the dry arid soil of our selfishness had no blossom or green thing to give to any one of us; and it was when I told her this during one of the brief visits I used to pay her, and when through her own hand I was able to write short messages--it was, I say, when I told her that there was not one fair thing for me to look upon save only the picture of herself, that she asked that I might be given a flower from her, and this white rosebud was brought to my room by a spirit friend and left for me to find when I returned from earth and her. Ah! you who have so many flowers that you do not value them enough and leave them to wither unseen, you can scarce realize what joy this blossom brought to me nor how I have so treasured it and her picture and some loving words she once wrote to me, that I have carried them with me from sphere to sphere as I have risen, and shall, I hope, treasure them evermore.

From this Twilight Land I took many journeys and saw many strange and different countries, but all bore the same stamp of coldness and desolation.

One place was a great valley of grey stones, with dim, cold, grey hills shutting it in on every side, and this twilight sky overhead. Here again not a blade of grass, not one poor stunted shrub was to be seen, not one touch of color or brightness anywhere, only this dull desolation of grey stones. Those who dwelt in this valley had centered their lives and their affections in themselves and had shut up their hearts against all the warmth and beauty of unselfish love. They had lived only for themselves, their own gratification, their own ambitions, and now they saw nothing but themselves and the grey desolation of their hard selfish lives around them. There were a great many beings flitting uneasily about in this valley, but strange to say they had been so centered in themselves that they had lost the power to see anyone else.

These unhappy beings were invisible to each other until such time as the thought of another and the desire to do something for some one besides themselves should awaken, when they would become conscious of those near to them, and through their efforts to lighten another's lot they would improve their own, till at last their stunted affections would expand and the hazy valley of selfishness would hold them in its chains no more.

Beyond this valley I came upon a great, dry, sandy-looking tract of country where there was a scanty straggling vegetation, and where the inhabitants had begun in some places to make small attempts at gardens near their habitations. In some places these habitations were clustered so thickly together that they formed small towns and cities. But all bore that desolate ugly look which came from the spiritual poverty of the inhabitants. This also was a land of selfishness and greed, although not of such complete indifference to others' feelings as in the grey valley, and therefore they sought for a certain amount of companionship even with those around them. Many had come from the grey valley, but most were direct from the earth life and were now, poor souls, struggling to rise a little higher, and wherever this was the case and an effort was made to overcome their own selfishness, then the dry soil around their homes would begin to put forth tiny blades of grass and little stunted shoots of shrubs.

Such miserable hovels as were in this land! such ragged, repulsive, wretched-looking people, like tramps or beggars, yet many had been amongst earth's wealthiest and most eminent in fashionable life, and had enjoyed all that luxury could give! But because they had used their wealth only for themselves and their own enjoyments, giving to others but the paltry crumbs that they could spare from their own wealth and hardly notice that they had given them--because of this, I say, they were now here in this Twilight Land, poor as beggars in the true spiritual wealth of the soul which may be earned in the earthly life alike by the richest king or the poorest beggar, and without which those who come over to the spirit land--be they of earth's greatest or humblest--must come here to dwell where all are alike poor in spiritual things.

Here some of the people would wrangle and quarrel and complain that they had not been fairly treated in being in such a place, seeing what had been their positions in earth life. They would blame others as being more culpable than themselves in the matter, and wake a thousand excuses, a thousand pretences, to anyone who would listen to them and the story of what they would call their wrongs. Others would still be trying to follow out the schemes of their earthly lives and would try to make their hearers believe that they had found means (at the expense of someone else) of ending all this weary life of discomfort, and would plot and plan and try to carry out their own schemes, and spoil those of others as being likely to interfere with theirs, and so on would go the weary round of life in this Land of Unrest.

To all whom I found willing to listen to me I gave some word of hope, some thought of encouragement or help to find the true way out of this country, and so passed on through it and journeyed into the Land of Misers--a land given over to them alone, for few have sympathy with true misers save those who also share their all-absorbing desire to hoard simply for the pleasure of hoarding.

In this country were dark crooked-looking beings with long claw-like fingers, who were scratching in the black soil like birds of prey in search of stray grains of gold that here and there rewarded their toil; and when they had found any they would wrap them up in little wallets they carried and thrust them into their bosoms that they might lie next to their hearts, as the thing of all things most dear to them. As a rule they were lonely, solitary beings, who avoided each other by instinct lest they should be robbed of their cherished treasure.

Here I found nothing that I could do. Only one solitary man listened for a brief moment to what I had to say ere he returned to his hunt in the earth for treasure, furtively watching me till I was gone lest I should learn what he had already got. The others were all so absorbed in their search for treasure they could not even be made conscious of my presence, and I soon passed on from that bleak land.

From the Misers' Country I passed downwards into a dark sphere, which was really below the earth in the sense of being even lower in its spiritual inhabitants than parts of the earth plane.

Here it was very much like the Land of Unrest, only that the spirits who dwelt here were worse and more degraded looking. There was no attempt made at cultivation, and the sky overhead was almost dark like night, the light being only such as enabled them to see each other and the objects near them. Whereas in the Land of Unrest there were but wranglings and discontent and jealousy, here there were fierce fights and bitter quarrels. Here were gamblers and drunkards. Betting men, card sharpers, commercial swindlers, profligates, and thieves of every kind, from the thief of the slums to his well-educated counterpart in the higher circles of earth life. All whose instincts were roguish or dissipated, all who were selfish and degraded in their tastes were here, as well as many who would have been in a higher condition of spiritual life had not constant association on earth with this class of men deteriorated and degraded them to the level of their companions, so that at death they had gravitated to this dark sphere, drawn down by ties of association. It was to this last class that I was sent, for amongst them there was hope that all sense of goodness and right was not quenched, and that the voice of one crying to them in the wilderness of their despair might be heard and lead them back to a better land.

The wretched houses or dwellings of this dark Land of Misery were many of them large spacious places, but all stamped with the same apalling look of uncleanness, foulness and decay. They resembled large houses to be seen in some of our slums, once handsome mansions and fine palaces, the abodes of luxury, which have become the haunts of the lowest denizens of vice and crime. Here and there would be great lonely tracts of country with a few scattered wretched houses, mere hovels, and in other places the buildings and the people were huddled together in great gloomy degraded-looking copies of your large cities of earth. Everywhere squalor and dirt and wretchedness reigned; nowhere was there one single bright or beautiful or gracious thing for the eye to rest upon in all this scene of desolation, made thus by the spiritual emanations from the dark beings who dwelt there.

Amongst these wretched inhabitants I wandered with my little star of pure light, so small that it was but a bright spark flickering about in the darkness as I moved, yet around me it shed a soft pale light as from a star of hope that shone for those not too blinded by their own selfish evil passions to behold it. Here and there I would come upon some crouched in a doorway or against a wall, or in some miserable room, who would arouse themselves sufficiently to look at me with my light and listen to the words I spoke to them, and would begin to seek for the better way, the returning path to those upper spheres from which they had fallen by their sins. Some I would be able to induce to join me in my work of helping others, but as a rule they could only think of their own miseries, and long for something higher than their present surroundings, and even this, small as it seems, was one step, and the next one of thinking how to help others forward as well would soon follow.

One day in my wanderings through this country I came to the outskirts of a large city in the middle of a wide desolate plain. The soil was black and arid, more like those great cinder heaps that are seen near your iron works than anything I can liken it to. I was amongst a few dilapidated, tumble-down little cottages that formed a sort of fringe between the unhappy city and the desolate plain, when my ears caught the sound of quarreling and shouting coming from one of them, and curiosity made me draw near to see what the dispute might be about and if even here there might not be someone whom I could help.

It was more like a barn than a house. A great rough table ran the length of the room, and round it upon coarse little wooden stools were seated about a dozen or so of men.

Such men! It is almost an insult to manhood to give them the name. They were more like orangutangs, with the varieties of pigs and wolves and birds of prey expressed in their coarse bloated distorted features. Such faces, such misshapen bodies, such distorted limbs, I can in no way describe them! They were clothed in various grotesque and ragged semblances of their former earthly finery, some in the fashion of centuries ago, others in more modern garb, yet all alike ragged, dirty, and unkempt, the hair disheveled, the eyes wild and staring and glowing now with the fierce light of passion, now with the sullen fire of despair and vindictive malice. To me, then, it seemed that I had reached the lowest pit of hell, but since then I have seen a region lower still--far blacker, far more horrible, inhabited by beings so much fiercer, so much lower, that beside them these were tame and human. Later on I shall describe more fully these lowest beings, when I come to that part of my wanderings which took me into their kingdoms in the lowest hell, but the spirits whom I now saw fighting in this cottage were quarreling over a bag of coins which lay on the table. It had been found by one of them and then given to be gambled for by the whole party. The dispute seemed to be because each wanted to take possession of it himself without regard to the rights of anyone else at all. It was simply a question of the strongest, and already they were menacing each other in a violent fashion. The finder of the money, or rather the spiritual counterpart of our earthly money, was a young man, under thirty I should say, who still possessed the remains of good looks, and but for the marks that dissipation had planted on his face would have seemed unfit for his present surroundings and degraded associates. He was arguing that the money was his, and though he had given it to be played for fairly he objected to be robbed of it by anyone. I felt I had no business there, and amidst a wild chorus of indignant cries and protestations that they "supposed they were as well able to say what was honest as he was," I turned and left them. I had proceeded but a short way, and was almost opposite another deserted little hovel when the whole wild crew came struggling and fighting out of the cottage, wrestling with each other to get near the young man with the bag of money whom the foremost of them were beating and kicking and trying to deprive of it. This one of them succeeded in doing, whereupon they all set upon him, while the young man broke away from them and began running towards me. In a moment there was a wild yell set up to catch him and beat him for an imposter and a cheat, since the bag was empty of gold and had only stones in it, the money, like the fairy gold in the stories, having turned, not into withered leaves, but into hard stones.

Almost before I realized it the wretched young man was clutching hold of me and crying out to me to save him from those devils; and the whole lot were coming down upon us in hot pursuit of their victim. Quick as thought I sprang into the empty hovel which gave us the only hope of asylum, dragging the unfortunate young man with me, and slamming the door I planted my back against it to keep our pursuers out. My Goodness! how they did yell and stamp and storm and try to batter in that door; and how I did brace myself up and exert all the force of mind and body to keep them out! I did not know it then, but I know now that unseen powers helped me and held fast that door till, baffled and angry that they could not move it, they went off at last to seek for some fresh quarrel or excitement elsewhere.

When they had gone I turned to my companion who sat huddled in a heap, and almost stunned, in one corner of the hut, and, helping him to rise, I suggested that if he could make shift to walk a little, it would be well for us both to leave the place in case those men should think fit to return. With much pain and trouble I got him up and helped him slowly to a place of safety on the dark plain where, if we were without shelter, we were at least free from the danger of being surrounded. Then I did my best to relieve his sufferings by methods I had learned during my stay in the House of Hope, and after a time the poor fellow was able to speak and tell about himself and how he came to be in that dark country. He was, it seemed, but recently from earth life, having been shot by a man who was jealous of his attentions to his wife, and not without reason. The one redeemeing feature about this poor spirit's story was that he, poor soul, did not feel any anger or desire for revenge upon the man who had hurried him out of life, but only sorrow and shame for it all. What had hurt him most and had opened his eyes to his degradation, was the discovery that the woman for whose love it had all been done, was so callous, so selfish, so devoid of all true sense of love for either of them, that she was only occupied in thinking how it would affect herself and her social position in the world of fashion, and not one thought, save of anger and annoyance, had she given to either her unhappy husband or the victim of his jealous anger.

"When," said the young man, whom I shall call Raoul, "when I knew that I was truly dead and yet possessed the power to return to earth again, my first thought was to fly to her and console her if possible, or at least make her feel that the dead yet lived, and that even in death I thought of her. And how do you think I found her? Weeping for me? Sorrowing for him? No! not one atom. Only thinking of herself and wishing she had never seen us, or that she could blot us both out from her life by one coup-de-main, and begin life again with someone else higher in the social scale than either of us had been. The scales fell from my eyes, and I knew she had never loved me one particle. But I was rich, I was of the noblesse, and through my help she had hoped to climb another rung of the social ladder, and had willingly sunk herself into an adulteress, not for love of me, but to gain the petty triumph of queening it over some rival woman. I was nothing but a poor blind fool, and my life had paid the penalty of my folly. To her I was but an unpleasant memory of the bitter shame and scandal that had fallen upon her. Then I fled from earth in my bitterness, anywhere, I cared not where it was. I said I would believe no more in goodness or truth of any kind, and my wild thoughts and desires drew me down to this dark spot and these degraded revellers, amongst whom I found kindred spirits to those who had been my parasites and flatterers on earth, and amongst whom I had wasted my substance and lost my soul."

"And now, oh! unhappy friend," I said, "would you not even now seek the path of repentance that would lead you back to brighter lands and help you to regain the lost inheritance of your manhood and your higher self?"

"Now, alas! it is too late," said Raoul. "In hell, and surely this is hell, there is no longer hope for any."

"No hope for any?" I answered. "Say not so, my friend; those words are heard all too often from the lips of unhappy souls, for I can testify that even in the darkest despair there is ever given hope. I, too, have known a sorrow and bitterness as deep as yours; yet I had ever hope, for she whom I loved was as the pure angels, and her hands were ever stretched out to give me love and hope, and for her sake I work to give to others the hope given to myself. Come, let me lead you and I will guide you to that better land."

"And who art thou, oh! friend, with the kind words and still kinder deeds to whom in truth I might say I owed my life; but had I not learned that in this place, alas! one cannot die--one can suffer to the point of death and even all its pains, yet death comes not to any, for we have passed beyond it, and it would seem must live through an eternity of suffering? Tell me who you are and how you come to be here, speaking words of hope with such confidence. I might fancy you an angel sent down to help me, but that you resemble myself too much for that."

Then I told him my history, and how I was working myself upwards even as he might do, and also spoke of the great hope I had always before me, that in time I should be fit to join my sweet love in a land where we should be no more parted.

"And she?" he said, "is content, you think, to wait for you? She will spend all her life lonely on earth that she may join you in heaven when you shall get there? Bah! mon ami, you deceive yourself. It is a mirage that you pursue. Unless she is either old or very plain, no woman will dream of living forever alone for your sake. She will for a time, I grant you, if she is romantic, or if no one come to woo her, but unless she is an angel she will console herself by and by, believe me. If your hopes are no more well founded than that I shall feel only sorry for you."

I confess his words angered me somewhat; they echoed the doubts that always haunted me, and were like a cold shower bath upon all the warmth of romance with which I had buoyed myself up. It was partly to satisfy my own doubts as well as his that I said, with some heat:

"If I take you to earth and we find her mourning only for me, thinking only of me, will you believe then that I know what I speak about and am under no delusion? Will you admit that your experience of life and of women may not apply to all, and that there is something that even you can learn on this as on other matters?"

"My good friend, believe me that I ask your pardon with all my soul if my unbelief has pained you. I admire your faith and would I could have but a little of it myself. By all means let us go and see her."

I took his hand and then "willing" intently that we should go to my beloved, we began to rise and rush through space with the speed of thought almost, till we found ourselves upon earth and standing in a room. I saw her guardian spirit watching over my beloved, and the dim outline of the room and its furniture, but my friend Raoul saw nothing but the form of my darling seated in her chair, and looking like some of the saints from the brightness of her spirit and the pale soft aureole of light that surrounded her, a spiritual light invisible to you of earth but seen by those on the spiritual side of life around those whose lives are good and pure, just as a dark mist surrounds those who are not good.

"Mon Dieu!" cried Raoul, sinking upon his knees at her feet. "It is an angel, a saint you have brought me to see, not a woman. She is not of earth at all."

Then I spoke to her by name, and she heard my voice and her face brightened and the sadness vanished from it, and she said softly: "My dearest, are you indeed there? I was longing for you to come again. I can think and dream of nothing but you. Can you touch me yet?" She put out her hand and for one brief moment mine rested in it, but even that moment made her shiver as though an icy wind had struck her.

"See, my darling one, I have brought an unhappy friend to ask your prayers. And I would have him to know that there are some faithful women on earth--some true love to bless us with were we but fit to enjoy it."

She had not heard clearly all that I said, but her mind caught its sense, and she smiled, so radiant a smile, and said: "Oh! yes, I am ever faithful to you, my beloved, as you are to me, and some day we shall be so very, very happy."

Then Raoul who was still kneeling before her, held out his hands and tried to touch hers, but the invisible wall kept him away as it had done me, and he drew back, crying out to her: "If your heart is so full of love and pity, spare some to me who am indeed unhappy and need your prayers. Pray that I, too, may be helped, and I shall know your prayers are heard where mine were not worthy to be, and I shall hope that even for me pardon may yet be possible."

My darling heard the words of this unhappy man, and kneeling down beside her chair offered up a little simple prayer for help and comfort to us all. And Raoul was so touched, so softened, that he broke down completely, and I had to take him by the hand and lead him back to the spirit land, though not now to a region devoid of hope.

From that time Raoul and I worked together for a little in the dark land he had now ceased to dwell in, and from day to day he grew more hopeful. By nature he was most vivacious and buoyant, a true Frenchman, full of airy graceful lightness of heart which even the awful surroundings of that gloomy spot could not wholly extinguish. We became great friends, and our work was pleasanter from being shared. Our companionship was, however, not destined to last long then, but we have since met and worked together many times, like comrades in different regiments whom the chances of war may bring together or separate at any time.

CHAPTER VIII.--Temptation.

I was again called upon to go to earth upon a mission of help, and to leave for a time my wanderings in the spirit spheres; and now it was that the greatest and most terrible temptation of my life came to me. In the course of my work I was brought across one still in the earth body, whose influence over my earthly life had done more than aught else to wreck and spoil it, and though I also had not been blameless--far indeed from it--yet I could not but feel an intense bitterness and thirst for revenge whenever I thought of this person and all the wrongs that I had suffered--wrongs brooded over till at times I felt as if my feelings must have vent in some wild burst of passionate resentment.

In my wanderings upon the earth plane I had learned many ways in which a spirit can still work mischief to those he hates who are yet in the flesh. Far more power is ours than you would dream of, but I feel it is wiser to let the veil rest still upon the possibilities the world holds even after death for the revengeful spirit. I could detail many terrible cases I know of as having actually taken place--mysterious murders and strange crimes committed, none knew why or how, by those on earth whose brains were so disordered that they were not themselves responsible for their actions, and were but the tools of a possessing spirit. These and many kindred things are known to us in the spirit spheres where circumstances often wear a very different aspect from the one shown to you. The old beliefs in demoniacal possession were not so visionary after all, only these demons or devils had themselves been once the denizens of earth.

It so happened to me then, that when I came once more, after long years of absence, across this person whom I so hated, all my old feelings of suffering and anger revived, but with tenfold more force than is possible in earth life, for a spirit has far, far greater capabilities of suffering or enjoyments, of pleasure or pain, love or hate, than one whose senses are still veiled and deadened by the earthly envelope, and thus all the senses of a dismbodied spirit are tenfold more acute.

Thus when I once more found myself beside this person, the desire for my long-suspended revenge woke again, and with the desire a most devilish plan for its accomplishment suggested itself to me. For my desire of vengeance drew up to me from their haunts in the lowest hell, spirits of so black a hue, so awful a type, that never before had I seen such beings or dreamed that out of some nightmare fable they could exist. These beings cannot live upon the earth plane nor even in the lower spheres surrounding it, unless there be congenial mortals or some strong magnetic attraction to hold them there for a time, and though they often rise in response to an intensely evil desire upon the part of either a mortal or spirit on the earth plane, yet they cannot remain long, and the moment the attracting force becomes weakened, like a rope that breaks, they lose their hold and sink down again to their own dark abodes.

At times of great popular indignation and anger, as in some great revolt of an oppressed people in whom all sense but that of suffering and anger has been crushed out, the bitter wrath and thirst for revenge felt by the oppressed will draw around them such a cloud of these dark beings, that horrors similar to those witnessed in the great French Revolution and kindred revolts of down-trodden people, will take place, and the maddened populace are for a time completely under the control of those spirits who are truly as devils.

In my case these horrible beings crowded round me with delight, whispered in my ears and pointed out a way of revenge so simple, so easy, and yet so horrible, so apalling in its wickedness, that I shall not venture to write it down lest the idea of it might be given to some other desperate one, and like seed falling into a fruitful soil bring forth its baleful blossoms.

At any other time I should have shrunk back in horror from these beings and their foul suggestions. Now in my mad passion I welcomed them and was about to invoke their aid to help me to accomplish my vengeance, when like the tones of a silver bell there fell upon my ears the voice of my beloved, to whose pleadings I was never deaf and whose tones could move me as none else could The voice summoned me to come to her by all that we both held sacred, by all the vows we had made and all the hopes we had cherished, and though I could not so instantly abandon my revenge, yet I was drawn as by a rope to the one I loved from the one I hated.

And the whole wild crew of black devils came with me, clinging to me and trying to hold me back, yet with an ever feebler hold as the voice of love and purity and truth penetrated more and more deeply to my heart.

And then I saw my beloved standing in her room, her arms stretched out to draw me to her, and two strong bright spirit guardians by her side, while around her was drawn a circle of flaming silver light as though a wall of lightning encircled her; yet at her call I passed through it and stood at her side.

The dark crowd sought to follow, but were kept back by the flaming ring. One of the boldest made a rush at me as I passed through, and tried to catch hold, but his hand and arm were caught by the flame of light and shriveled up as though thrust into a furnace. With a yell of pain and rage he drew back amidst a wild howl of derisive laughter from the rest.

With all the power of her love my darling pleaded with me that I should give up this terrible idea, and promise her nevermore to yield to so base a thought. She asked me if I loved my revenge so much better than I loved her, that to gratify it I would raise up between us the insurmountable barrier of my meditated crime? Was her love indeed so little to me after all?

At first I would not, could not yield, but at last she began to weep, and then my heart melted as though her tears had been warm drops of her heart's blood falling on it to thaw its ice, and in bitter anguish of soul that I should have caused her to shed tears I knelt at her feet and prayed to be forgiven my wicked thought--prayed that I might still be left with her love to cheer me, still with her for my one thought, one hope, my all. And as I prayed the circle of dark spirits, who had been fighting to get in and beckoning to me and trying to draw me out, broke like a cloud of black mist when the wind scatters it, and they sank away down to their own abode again, while I sank exhausted at my darling's feet.

At times after this I saw the dark spirits draw near to me, though never again could they come close, for I had an armor in my darling's love and my promise to her which was proof against all their attacks.

I was next sent to visit what will indeed seem a strange country to exist in the spirit world. The Land of Ice and Snow--the Frozen Land--in which lived all those who had been cold and selfishly calculating in their earthly lives. Those who had crushed out and chilled and frozen from their own lives and the lives of others, all those warm sweet impulses and affections which make the life of heart and soul. Love had been so crushed and killed by them that its sun could not shine where they were, and only the frost of life remained.

Great statesmen were amongst those whom I saw dwelling in this land, but they were those who had not loved their country nor sought its good. Only their own ambitions, their own aggrandizement had been their aim, and to me they now appeared to dwell in great palaces of ice and on the lofty frozen pinnacles of their own ambitions. Others more humble and in different paths in life I saw, but all alike were chilled and frozen by the awful coldness and barrenness of a life from which all warmth, all passion, was shut out. I had learned the evils of an excess of emotion and of passion, now I saw the evils of their entire absence. Thank God this land had far fewer inhabitants than the other, for terrible as are the effects of mis-used love, they are not so hard to overcome as the absence of all the tender feelings of the human heart.

There were men here who had been prominent members of every religious faith and every nationality on your earth. Roman Catholic cardinals and priests of austere and pious but cold and selfish lives, Puritan preachers, Methodist ministers, Presbyterian divines, Church of England bishops and clergymen, missionaries, Brahmin priests, Parsees, Egyptians, Mohammedans--in short all sorts and all nationalities were to be found in the Frozen Land, yet in scarcely one was there enough warmth of feeling to thaw the ice around themselves even in a small degree. When there was even a little tiny drop of warmth, such as one tear of sorrow, then the ice began to melt and there was hope for that poor soul.

There was one man whom I saw who appeared to be enclosed in a cage of ice; the bars were of ice, yet they were as bars of polished steel for strength. This man had been one of the Grand Inquisitors of the Inquisition in Venice, and had been one of those whose very names sent terror to the heart of any unfortunate who fell into their clutches; a most celebrated name in history, yet in all the records of his life and acts there was not one instance where one shade of pity for his victims had touched his heart and caused him to turn aside, even for one brief moment, from his awful determination in torturing and killing those whom the Inquisition got into its toils. A man known for his own hard austere life, which had no more indulgence for himself than for others. Cold and pitiless, he knew not what it was to feel one answering throb awake in his heart for another's sufferings. His face was a type of cold unemotional cruelty; the long thin high nose, the pointed sharp chin, the high and rather wide cheek bones, the thin straight cruel lips like a thin line across the face, the head somewhat flat and wide over the ears, while the deep-set penetrating eyes glittered from their penthouse brows with the cold steely glitter of a wild beast's.

Like a procession of spectres I saw the wraiths of some of this man's many victims glide past him, maimed and crushed, torn and bleeding from their tortures--pallid ghosts, wandering astral shades, from which the souls had departed forever, but which yet clung around this man, unable to decay into the elements whilst his magnetism attached them, like a chain, to him. The souls and all the higher elements had forever left those--which were true astral shells--yet they possessed a certain amount of vitality--only it was all drawn from this man, not from the released spirits which had once inhabited them. They were such things as those ghosts are made of which are seen haunting the spot where some one too good and innocent to be so chained to earth, has been murdered. They seem to their murderers and others to live and haunt them, yet the life of such astrals (or ghosts) is but a reflected one, and ceases as soon as remorse and repentance have sufficed to sever the tie that links them to their murderers.

Other spirits I saw haunting this man, and taunting him with his own helplessness and their past sufferings, but these were very different looking; they were more solid in appearance and possessed a power and strength and intelligence wanting in those other misty-looking shades. These were spirits whose astral forms still held the immortal souls imprisoned in them, though they had been so crushed and tortured that only the fierce desire of revenge remained. These spirits were incessant in their endeavor to get at their former oppressor and tear him to pieces, and the icy cage seemed to be regarded by him as being as much a protection from them as a prison for himself. One more clever than the rest had constructed a long, sharp-pointed pole which he thrust through the bars to prod at the man within, and wonderful was the activity he displayed in trying to avoid its sharp point. Others had sharp short javelins which they hurled through the bars at him. Others again squirted foul, slimy water, and at times the whole crowd would combine in trying to hurl themselves en masse upon the sheltering bars to break through, but in vain. The wretched man within, whom long experience had taught the impregnability of his cage, would taunt them in return with a cold crafty enjoyment of their fruitless efforts.

To my mental query as to whether this man was ever released, an answer was given to me by that majestic spirit whose voice I had heard at rare times speaking to me, from the time when I heard it first at my own grave. On various occasions when I had asked for help or knowledge, this spirit had spoken to me, as now, from a distance, his voice sounding to me as the voice spoken of by the prophets of old when they thought the Lord spoke to them in the thunder. This voice rang in my ears with its full deep tones, yet neither the imprisoned spirit nor those haunting him heard it; their ears were deaf so that they could not hear, and their eyes blind so that they could not see.

And to me the voice said: "Son, behold the thoughts of this man for one brief moment--see how he would use liberty were it his."

And I saw, as one sees images reflected in a mirror, the mind of this man. First the thought that he could get free, and when once free he could force himself back to earth and the earth plane, and once there he could find some still in the flesh whose aspirations and ambitions were like his own, and through their help he would forge a still stronger yoke as of iron to rivet upon men's necks, and found a still crueller tyranny--a still more pitiless Inquisition, if that were possible, which should crush out the last remnant of liberty left to its oppressed victims. He knew he would sway a power far greater than his earthly power, since he would work with hands and brain freed from all earthly fetters, and would be able to call up around him kindred spirits, fellow workers with souls as cold and cruel as his own. He seemed to revel in the thought of the fresh oppressions he could plan, and took pride to himself in the recollection that he had ever listened unmoved to the shrieks and groans and prayers of the victims he had tortured to death. From the love of oppression and for his own relentless ambition had he worked, making the aggrandizement of his order but the pretext for his actions, and in no single atom of his hard soul was there awakened one spark of pity or remorse. Such a man set free to return to earth would be a source of danger far more deadly than the most fierce wild beast, since his powers would be far less limited. He did not know that his vaunted Inquisition, which he still sought to strengthen in all its deadly powers, had become a thing of the past, swept away from the face of God's earth by a power far mightier than any he could wield; and that, like the dark and terrible age in which it had sprung up like a noisome growth, it had gone nevermore to return--thank God!--never again to disgrace humanity by the crimes committed in the name of him who came only to preach peace and love on earth-- gone, with its traces and its scars left yet upon the human mind in its shaken and broken trust in a God and an immortality. The recoil of that movement which at last swept away the Inquisition is yet felt on earth, and long years must pass before all which was good and pure and true and had survived throughout even those dark ages shall reassert its power and lead men back to their faith in a God of Love, not a God of Horrors, as those oppressors painted him.

From this Frozen Land I turned away chilled and saddened. I did not care to linger there or explore its secrets, though it may be that again at some future time I may visit it. I felt that there was nothing I could do in that land, none I could understand, and they but froze and revolted me without my doing them any good.

On my way back from the Frozen Land to the Land of Twilight, I passed a number of vast caverns called the "Caverns of Slumber," wherein lay a great multitude of spirits in a state of complete stupor, unconscious of all around them. These, I learned, were the spirits of mortals who had killed themselves with opium eating and smoking, and whose spirits had thus been deprived of all chance of development, and so had retrograded instead of advancing and growing--just as a limb tied up and deprived of motion withers away--and now they were feebler than an unborn infant, and as little able to possess conscious life.

In many cases their sleep would last for centuries; in others, where the indulgence in the drug had been less, it might only last for twenty, fifty, or a hundred years. These spirits lived, and that was all, their senses being little more developed than those of some fungus growth which exists without one spark of intelligence; yet in them the soul germ had lingered, imprisoned like a tiny seed in the wrapping of some Egyptian mummy, which, long as it may lie thus, is yet alive, and will in a kindly soil sprout forth at last. These caverns, in which kind spirit hands had laid them, were full of life-giving magnetism, and a number of attendant spirits who had themselves passed through a similar state from opium poisoning in their own earth lives, were engaged in giving what life they could pour into those comatose spirit bodies which lay like rows of dead people all over the floor.

By slow degrees, according as the spirit had been more or less injured by the drug taken in the earthly life, these wretched beings would awake to consciousness and all the sufferings experienced by the opium eater when deprived of his deadly drug. By long and slow degrees the poor spirits would awaken, sense by sense, till at last like feeble suffering children they would become fit for instruction, when they would be sent to institutions like your idiot asylums, where the dawning intellect would be trained and helped to develop, and those faculties recovered which had been all but destroyed in the earth life.

These poor souls would only learn very slowly, because they had to try to learn now, without the aids of the earthly life, those lessons which it had been designed to teach. Like drunkards (only more completely) they had paralyzed brain and senses and had avoided, not learned, the lessons of the earthly life and its development of the spirit.

To me these Caves of Slumber were inexpressibly sad to behold--not less so that those wretched slumberers were unconscious for so long of the valuable time they lost in their dreamless, hopeless sleep of stagnation.

Like the hare in the fable, while they slept others less swift won the race, and these poor souls might try in vain through countless ages to recover the time which they had lost.

When these slumberers shall at last awake, to what a fate do they not waken, through what an awful path must they not climb to reach again that point in the earth life from which they have fallen! Does it not fill our souls with horror to think that there are those on earth who live, and pile up wealth through the profits made from that dreadful trade in opium, which not alone destroys the body, but would seem to desroy even more fatally the soul, till one would despondently ask if there be indeed hope for these its victims?

These awful caves--these terrible stupified spirits--can any words point a fate more fearful than theirs? To awaken at last with the intellects of idiots, to grow, through hundreds of years, back at last to the possession of the mental powers of children--not of grown men and women. Slow, slow, must be their development even then, for unlike ordinary children they have almost lost the power to grow, and take many generations of time to learn what one generation on earth could have taught them. I have heard it said that many of the unhappy beings when they have attained at last to the development of infants, are sent back to earth to be reincarnated in an earthly body, that they may enjoy again the advantages they have misused before. But of this I only know by hearsay, and cannot give any opinion of my own upon its truth. I only know that I should be glad to think of any such possibility for them which could shorten the process of development or help them to regain all that they had lost.

In my home in the Twilight Land I rested now for a time, studying to learn more of myself and the powers I had within me, and seeking to apply the lessons I had learned in my wanderings. My chief instructor at this time was a man like myself in many respects, who had lived a similar life on earth and had passed through the lower spheres, as I was now doing, and who had become a dweller in a bright land of sunshine from which he came constantly to teach and help those of the Brotherhood who, like myself, were his pupils.

There was likewise another teacher or guide whom I sometimes saw, whose influence over me was even greater, and from whom I learned many strange things, but as he was in a much more advanced sphere than the other, it was but seldom that I could see him as a distinct personality. His teachings came to me more as mental suggestions or inspirational discourses in answer to some questioning thought on my part. This spirit I shall not now describe to you, as at this time of my sojourn in the Twilight Land I saw him but very dimly, and only clearly when my progression had carried me into a brighter state.

Though this man was not fully visible to me I was often conscious of his presence and his aid, and when later on I learned that he had been my principal guardian spirit during my earthly life, I could easily trace many thoughts and suggestions, many of my higher aspirations, to his influence; and it was his voice that had so often spoke to me in warning or in comfort when I struggled on almost overwhelmed with my terrible position on first entering the spirit world. In the days of darkness I had been faintly conscious of his form flitting in and out of my little cell, and soothing my terrible sufferings with his magnetism and his wonderful knowledge and power.

On returning to the Twilight Land from the darker spheres I had visited, I felt almost like returning to a home, for, bare and shabby as my room looked, and small and narrow as it was, it yet held all my greatest treasures: my picture mirror in which I could see my beloved, and the rose, and the letter she had sent to me. Moreover I had friends there, companions in misfortune like myself, and though we were as a rule much alone, meditating upon our past mistakes and their lessons, yet at times it was very pleasant to have one friend or another come in to see you, and since we were all alike men who had disgraced ourselves by our earthly lives and were now seeking to follow the better way, there was even in that a bond of sympathy. Our life, could I make you fully realize it, would indeed seem strange to you. It was like and yet unlike an earthly life. For instance, we ate at times a simple sort of food provided for us, it would seem, by magic whenever we felt hungry, but often for a week at a time we would not think of food, unless indeed it was one of us who had been fond of good eating on earth, and in that case the desire would be much more frequent and

50

troublesome to satisfy. For myself my tastes had been somewhat simple, and neither eating nor drinking had in themselves possessed special attractions for me.

There was always around us this twilight, which was never varied with dark night or bright day, and which was most especially trying to me in its monotony. I so love light and sunshine. To me it was ever as a life-giving bath. I had been born in a land of earth where all is sunshine and flowers.

Then although we usually walked about this building and the surrounding country much as you do, we could float a little at will, though not so well as more advanced spirits do, and if we were in a great hurry to go anywhere our wills seemed to carry us there with the speed almost of thought.

As for sleep, we could spend long intervals without feeling its need, or, again, we could lie and sleep for weeks at a time, sometimes semi-conscious of all that passed, at others in the most complete of slumbers. Another strange thing was our dress-- which never seemed to wear out and renewed itself in some mysterious fashion. All through this period of my wanderings and while I was in this abode it was of a dark--a very dark--blue color, with a yellow girdle round the waist, and an anchor worked in yellow on the left sleeve, with the words, "Hope is Eternal," below it. There were close-fitting undergarments of the same dark color. The robe was long and such as you see penitent brotherhoods or monks wear on earth, with a hood hung from the shoulders, which could be used to cover the head and face of any who desired to screen their features from view; and indeed there were often times when we wished to do so, for suffering and remorse had made such changes in us that we were often glad to hide our faces from the gaze of those we loved. The hollow eyes, sunken cheeks, wasted and bent forms, and deep lines suffering had traced upon each face told their own story but too well, and such of us as had dear friends on earth or in the spirit land still grieving for our loss, sought often at times to hide from their eyes our disfigured forms and faces.

Our lives had somewhat of monotony about them in the regular order in which our studies and our lectures followed each other like clockwork. At certain stages--for they did not count time by days or weeks, but only as advance was made in the development of each spirit--when a lesson had been learned, in a longer or shorter time according to the spiritual and intellectual development, the spirit was advanced to a higher branch of the subject studied.

Some remain a very long time before they can grasp the meaning of the lesson shown to them; if so, the spirit is in no way hurried or pressed on as is done in earth education, where life seems all too short for learning. As a spirit a man has all eternity before him and can stand still or go on as he pleases, or he may remain where he is till he has thought out and grasped clearly what has been shown, and then he is ready for the next step, and so on. There is no hurrying anyone faster than he chooses to go; no interference with his liberty to live on in the same state of undevelopment if he wishes, so long as he interferes with the liberty of no one else and conforms to the simple rule which governs that great Brotherhood, the rule of freedom and sympathy for all. None were urged to learn, and none were kept back from doing so; it was all voluntary, and did anyone seek (as many did) to leave this place, he was free to go where he would, and to return again if he wished; the doors were closed to none, either in going or returning, and none ever sought to reproach another with his faults or shortcomings, for each felt the full depth of his own.

Some had been years there, I learned, for to them the lessons were hard and slow to be learned. Others, again, had broken away and gone back to the life of the earth plane so many times that they had descended to the lowest sphere at last, and gone through a course of purification in that other House of Hope where I had first been. They had appeared to go back instead of forward, yet even this had not been in truth a retrogression, but only a needful lesson, since they were thus cured of the desire to try the pleasures of the earth plane again. A few, like myself, who had a strong and powerful motive to rise, made rapid progress, and soon passed on from step to step, but there were, alas! too many who required all the hope and all the help that could be given to sustain and comfort them through all their trials; and it was my lot to be able, out of the storehouse of my own hopefulness, to give a share to others less fortunate who were not blessed, as I was, with a stream of love and sympathy flowing ever to me from my beloved on earth, cheering me on to fresh efforts with its promise of joy and peace at last.

CHAPTER XI.--Ahrinziman.

To these meetings for materialization I was always accompanied by that majestic spirit of whom I have already spoken, and whom I now knew by his name, Ahrinziman, "the Eastern Guide." As I was now beginning to see him more clearly I will describe him to you.

He was a tall, majestic-looking man with long flowing white garments bordered with yellow, and a yellow girdle around his waist. His complexion was that of an Eastern, of a pale dusky tint. The features were straight and beautifully molded, as one sees them in the statues of Apollo, though their peculiar Eastern cast caused them to vary a little from the perfect Grecian type. His eyes were large, dark, soft and tender as a woman's, yet with a latent fire and force of passion in their depths which, though subdued and controlled by his strong will, yet gave a warmth and intensity to his looks and manner, from which I could easily believe that in his earth life he had known all the sweetness and all the passion of violent love and hate. Now his passions were purified from all earthly dross, and served but as links of sympathy between him and those who, like myself, were still struggling to subdue their lower natures, and conquer their passions. A short silky black beard covered his cheeks and chin, and his soft wavy black hair hung somewhat long upon his shoulders. His figure, though tall and powerful, had all the litheness and supple grace of his Eastern race, for so marked are the types of each race that even the spirit bears still the impress of its earthly nationality, and although centuries had passed since Ahrinziman had left the earthly body he retained all the peculiarities which distinguished the Eastern from the Western people. The spirit was strangely like an earthly mortal man, and yet so unlike in that peculiar dazzling brightness of form and feature which no words can ever paint, nor pen describe, that strange and wonderful ethereality, and yet distinct tangibility, which only those who have seen a spirit of the higher spheres can truly understand. In his earth life he had been a deep student of the occult sciences, and since his entry into the spirit world he had expanded and increased his knowledge till to me it seemed there was no limit to his powers. Like myself, of a warm and passionate nature, he had learned during long years of spirit life to overcome and subdue all his passions, till now he stood upon a pinnacle of power whence he stooped down ever to draw up strugglers like myself, whom his sympathy and ready understanding of our weaknesses made ready to receive his help, while one who had never himself fallen would have spoken to us in vain. With all his gentleness and ready sympathy, however, he had also a power of will against which, when he chose to exert it, one sought in vain to fight, and I have beheld on more than one occasion some of the wild passionate beings amongst whom he worked, brought to a stop in something they were about to do which would have harmed themselves or others. They would be spellbound and unable to move a limb, yet he had never touched them. It was but by his own powerful will, which was so much stronger than theirs that for the time they were paralyzed. Then he would argue the matter with them, kindly and frankly, and show to them in some of his wonderful ways the full consequences to themselves and others of what they were about to do, and when he had done so he would lift from them the spell of his will and leave them free to act as they desired, free to commit the meditated sin now that they knew its consequences; and seldom have I known any who, after so solemn a warning, would still persist in following their own path. I myself have always been considered one whose will was strong, and who could not readily give it up to any other's, but beside this spirit I have felt myself a child, and have bowed more than once to the force of his decisions. And here let me say that in all things in the spirit world man is free--free as air--to follow his own inclinations and desires if he wishes, and does not choose to take the advice offered to him. The limitations to a man's own indulgence and the extent to which he can infringe upon the rights of others, are regulated by the amount of law and order existing in the sphere to which he belongs.

For example, in the lowest sphere of all, where no law prevails but the law of the strongest oppressor, you may do what you please; you may injure or oppress another to the very last limits of his endurance, and those who are stronger than you will do the same to you. The most oppressed slaves on earth are less unhappy than those whom I have seen in the lowest sphere of all, where no law prevails and where only those spirits are to be found who have defied all laws of God or man and have been a law to themselves, exercising the most boundless oppression and wrong towards their neighbors. In those spheres which I shall shortly describe, it seems that strong, cruel and oppressive as a spirit may be, there is always found someone still stronger to oppress him, some one still crueller, still wickeder, still more oppressive, till at last you arrive at those who may truly be said to reign in hell--Kings and Emperors of Evil! And it goes on till at last the very excess of evil will work its own cure. The worst and most tyrannical will long for some other state of things, some laws to restrain, some power to control; and that feeling will be the first step, the first desire for a better life, which will give the Brothers of Hope sent to work in those dark spheres, the little loophole through which to give the idea of improvement, and the hope that it is still possible for them. As the spirit progresses upwards there will be found in each circle of the ladder of progress an increased degree of law and order prevailing, to which he will be ready to conform himself, as he expects others to conform where the laws affect him. The perfect observance of the highest moral laws is found only in the highest spheres, but there are many degrees of observance, and he who respects the rights of others will find his rights respected, while he who tramples upon his neighbor will in turn be trampled upon by the stronger ones.

In all respects man in the spirit world is free to work or to be idle, to do good or to do evil, to win a blessing or a curse. Such as he is, such will be his surroundings, and the sphere for which he is fitted must ever be the highest to which he can attain till his own efforts fit him to become a dweller in one higher. Thus the good need no protection against the evil in the spirit world. Their own different states place an insurmountable barrier between them. Those above can always descend at will to visit or help those below them, but between them and the lower spirits there is a great gulf which the lower ones cannot pass. Only upon your earth and on other planets where material life exists, can there be the mixture of good and evil influences with almost equal power. I say almost equal, since even on earth the good have the greater power, unless man shuts himself out from their aid by the indulgence of his lower passions.

In days of old when men's hearts were simple as little children's, the spirit world lay close at their doors and they knew it not, but now men have drifted far from it, and are like mariners upon a raft, who are seeking now again through fog and mist to find it. Kind pilots of the spirit world are striving to guide and help them to reach that radiant land that they may bring back a bright store of hope and light for the weary strugglers upon earth.

CHAPTER XII.--My Second Death.

The meetings for materialization were held once a fortnight, and from the number of them I judged that about three months had passed, when I was told by Ahrinziman to prepare myself for a great change which was about to take place in myself and my surroundings, and which would mean my passing into a higher sphere. I have heard the spheres divided differently by different spirit teachers, and it is not very important that they should be all divided by the same standard, since these divisions are very similar to mapping out a country where the boundaries melt so imperceptibly into one another that it is not very essential to have the limits defined with perfect exactitude, since the changes in the countries and the people will of themselves mark their different states as you progress on your journey. Thus, then, some will tell you there are seven spheres and that the seventh means the heaven spoken of in the Bible; others say there are twelve spheres; others again extend the number. Each sphere is, however, divided into circles, usually twelve to a sphere, though here again some spirits will reckon them differently, just as your standards of measurement on earth differ in different countries, yet the thing they measure remains the same. For myself, I have been used to count that there are seven spheres above the earth and seven below it--using the terms above and below as signifying the nearness to, or distance from, the great central sun of our solar system, the nearest point of attraction towards that sun being considered to be our highest point of attainment (while in the limits of the earth spheres), and the farthest away being regarded as our lowest or most degraded sphere. Each sphere, then, being subdivided into twelve circles, which are blended so closely into each other that you appear to pass almost insensibly from one to the other. I had hitherto been in what is called the earth plane, which like a great broad belt circles around the earth and permeates its atmosphere. This earth plane may be said to comprehend within its bounds the first of the seven spheres above and the first of those below the earth, and is used commonly in describing the habitations of those spirits who are said to be earth-bound in a greater or less degree because they are not able to sink below the earth attractions nor to free themselves from its influences.

I was now told that I had so far freed myself from the earth's attractions and overcome my desires for earthly things, that I was able to pass into the second sphere. The passing from the body of a lower sphere into that of a higher one is often, though not invariably, accomplished during a deep sleep which closely resembles the death-sleep of the spirit in leaving the earthly body. As a spirit grows more elevated, more etherealized, this change is accompanied by a greater degree of consciousness, till at last the passing from one high sphere to another is simply like changing one garb for another a little finer, discarding one spiritual envelope for a more ethereal one. Thus the soul passes onward, growing less and less earthly (or material) in its envelopment, till it passes beyond the limits of our earth spheres into those of the solar systems.

It happened, then, that upon my return from one of my visits to the earth, I felt overpowered by a strange unusual sense of drowsiness, which was more like paralysis of the brain than sleep.

I retired to my little room in the Twilight Land, and throwing myself upon my couch, sank at once into a profound dreamless slumber like unto the unconscious sleep of death.

In this state of unconsciousness I lay for about two weeks of earthly time, and during it my soul passed from the disfigured astral body and came forth like a newborn child, clothed in a brighter, purer spiritual envelope, which my efforts at overcoming the evil in myself had created for it. Only I was not born as an infant but as a full grown man, even as my experience and knowledge had been those of a mature spirit. There are some mortals whose knowledge of life is so limited, whose minds have been so little cultivated, and whose natures are so simple and childlike, that they are born into the spirit world as mere children, however many years of earth life they may have known, but it was not so with me, and in assuming my new condition I also possessed the development in age which my earth life had given me.

In a state of perfect unconsciousness my newborn soul was borne by the attendant spirit friends into the second sphere, where I lay sleeping my dreamless sleep till the time came for my awakening.

The discarded astral envelope I had left was by the power of attendant spirits dissolved into the elements of the earth plane, even as my earthly body left at my first death would decay into the earthly material from which it had been taken,--dust returning unto dust again, while the immortal soul passed on to a higher state.

Thus did I pass through my second death and awake to the resurrection of my higher self.

PART II.
The Dawn of Light.

On my awakening for the second time from a sleep of death to consciousness in the spirit world, I found that I was in much pleasanter surroundings. There was daylight at last, though it was as that of a dull day without sun, yet what a blessed change from the dismal twilight and the dark night!

I was in a neat little room quite like an earthly one, lying upon a little bed of soft white down. Before me was a long window looking out upon a wide stretch of hills and undulating country. There were no trees or shrubs to be seen, and hardly any flowers, save here and there some little simple ones like flowering weeds, yet even these were refreshing to the eyes, and there were ferns and grass clothing the ground with a carpet of verdure instead of the hard bare soil of the Twilight Land.

This region was called the "Land of Dawn," and truly the light was as the day appears before the sun has arisen to warm it. The sky was of a pale blue grey, and white cloudlets seemed to chase each other across it and float in quiet masses on the horizon. You who think that there are no clouds and no sunshine in the spirit lands hardly know how beautiful a thing you would shut out, unless you have spent, as I did, a long monotonous time without seeing either of them.

The room I was in, though by no means luxurious, was yet fairly comfortable in appearance, and reminded me of some cottage interior upon earth. It held all that was needful to comfort, if nothing that was specially beautiful, and it had not that bare prison-like look of my former dwellings. There were a few pictures of scenes of my earth life which had been pleasant, and the recollections they called up gave me a fresh pleasure; there were also some pictures of spirit life and oh! joy, there was my picture mirror, and my rose, and the letter--all my treasures! I stopped my explorations to look into that mirror and see what my beloved was doing. She was asleep, and on her face was a happy smile as if even in her dreams she knew some good had befallen me. Then I went to the window and looked out over the country and those long rolling hills, treeless and somewhat bare, save for their covering of grass and ferns. I looked long upon this scene, it was so like and yet so unlike earth, so strangely bare and yet so peaceful. My eyes, long wearied with those lower spheres, rested in joy and peace upon this new scene, and the thought that I had thus risen to a new life filled me with a thankfulness of heart unspeakable.

At last I turned from the window, and seeing what was like a small mirror near me, I looked to see what change there might be in myself. I started back with an exclamation of joy and surprise. Was it possible? Could this be as I appeared now? I gazed and gazed again. This myself? Why, I was young again! I looked a man of about thirty or thirty-five, not more certainly, and I beheld myself as I had been in my prime on earth! I had looked so old, so haggard, so miserable in that Twilight Land that I had avoided to look at myself. I had looked twenty times worse than I could ever have looked on earth, had I lived to be a hundred years old. And now, why, I was young! I held out my hand, it was firm and fresh-looking like my face. A closer inspection of myself pleased me still more. I was in all respects a young man again in my prime of vigor, yet not quite as I had been; no! there was a sadness in my look, a certain something more in the eyes than anywhere else that showed the suffering through which I had passed. I knew that never again could I feel the heedless buoyant ecstasy of youth, for never again could I go back and be quite as I had been. The bitter past of my life rose up before me and checked my buoyant thoughts. The remorse for my past sins was with me yet, and cast still its shadow over even the joy of this awakening. Never, ah! never can we undo all the past life of earth, so that no trace of it will cling to the risen spirit, and I have heard that even those who have progressed far beyond what I have even yet done, bear still the scars of their past sins and sorrows, scars that will slowly, very slowly, wear away at last in the great ages of eternity. For me there had come joy, great joy, wonderful fulfillment of my hope, yet there clung to me the shadow of the past, and its dark mantle clouded even the happiness of this hour.

While I yet mused upon the change which had passed over me, the door opened and a spirit glided in, dressed (as I now was) in a long robe of a dark blue color with yellow borderings, and the symbol of our order on the sleeve. He had come to invite me to a banquet which was to be given to myself and others who were newly arrived from the lower sphere. "All is simple here," said he, "even our festivals, yet there will be the salt of friendship to season it and the wine of love to refresh you all. Today you are our honored guests, and we all wait to welcome you as those who have fought a good fight and gained a worthy victory."

Then he took me by the hand and led me into a long hall, with many windows looking out upon more hills and a great peaceful quiet lake. Here there were long tables spread for the banquet, and seats placed round for us all. There were about five or six hundred brothers newly arrived, like myself, and about a thousand more who had been there for some time and who were going about from one to another introducing themselves and welcoming the new-comers cordially. Here and there someone would recognize an old friend or comrade, or one who had either assisted them or been assisted by them in the lower spheres. They were all awaiting the arrival of the presiding spirit of the order in this sphere, who was called "The Grand Master."

Presently the large doors at one end of the hall were seen to glide apart of themselves, and a procession entered. First came a most majestic, handsome spirit in robes of that rich blue color one sees in the pictures of the Virgin Mary. These robes were lined with white and bordered with yellow, while a hood of yellow lined with white hung from the shoulders, and on the sleeve was embroidered the symbol of the Order of Hope. Behind this man were about a hundred or so of youths, all in white and blue robes, who bore in their hands wreaths of laurel. At the upper end of the hall there was a handsome chair of state, with a white, blue and yellow canopy over it, and after saluting us all the Grand Master seated himself in it, while the youths ranged themselves in a semicircle behind him. After a short prayer of thanksgiving to Almighty God for us all he addressed us in these terms:

"My Brethren, you who are assembled to welcome these wanderers who are to find for a time rest and peace, sympathy and love, in this our House of Hope, and you our wandering brothers, whom we are all assembled to welcome and to honor as conquerers in the great battle against selfishness and sin, to you we give our heartiest greeting, and bid you accept, as members of our great brotherhood, these tributes of our respect and honor, which we offer and which you have fairly won. And from the increased happiness of your own lives we bid you stretch forth your hands in brotherly love to all the sorrowing ones whom you have left still toiling in the darkness of the earth life and in the spheres of the earth plane, and as you shall yourselves know yet more perfect triumphs, yet nobler conquests, so seek ye to give to others yet more and more of the perfect love of our great brotherhood, whose highest and most glorious masters are in the heavens, and whose humblest members are yet struggling sinners in the dark earth plane. In one long and unbroken chain our great order shall stretch from the heavens to the earth while this planet shall support material life, and each and every one of you must ever remember that you are links of that great chain, fellow workers with the angels, brother workers with the most oppressed. I summon you now, each in your turn, to receive and to cherish as a symbol of the honor you have won, these wreaths of fadeless laurel which shall crown the victors' brows. In the name of the Great Supreme Ruler of the Universe, in the name of all Angels and of our Brotherhood, I crown each one and dedicate you to the cause of Light and Hope and Truth."

Then at a signal we, the new arrivals, many of us almost overcome by these kindly words and this mark of honor, drew near, and, kneeling down before the Grand Master, had placed upon our heads these laurel crowns which the youths handed to the Master, and with which he crowned us with his own hands.

When the last one had received his crown, such a shout of joy went up from the assembled Brothers, such cheers, and then they sang a most beautiful song of praise, with so lovely a melody and such poetical words that I would I could reproduce it all for you. When this was over we were each led to a seat by an attendant brother and the banquet began.

You will wonder how such a banquet could be in the spirit world, but do you think that even on earth your all of enjoyment at such a scene is in the food you eat, the wine you drink, and do you imagine that a spirit has no need for food of any kind? If so, you are in error. We need, and we eat, food, though not of so material a substance as is yours. There is no animal food of any sort, nor anything like it, save only in the lowest spheres of earth-bound spirits, where they enjoy through others yet in the flesh the satisfaction of the animal apetites.

But there are in this second sphere the most delicious fruits, almost transparent to look at, which melt in your mouth as you eat them. There is wine like sparkling nectar, which does not intoxicate or create a thirst for more. There are none of those things which would gratify coarse apetites, but there are delicate cakes and a sort of light bread. Of such fare and such wine did this banquet consist, and I for one confess I never enjoyed anything more than the lovely fruits, which were the first I had seen in the spirit world, and which I was told were truly the fruits of our own labors grown in the spirit land by our efforts to help others.

After the banquet was over there was another speech, and a grand chorus of thanks in which we all joined. Then we dispersed, some of us to see our friends upon earth and try to make them feel that some happy event had befallen us. Many of us, alas! were being mourned as among the lost souls who had died in sin, and it was a great grief to us that these earthly friends could not be made conscious how great were now our hopes. Others of the Brothers turned to converse with newly-found spirit friends, while for my part I went straight to earth to tell the good news to my beloved. I found her about to attend one of those meetings for materialization, and, trembling with joy and eagerness, I followed her there, for now I knew there was no longer any reason why I should not show my face to her who had been so faithful and so patient in waiting for me--no longer would the sight of me give pain or shock her.

Ah, what a happy night that was! I stood beside her all the time. I touched her again and again. I stood there, no more the dark shrouded figure hiding his face from all eyes. No! I was there in my new dress with my new hopes, my risen body, and the ashes of my dead past were there no more to give me such shame and sorrow of heart as I had known. And then--oh! crowning joy to that most joyful day--I showed myself to her wondering eyes, and they gazed into my own. But she did not know me at once; she was looking for me as she had seen me last on earth, with face of care and wrinkled brow, and the young man's face looked strange to her. Yet not quite strange, she smiled and looked with a puzzled wondering look which, could I but have held the material particles of my form together for but a few more minutes, must have changed to recognition. But, alas! all too soon I felt my material form melting from me like soft wax, and I had to turn and go as it faded away. But as I went I heard her say: "It was so like, so very like what my dear friend must have been in youth. It was so like and yet so unlike him, I hardly know what to think."

Then I went behind her and whispered in her ear that it was I myself, and no other. And she heard my whisper and laughed and smiled, and said she had felt sure it must be so. Then indeed the cup of my joy was full, then indeed was the crown of my day complete.

CHAPTER XIV.--A Father's Love.

After this there came for me a time of happiness, a season of rest and refreshment upon which I shall not dwell; its memories are all too sacred to me, for those days were spent near to her I loved, and I had the happiness of knowing that she was conscious of much, though not all, I said to her, and I spent so much of my time on earth that I had none to explore the wonders of that Land of Dawn of which I had become an inhabitant.

And now a fresh surprise awaited me. In all my wanderings since my death I had never once seen any of my relatives nor the friends who had passed before me into the spirit land. But one day when I came as usual to see my beloved, I found her full of some mysterious message she had received, and which she was to give me herself. After a little she told me that it was from a spirit who had come to visit her, and who said he was my father and that he wished her to give his message to me. I was so overcome when she said this that I could scarcely speak--scarcely ask what his message was. I had so loved my father upon earth, for my mother had died when I was so young that she was but a faint tender memory to me. But my father! he had been everything to me. He had had such pride and joy in all my successes, such hopes for my future; and, then, when I had made shipwreck of my life, I knew that I had broken his heart. He did not long survive the crushing of all his hopes, and since his death I had only thought of him with pain and shame of heart. And now when I heard that from beyond the gates of Death he had come to my beloved and spoken to her of me, I feared lest his words might be but a lament over his buried hopes, his degraded son, and I cried out that I could not dare to meet him, yet I longed to hear what he had said, and to know if there was in it a word of forgiveness for me, his son, who had so deeply sinned.

How shall I tell what his words had been? How say what I felt to hear them? They fell upon my heart as dew upon a thirsty land, those words of his, and are far, far too precious to be given to the world, but surely the father in the parable must have welcomed back his prodigal son in some such words as these! Ah! how I cried out to my beloved when I heard those words, and how I longed to see that father again and be taken once more to his heart as when I was a boy! And as I turned away I beheld his spirit standing by us, just as I had seen him last in life, only with a glory of the spirit world upon him such as no mortal eyes have ever seen. My father--so long parted from me, and to meet again thus! We had no words to greet each other with but "My father" and "My son," but we clasped each other to the heart in a joy that required no words.

When our feelings had calmed down again we began to speak of many things, and not least of her whose love had led me so far upon my upward path, and then I learned that this beloved father had helped, watched over, and protected us both; that he had followed me during all my wanderings both on earth and in the spirit land, and had protected and comforted me in my struggles. Unseen himself he had yet been near, and unceasing in his efforts and his love. All this time when I had so shrunk from the thought of meeting him he had been there, only waiting an opportunity to make himself known, and he had come at last through her who had so much of my love, in order that he might thereby link us all three more closely together in the joy of this reunion.

CHAPTER XV.--A New Expedition Proposed.

When I returned to the spirit land, my father went with me and we spent a long time together. In the course of our conversation he told me that an expedition was about to be sent from this sphere to work as "Rescuers" in the lowest sphere of all, a sphere below any I had yet seen and which was in truth the hell believed in by the church. How long the expedition would be absent was not known, but a certain work had to be accomplished, and like an invading army we would remain till we had attained our object.

My Eastern guide advised me to join this band of workers, and as my father had in earth life sent his sons forth to fight for their beloved country, so did he now wish me to go forth with this army of soldiers in the cause of Truth and Light and Hope. To fight successfully against these powers of evil, it was necessary to be beyond the temptations of the earth plane and lower spheres, and to help the unhappy ones by a visible help which they could see and take hold of; one must not belong to the higher spheres, for spirits more advanced than the Brothers of Hope in this, the first circle of the second sphere, would be quite invisible to the unhappy ones who could neither see nor hear them. Also in entering these lowest spheres we would, in order to be visible, have to clothe ourselves in a certain portion of their material elements, and this a more advanced spirit could not do. So that although unseen helpers from the higher spheres would accompany the expedition to protect and assist us, they would be invisible alike to ourselves and those we had come to help.

Those who were to go upon this expedition with me were similar to myself in disposition, and it was felt that we would all learn much from seeing to what our passionate feelings would have sunk us, had we indulged in them. At the same time we would be able to rescue from those dark spheres many poor repentant souls. Those whom we rescued would be taken to where I had been on my first passing over from earth life, where there were numerous institutions specially set apart for such poor spirits, presided over and attended by spirits who had themselves been rescued from the Kingdoms of Hell and who were therefore best fitted to aid these poor wanderers.

Besides the Brothers of Hope from the Land of Dawn, there were other similar bands from other brotherhoods always being sent down to the dark spheres, such expeditions being, in fact, part of the great system of help for sinners ever being carried on in the name of the Eternal Father of all, who dooms none of his children to an eternity of misery.

A number of friends would accompany us a part of our journey, and our expedition would be commanded by a leader who had himself been rescued from the dark spheres and who knew their especial dangers.

As we would pass through the earth plane and lower spheres we would see them in a way we had not done before, and my Eastern guide said he would send one of his pupils to accompany me as far as the lowest sphere, in order that he might explain to me and make visible some of the mysteries of the astral plane which we would see as we passed. Hassein (as the student was named) was studying those mysteries of nature which have been classed under the name of magic and as such deemed evil, whereas it is their abuse only which is evil. A more extended intelligent knowledge of them would tend to prevent many existing evils and counteract some of those evil powers brought to bear upon man, often very injuriously, in his present ignorance. This student spirit had been a Persian and a follower of Zoroaster in his earth life, as Ahrinziman himself had been, and they belonged still to that school of thought of which Zoroaster was the great exponent.

"In the spirit world," said Ahrinziman, "there are a great number of different schools of thought, all containing the great fundamental eternal truths of nature, but each differing in many minor details, and also as to how these great truths should be applied for the advancement of the soul; they likewise differ as to how their respective theories will work out, and the conclusions to be drawn from the undoubted knowledge they possess, when it is applied to subjects upon which they have no certain knowledge and which are still with them as with those on earth, the subject of speculation, theory, and discussion. It is a mistake to suppose that in the spirit world of our planet there is any absolute knowledge which can explain all the great mysteries of Creation, the why and wherefore of our being, the existence of so much evil mixed with the good, or the nature of the soul and how it comes from God.

"The waves of truth are continually flowing from the great thought centers of the Universe, and are transmitted to earth through chains of spirit intelligences, but each spirit can only transmit such portions of truth as his development has enabled him to understand, and each mortal can only receive as much knowledge as his intellectual faculties are able to assimilate and comprehend.

"Neither spirits nor mortals can know everything, and spirits can only give you what are the teachings which their own particular schools of thought and advanced teachers give as their explanations. Beyond this they cannot go, for beyond this they do not themselves know; there is no more absolute certainty in the spirit world than on earth, and those who assert that they have the true and only explanation of these great mysteries are giving you merely what they have been taught by more advanced spirits, who, with all due deference to them, are no more entitled to speak absolutely than the most advanced teachers of some other school. I assert with knowledge not my own, but from another who is indeed regarded in the spirit world as a leader of most advanced thought, that it is in no way possible to give a final answer to or explanation of subjects which are beyond the powers of any spirit of our entire solar system to solve, and still more beyond those of the spirits of our earth spheres. In these subjects and their explanation are involved and required a knowledge of the limits of the universe itself which has no limits, and the nature of that Supreme Being of whom no man or spirit can know the nature, save in so far as we can grasp the great truth that he is Infinite Spirit, limitless in all senses, Unknowable and Unknown.

"Let men and spirits, then, argue or explain, they can only teach you to the limits of their own knowledge and beyond that again are limits none can reach. How can any pretend to show you the ultimate end of that which has no end, or sound the great depths of an infinite thought which has no bottom? Thought is as eternal as life and as fathomless. Spirit is infinite and all-pervading. God is in all and over and above all, yet none know his nature nor what manner of essense he is of, save that he is in everything and everywhere. The mind of man must pause on the very threshold of his inquiries, appalled by the sense of his own littleness, and the most he can do is to learn humbly and study cautiously, that each step be assured before he essays again to climb. The most lofty, the most daring minds cannot grasp all at once, and can man on earth hope that all can be explained to him with his limited range of vision, when the most advanced minds in the spirit world are ever being checked in their explorations after truth by the sense of their limited powers?"

The friend whom Ahrinziman sent to accompany and instruct me, appeared to my eyes as a youth of about five-and-twenty to thirty years of age, judging by earth's standard in such matters, but he told me he had lived to upwards of sixty years on earth. His present appearance was that of his spiritual development, which alone constitutes the age of a spirit. As a spirit grows more highly developed in his intellectual powers, the appearance becomes more matured, till at last he assumes that of a sage, without, however, the wrinkles and defects of age in earth life, only its dignity, its power, and its experience. Thus, when a spirit has attained to the highest possible development of the earth (or any other planet's) spheres he would possess the appearance of one of its patriarchs, and would then pass into the higher and more extended spheres of the solar system of that planet, beginning there as a youth again since his development compared to that of the advanced spirits of those higher spheres would be but that of a youth.

Hassein told me that he was at present studying the various powers and forms of nature in those stages which were below soul life, and would be able to make visible and explain to me many curious things we should see upon our journey.

"Many spirits," he said, "pass through the sphere of the astral plane without being conscious of its spectral inhabitants, by reason of the fact that their senses are not developed in such a way as to enable them to become conscious of their surroundings in all their entirety, just as in earth life there are many persons quite unable to see the spirits around them, although to others again they are perfectly visible. There are upon earth persons who can see not alone the spirits of human beings but also these astral and elementary beings who are not truly 'spirits,' since that word should be used to denote only those which possess within them the soul germ. Now many of these beings which we shall see never possessed any soul, and others again are only the empty shells from which the soul germ has departed. To distinguish between the soul spirit and the soulless astral one must possess a double power of soul-sight or clairvoyance as it is termed, and many who possess only an imperfect degree of this double power will be able to see elementals and astrals, but without being able to distinguish them clearly from the soul-enveloping spirit forms. Hence much confusion and many mistakes have arisen amongst these imperfect clairvoyants as to the nature and attributes of these classes of beings. There are seven degrees of the soul-sight found in persons yet in the earth life; and in the next stage of life the spiritual part or soul being freed from the gross elements of material life, there will be found seven more expansions of this gift, and so on in progressive succession as the soul casts off one by one the envelopes of matter--first the most gross or earthly matter, then succeeding degrees of refined or sublimated matter, for we hold that there can be no such thing as entire severance between soul and matter--that is so long as it is conscious of existence in any of our solar systems. Beyond these limits we have no knowledge to guide us, and it is a matter of pure speculation. It is only a question of the degree and quality of the matter which is more or less refined and etherealized as the soul is in a higher or lower state of development. It is of the first stage of earthly conscious soul life that I shall now speak in speaking of the clairvoyant sight, leaving till another time the theories and beliefs involved in the study of what has passed before man's present conscious stage of existence and what may happen when he passes beyond the limits of our present knowledge.

"We find, then, in the earthly stage of life persons--most often women or very young boys--who are endowed with some or all of these seven degrees of soul-sight. The first three degrees are very often found, the fourth and fifth more rarely, while the sixth and seventh are hardly ever met with except in persons endowed with certain peculiarities of organization, due to those astrological influences under which they are born--particularly to those prevailing at the exact moment the child sees the light of earth life. So rare are these perfect sixth and seventh degrees that very few possess them, though some are found with an imperfect sixth and none of the seventh, in which case they can never attain to the perfection of soul-sight, and as with imperfect glasses, the defect in their sight will cause them to have an imperfect vision of celestial things, and although they will see into the sixth sphere in a sense, yet their defective power will greatly impair the value of what they see.

"Those, however, who have the perfect sixth and seventh degrees can be taken in spirit into the seventh sphere itself, which is the highest, or heaven of the earth spheres, and like St. John of old they shall see unspeakable things. To do this the soul requires to be freed from all ties to the material body, save only the slender thread without which connecting link, body and soul would part forever. Thus they may be said to be out of the body at such times, and so difficult and dangerous is it to thus take the soul into the seventh sphere, that only with exceptional persons and under very exceptional circumstances can it be done even where the power exists. Of the clairvoyants of the lower degrees of power the same may be said, except that the less celestial their powers, the more safely and easily may they be used, each clairvoyant being able to see into that sphere which corresponds to the degree of power which they possess. It is, however, a curious fact that many clairvoyants possess one or more perfect degrees of soul-sight with at the same time an imperfect form of a degree still higher, and when this is so it will be found that the medium mixes the visions seen and is not reliable, since the defective degree (if used) will act like a defective eye and cause that which is beheld by both eyes at the same time to partake of its imperfections. It is, therefore, far better to have the entire absence of a degree than to possess an imperfect form of it, since the imperfect one only causes confusion in using the perfect ones, unless indeed you do with these powers as you might do with the defective eye, and close it altogether in order that the vision, though limited, may be correct. Thus the ancients when they found the highest amount of perfect vision of one or more degrees in their pupils, arrested their further development at that degree before the imperfect sight of a higher one could in any way impair the value of those they possessed. In this way they were able to train as reliable clairvoyants of moderate powers many who by a further effort at development would have lost far more than they could gain. In olden days seers were divided into classes even as they still are amongst certain schools of prophets in the East, though now the art is not studied to the perfection it once was when the Eastern nations were a power upon earth.

"Each class underwent a special training adapted to their special degrees of power and class of gifts, and there was not the present curious mixture of great gifts and entire ignorance of how to use them wisely, which in many instances results in so many inaccuracies and so much harm both to mediums and to those who go to them for spiritual knowledge. As well might a trainer of young gymnasts think that he could overtax and strain the growing muscles without lasting harm to them, as those who make an ignorant, unlimited, and indiscriminate use and development of the mediumistic powers. A young fledgling cast from the nest too soon flutters and falls to the ground, while if left till the wings are strong enough to bear its flight it will soar to heaven itself. With more extended knowledge upon earth there will be given to certain sensitives endowed with the needful mediumistic powers the knowledge by which under the guidance of those higher intelligences who are directing the great spiritual movement, they can judge between the spirits of low and degraded states and those of a higher degree of advancement, and thus much of the confusion and danger which still hampers the movement will be gradually eliminated from it.

"On the spirit side of life are many teachers who for centuries have made a study of these subjects--of all forms of life--and of the mediumistic powers of those who are incarnated upon earth, and they are even now seeking on all sides for open doors through which to impart such knowledge as may be of use to man. Much which they know could not yet be imparted, but there are things which could, and with this subject as with all others the minds upon earth will expand and develop as knowledge is given."

I thanked my new friend for his information and promised help, and as the expedition was soon to start I went to earth to bid adieu for a time to my beloved. Upon our parting I shall not dwell, nor say how much we both felt we should miss our constant little intercourse; for even restricted as it was by the barrier between us, it had been been a great joy to both.

I found on my return that the preparations for our journey were now complete, and I was summoned to bid my father and others adieu, and to join my companions in the great hall where they were now assembled to receive the farewell benediction of our Grand Master.

After this our band started amidst the cheers and good wishes of all the assembled Brotherhood.

I can hardly give you a better idea of the course of our journey than by asking you to imagine a vast spiral or corkscrew winding upwards and downwards in circling rings. A tiny speck no bigger than a pin's head in the middle of a large cart-wheel might represent the earth in the centre of these circling rings, an equal number of which are above and below the earth, all winding in a connected series from the lowest to the highest around this speck, and the head of the spiral pointing towards our central sun-- this being regarded as the highest point of the most advanced sphere.

This will give you a faint idea of the earth and its attendant spirit spheres, and help you to understand how in our journey we passed from the second into the lowest sphere, and in doing so passed through the earth plane. As we entered it I perceived many spirits of mortals hurrying to and fro just as I had been wont to see them, but now for the first time I also saw that mingling with them were many floating spectral shapes similar to those wraiths I had seen haunting the spirit in the icy cage in the Frozen Land. These wraiths seemed to be floating to and fro like driftweed upon a seashore, borne here and there by the different astral currents which revolve and circle round the earth.

Some were very distinct and life-like till a closer inspection revealed to me that the light of intelligence was wanting in their eyes and expressions, and there was a helpless collapsed look about them like wax dolls from which the stuffing has run out. For the life of me I can think of nothing that will so well express their appearance.

In my former wanderings through the earth plane I had not been conscious of any of these beings, and on asking Hassein the reason of this he answered: "First, because you were so much absorbed in your work, and secondly, your powers of sight were not sufficiently developed. Now look," he added, pointing to a strange little group of beings like elves which were approaching us hand in hand, gamboling like children. "Look at those; they are the mental and bodily emanations cast off from the minds and bodies of children which consolidate into these queer, harmless little elementals when brought into contact with any of the great life currents that circle around the earth, and which bear upon their waves the living emanations cast off from men, women and children. These curious little beings have no real separate intelligent life such as a soul would give, and they are so evanescent and ethereal that they take their shapes and change them, as you will observe, like the clouds on a summer sky. See how they are all dissolving and forming again afresh."

As I looked I saw the whole little cloud of figures shift into a new form of grotesque likeness, and whereas they had looked like tiny fairies in caps and gowns made from flowers, they now took wings, becoming like a species of half butterflies, half imps, with human bodies, animal's heads, and butterflies' wings. Then as a fresh strong wave of magnetism swept over them, lo! they were all broken up and carried away to form fresh groups elsewhere with other particles.

I was so astonished at this, the real living appearance and the unreal disappearance, that I suppose Hassein read my puzzled state of mind, for he said, "What you have now beheld is only an ethereal form of elemental life, which is not material enough for a long continued existence on the earth plane, and is like the foam of the sea thrown up by the wave motions of pure earthly lives and thoughts. See now how much stronger on the astral plan can be the consistency of that which is not pure."

I beheld approaching us a great mass of aerial forms, dark, misshapen, human, yet inhuman, in appearance. "These," said he, "are the beings which haunt the delirium of the drunkard, which gather round him, drawn by his corrupted magnetism and unable to be repelled by one who has lost the will-force needful to protect him from such creatures which cling like barnacles to him, and like leeches suck his animal vitality with a strange ghoulish intelligence akin to that of some noisome plant which has fastened itself upon a tree. For such a one as the unfortunate drunkard the best help which can be given is by obtaining some one upon the earth side of life who possesses a strong will and mesmeric powers, and let him place the drunkard under the protection of his will and the strong influence of his magnetism, till the last of these phantoms drops off from inability to hold on longer under the stream of healthy magnetism poured upon them and the unlucky man upon whom they have fastened. The healthy magnetism acts like a poison upon these creatures, and kills them so that they drop off, and their bodies, unable to hold together, decay into immaterial dust. Should these beings, however, not encounter such a strong dose of healthy magnetism they will go on for years floating about and drawing away the animal vitality of one human being after another, till at last they become endowed with a certain amount of independent animal life of their own. At this stage they can be used by higher, more intelligent beings to carry out such work as their peculiar organizations fit them for, and it is these soulless creatures, though created and earth-nourished, whom a certain class of practitioners of the so-called black magic made use of in some of their experiments, as well as for carrying out their evil designs against any one who had offended them. But like deadly weeds at the bottom of a dark pool, these astrals draw down and destroy in their soulless clutches those who venture to meddle with them unprotected by the higher powers."

"And now tell me, friend Hassein," said I, "if these astrals, when they fasten upon a drunkard, can or do influence him to drink more, as is the case when the earth-bound spirit of a departed drunkard controls one still in the flesh."

"No! These beings do not derive any pleasure from the drink a man swallows, except in so far as by corrupting his magnetism it makes him such that they can more readily feed upon him. It is his animal or earthly life-force they desire. It means existence for them and is much the same as water to a plant, and beyond the fact that by draining the victim of his vitality they cause a sense of exhaustion which makes him fly to stimulants for relief, they do not affect the question of his continuing to drink. They are mere parasites, and possess no intelligence of their own except of so rudimentary a character that we can scarcely give it that name.

"To originate a thought or to impress your thoughts upon another requires the possession of an intelligent soul germ or spark of the divine essence, and once this has been given the being becomes possessed of an independent individuality it can never again lose. It may cast off envelope after envelope, or it may sink into grosser and still grosser forms of matter, but once endowed with soul-life it can never cease to exist, and in existing must retain the individuality of its nature and the responsibility of its actions. This is alike true of the human soul and the intelligent soul-principle as manifested in the animals or lower types of soul existence. Whenever you see the power to reason and to act upon such reasoning manifested either in man, the highest type, or in animals, the lower type, you may know that a soul exists, and it is only a question of degree of purity of soul essence. We see in man and in the brute creation alike a power of reasoning intelligence differing only in degree, and from this fact the school of thought to which I belong draws the inference that both alike have a conscious individual immortality, differing, however, in the type and degree of soul essence, animals as well as men having an immortal future for development before them. What are the limits of the action of this law we cannot pretend to say, but we draw our conclusions from the existence in the spirit world of animals as well as men who have alike lived on earth, and both of whom are found in a more advanced state of development than they were in their earth existences.

"It is impossible for the soulless parasite to influence the mind of any mortal; and it is therefore undoubtedly the souls which have been incarnated in earthly bodies and have so indulged their lower passions in that state that they are not able to free themselves from the fetters of their astral envelopes, that haunt the earth and incite those yet in the flesh to indulgence in drink and similar vices. They, as you know, can control man in many ways, either partially or completely, and the most common way is for the spirit to partly envelop the man he controls with his spirit body until a link has been formed between them, somewhat after the nature of that uniting some twin children who possess distinct bodies, but are so joined to each other and interblended that all which one feels is felt by the other. In this fashion what is swallowed by the mortal is enjoyed by the spirit who controls the unfortunate man, and who urges him to drink as much as possible, and when he can no longer do so the spirit will then try to free himself and go elsewhere in search of some other weak-willed man or woman of depraved tastes. Not always, however, can either the spirit or the mortal free themselves from the strange link woven between them by the indulgence of their joint desires. After a long-continued connection of this sort it becomes very difficult for them to separate, and the spirit and the man may go on for years sick of each other yet unable to break the tie without help from the higher powers, who are always ready to assist those who call upon their aid. Should a spirit continue to control men for the purpose of self-gratification as I have described, he sinks lower and lower, and drags his victims down with him into the depths of hell itself, from which they will both have a bitter and weary task to climb when at last the desire for better things shall awaken. To a soul alone belongs the power to think and to will, and those other soulless creatures but obey the laws of attraction and repulsion, which are felt likewise by all the material atoms of which the universe is composed, and even when these astral parasites have, by long feeding upon the vital force of men or women, attained to a certain amount of independent life, they have no intelligence to direct their own or others' movements; they float about like fever germs generated in a foul atmosphere, attracted to one person more readily than to another, and like such germs may be said to possess a very low form of life.

"Another class of elemental astrals are those of the earth, air, fire, and water, whose bodies are formed from the material life germs in each element. Some are in appearance like the gnomes and elves who are said to inhabit mines and mountain caverns which have never been exposed to the light of day. Such, too, are the fairies whom men have seen in lonely and secluded places amongst primitive races of men. Such, with the variations caused by the different natures of the elements from which they are formed, are the water sprites and the mermaids of ancient fable, and the spirits of the fire and the spirits of the air.

"All these beings possess life, but as yet no souls, for their lives are drawn from and sustained by the lives of earthly men and women, and they are but reflections of the men amongst whom they dwell. Some of these beings are of a very low order of life, almost like the higher orders of plants, except that they possess an independent power of motion. Others are very lively and full of grotesque unmeaning tricks, with the power of very rapid flight from place to place. Some are perfectly harmless, while others again are more malignant in their instincts as the human beings from whom their life is drawn are of a more savage race. These curious earth elementals cannot exist long amongst nations where the more intellectual stage of development has been reached, because then the life germs thrown off by man contain too little of the lower or animal life to sustain them, and they die and their bodies decay into the atmosphere. Thus as nations advance and grow more spiritual, these lower forms of life die out from the astral plane of that earth's sphere, and succeeding generations begin at first to doubt and then to deny that they ever had an existence. Only amongst those ancient religions of the East who have kept still unbroken the threads of record, are there to be found accounts of these intermediate dependent races of beings and the causes of their existence.

"These soulless elementals of earth, air, fire and water, are a class distinct from those others which I have drawn you as emanating from the debased intelligence of man's mind and the evil actions of his body. Behold now, oh! man of a Western nation, the knowledge which your philosophers and learned men have shut out and locked away as being harmful fables, till man, shut into the narrow bounds of what he can with his physical senses alone see, hear, and feel, has begun to doubt if he has any soul at all; any higher, purer, nobler self than is sustained by the sordid life of earth. See now the multitudinous beings that surround man on every side, and ask yourself if it would not be well that he should have the knowledge which could help to keep him safe from the many pitfalls over which he walks in blind ignorance and unconsciousness of his danger. In the primitive ages of the earth man was content to look like a child for help and succor to his Heavenly Father, and God sent his angels and ministering spirits to protect his earthly children. In these latter ages man, like a full-grown troublesome youth, seeks in his self-conceit no higher help than his own, and rushes into danger with his eyes bandaged by his pride and ignorance. He scoffs at those things which he is too limited in his powers to understand, and turns aside from those who would instruct him. Because he cannot see his soul, cannot weigh it and analyze it, he says, forsooth, that man has no soul and had better enjoy this earthly life as one who shall some day die and turn to dust again, consciousness, individuality, all forever blotted out.

"Or, again, in abject fear of the unknown fate before him, man takes refuge in the vague superstitions, the shadowy creeds of those who profess to act as guides upon the pathway to the Unknown Land, with little more certain knowledge than man has himself.

"Thus, then, it is in pity to his wandering, struggling children that God has in these later days opened once more--and wider than ever before--the doors of communion between the two worlds. He is sending out again messengers to warn man, ambassadors, to tell him of the better way, the truer path to the happiness of a higher life, and to show him that knowledge and that power which shall yet be of right his inheritance. As the prophets of old spake, so speak these messengers now, and if they speak with clearer voice, with less veiled metaphor, it is because man is no longer in his infancy and needs now that he should be shown the reason and the science upon which his beliefs and hopes must be founded.

"Listen, then, unto this voice that calls, oh! ye toilers of the earth!" cried Hassein, turning and stretching out his hands towards a small dark ball that seemed to float far away on the horizon of our sight--a small dark globe that we knew to be the sorrowful planet called Earth. "Listen to the voices that call to you and turn not a deaf ear, and realize ere it be too late that God is not a God of the dead but of the living, for all things are alive for evermore. Life is everywhere and in everything; even the dull earth and the hard rocks are composed of living germs, each living according to its own degree. The very air we breathe and the boundless ether of universal space are full of life, and there is not one thought we think but lives for good or ill, not one act whose image shall not live to torture or to solace the soul in the days of its release from its incarnation in an earthly form. Life is in all things, and God is the central Life of All."

Hassein paused, then in a calmer voice he said to me: "Look yonder! What would you say those things were?"

He pointed to what seemed to me at first a mass of spirit forms which came sweeping towards us as though blown by a strong wind. As they came near I saw they were evidently soulless astral envelopes, but unlike those floating wraiths I had seen haunting the man in the icy cage, these were solid, and to my spiritual sight life-like and full of animal vigor; yet they were like automatons and did not seem to possess any intelligence. They were drifting and bobbing about like buoys at sea to which boats are anchored. As they drifted close to us my friend put forth his will-force and captured one, which then remained floating in mid air.

"Now look," said he, "you will observe this is somewhat like a great living doll. It is the result of countless little living germs which man is continually throwing off from his earthly body, emanations solely of his animal or lower life, material enough when brought into contact with the magnetic forces of the astral plane, to form into these imitations of earthly men and women, and immaterial enough to be invisible to man's purely material sight, although a very small degree of clairvoyant power would enable him to see them. A stronger and higher degree of clairvoyant power would enable him to see, as you do, that this is not a true spirit envelope, since the soul principle is wanting; and a yet higher degree of clairvoyant power would show that a soul has never been in this form, and that it has never had a conscious existence as a soul's astral envelope.

"Amongst ordinary clairvoyants the subject of astral spirits is not studied sufficiently to develop these degrees of soul-sight, therefore few clairvoyants in your earthly country could tell you whether this was a true soul-enveloping astral form or one from which the soul had departed, or yet again one in which the soul had never been present at all. Presently I shall show you an experiment with this astral form, but first observe that being such as it is, it is fresh and full of the animal life of the earth plane, and has not the collapsed appearance of those you saw before, which had once contained a soul and which were there in a state of rapid decay yet. And mark this carefully: this fresh looking astral will decay far faster than the others, for it has none of the higher principle of life clinging to it, which, in the case of an astral that has once contained a soul, often remains for a long time animating and keeping it from perfect decay. Astral forms must draw their life from a higher source (from soul germs in fact), or they soon cease to exist and crumble away."

"But," I asked, "how do they assume the shapes of men and women?"

"By the action of the spiritualized magnetic currents which flow through all the ether space continually, as the currents flow in the ocean. These magnetic life currents are of a more etherealized degree than those known to scientific mortals, being in fact their spiritual counterpart, and as such they act upon these cloud masses of human atoms in the same way that electricity acts upon the freezing moisture upon a window pane, forming them into the semblance of men and women as the electricity forms the freezing moisture into a likeness of trees, plants, etc.

"It is an acknowledged fact that electricity is an active agent in the formation of the shapes of leaves and trees, etc., in vegetable life, but few know that this refined form of magnetism has a similar share in the formation of human forms and animal life. I say animal life as applied to those types which are lower than man."

"Are there, then, also the astral forms of animals?"

"Certainly, and very queer, grotesque combinations some of them are. I cannot show them to you now, because your powers of sight are not yet fully developed, and also because we are traveling too rapidly to enable me to develop them for you, but some day I shall show you these, as well as many other curious things relating to the astral plane. I may tell you that atoms may be classed under different heads, and that each class will have a special attraction for others of its own kind; thus vegetable atoms will be attracted together to form astral trees and plants, while animal atoms will form into the semblance of beasts, birds, etc., and human atoms into men and women's forms. In some cases, where the human beings from whom the atoms come are very low in the scale of humanity and nearly akin to animals, their atoms will blend with those of the lower forms of life and create grotesque horrible creatures which resemble at once animals and men, and having been seen by clairvoyants in a semi-trance condition are described as nightmare visions. In the earth spheres an immense amount of these living atoms are thrown off continually from man's lower or animal life, and these sustain and renew the astral forms, but were we to transport one of these shells to a planet whose spheres had been spiritualized beyond the stage of material life, or in other words freed from all these lower germs, the astrals could not exist, they would become like a noxious vapor and be blown away. These astrals being, as I have said, created from the cloud masses of human atoms, and never having been the envelope of any soul, are very little more permanent in their nature than the frost flowers on a window pane, unless the power of some higher intelligence acts upon them to intensify their vitality and prolong their existence. They are, as you will see, expressionless and like wax dolls in appearance, and readily lend themselves to receive any individuality stamped upon them, hence their use in ancient times by magicians and others. Astral atoms, whether of trees, plants, animals, or human beings, must not be confounded with the true spirit or soul-clothing atoms which constitute the real spirit world and its inhabitants. Astrals of every kind are the intermediate degree of materiality between the gross matter of earth and the more etherealized matter of the spirit world, and we talk of a soul clothed in its astral envelope to express that earth-bound condition in which it is too refined or immaterial for earth existence, and too grossly clad to ascend into the spirit world of the higher spheres, or to descend to those of the lower."

"Then you mean that a spirit even in the lowest sphere is more spiritualized as regards its body than an earth-bound spirit?"

"Certainly I do. The astral plane extends like a belt around each planet and is, as I said, formed of the matter which is too fine for reabsorption by the planet, and too coarse to escape from the attraction of the planet's mass and pass into the spheres of the spirit world to form either matter in the course of disintegration or change from one form to another, and it is only the vitalizing power of such soul magnetism as it retains which enables it to cling together in any shape at all.

"In the case of human astral forms which have possessed individualized life as a soul's envelope, the astral atoms have absorbed a greater or less degree of the soul's magnetism, or true life essence, according as the earthly existence of the soul has been good or evil, elevated or degraded, and this soul magnetism animates it for a longer or shorter period, and forms a link between it and the soul which has animated it. In the case of a soul whose desires are all for higher things, the link is soon severed and the astral envelope soon decays, while with a soul of evil desires the tie may last for centuries and chain the soul to earth, making it in fact earth-bound. In some cases the astral of a soul of very evil life will have absorbed the lower or higher spheres. Astral matter is practically so much of the soul's vitality that after the soul itself has sunk into the lowest sphere of all, the empty shell will still float about the earth like a fading image of its departed owner. Such are sometimes seen by clairvoyants hanging about the places where they once lived, and are truly 'spooks.' They have no intelligence of their own, since the soul has fled, and they can neither influence mediums nor move tables, nor do any other thing except as mechanical agents of some higher intelligence, whether that intelligence be good or evil.

"The astral before us now has no soul magnetism in it; it never possessed any, therefore it will soon decay and its atoms be absorbed by others. But see to what use it can be turned when acted upon by my will power and animated for the time being by my individuality."

I looked as he spoke and saw the astral doll become suddenly animated and intelligent, and then glide to one of the Brotherhood whom Hassein had selected and touch him upon the shoulder, seeming to say, "Friend, Hassein Bey salutes you." Then bowing to the amused and wondering brother, it glided back to us as though Hassein had held it by a string like a performing monkey.

"Now you see," he said, "how if I chose I might use this astral as a messenger to execute some work I wished done at a distance from myself, and you will understand one of the means made use of by the old magicians to carry out some work at a great distance from themselves and without their appearing to take any share in it. These astrals, however, are only capable of being made use of upon the astral plane. They could not move any material object, although they would be visible to material sight at the will of the mortal using them. There are other astrals more material in substance who could be used to penetrate into the earth itself and to bring forth its hidden treasures, the precious metals and the gems deeply buried from the eyes of men. It would not, however, be lawful or right for me to explain to you the power by which this could be done, and those magicians who have discovered and made use of such powers have sooner or later fallen victims to those powers they could summon to their aid but rarely continue to control."

"Then were this astral to become animated by an evil intelligence it would be an actual danger to man?" I said.

"Yes, without doubt it might; and you will also observe that although I should not care to descend to clothe myself in this astral form, yet a spirit more ignorant than myself could easily do so in order to make himself felt and seen upon the earth in a more palpable form than possible to any spirit who has left the earth plane; but in doing so he would run a danger of creating a link between himself and the astral envelope not easily broken, and which might thus tie him to the astral plane for a considerable time. You will, therefore, see how the idea has arisen that men on earth, in seeking to see their departed friends, draw the spirits back into earthly conditions and do them harm. Many an ignorant spirit who is good and pure himself, has committed the mistake of reclothing himself in one of these fresh astral shells when he would have turned away from those which he knew to have been left by another spirit, and has found to his cost that he has thereby made of himself a prisoner upon the earth plane, till a higher intelligence comes to his aid and releases him.

"In a like manner spirits of a low type can clothe themselves in these empty astral garments, but in their case the very grossness of the spirit (or soul) prevents them from retaining possession long, the dense magnetism of the low spirit's own body acting as a strong noxious vapor or gas would do upon a covering made, say, of a spider's web of fine gossamer, and rending it into a thousand pieces. To a spirit above the astral plane an astral envelope appears almost as solid as iron, but to one below it these fragile shells are like a cloud or vapor. The lower the soul the stronger is its envelope and the more firmly does it hold the soul, limiting its powers and preventing it from rising into a more advanced sphere."

"You mean, then, that spirits sometimes use these astral shells as they do earthly mediums, and either control them independently or actually enter into the form?"

"Yes, certainly. A spirit above the earth plane, anxious to show himself to a clairvoyant of the lowest or first degree of power, will sometimes enter one of these shells which he at once stamps with his identity, and in that way the clairvoyant will truly see and describe him. The danger lies in the fact that when the good spirit of limited knowledge seeks to leave again the astral shell, he finds he cannot do so; he has animated it and its strong life holds him prisoner, and it is often difficult to release him. In similar manner the too complete, too long continued control of an earthly medium by a spirit, has been found to create a link between them which becomes at last a chain. To a spirit of the lowest spheres an astral envelope is but a convenient, all too evanescent cloak with which to hide his own degraded spirit body, and thus impose upon clairvoyants unable to see the vile spirit underneath; but to a good and pure spirit the astral envelope is as a suit of iron capable of imprisoning him."

"Then in the case of what are called personations by one spirit of another at seances upon earth, are these astrals made use of?"

"Very often they are, where the mischief-making spirit is of too low a type himself to come into direct contact with the medium. You must know by this time how wonderfully the thoughts of mortal men and women are mirrored upon the atmosphere of the astral plane, and as pictures they can be read and answered by spirits possessing the knowledge of how to read them. All spirits have not the power, just as all men and women on earth are not able to read a newspaper or a letter. It requires intellect and education with us as with those on earth. The spirits, then, of which men should most beware are not so much the poor ignorant half developed spirits of the earth plane and lower spheres, whose degraded lives have made them what they are and who are often glad of a helping hand to raise them, but it is of the intellectually evil, those who have great powers alike of mind and body and who have only used them for wrong purposes. These are the real dangers to guard against, and it is only by the increase of knowledge amongst the mediums incarnated in the earthly body that it will be successfully done, for then mortals and spirit workers will labor in unison, and mutually protect the spiritual movement from fraud and from the mistakes of the well meaning but half-ignorant spirits and mortals who are doing good work in directing the attention of mankind to the matter, but who often do harm both to themselves and others. They are like ignorant chemists and liable to bring destruction and harm upon others as well as on themselves in their experiments in search of knowledge."

"You do not think, then, that the purity of their motives will suffice to protect them?"

"Would purity of motive save a child from being burnt if it thrust its hands into a blazing furnace? No! then the only way is to keep the child as far from the fire as possible. This good and wise spirit guardians do in a great measure, but if the children are continually hovering near the danger, and try at all sorts of odd times and fashions to get just another peep at the dangerous thing, it is impossible but that some of them will get scorched."

"Then you would not advise the indiscriminate cultivation of mediumistic powers by all mortals?"

"Certainly not. I would have all men use the powers of those who have been carefully developed under wise guardians, and I would have all assisted to cultivate them who are truly anxious to develop their powers as a means of doing good to others. But when you consider how manifold and how selfish may be the motives of those mediumistically endowed, you will see how exceedingly difficult it would be to protect them. Perhaps my ideas are colored by the circumstances of race and my earthly education, but I confess I should wish to limit the practice of mediumship to those who have proved their readiness to give up more material advantages for its sake. I would, in fact, rather see them set apart as a body who have no share in the ambitions of mankind. But enough of our discussion. I am now about to let this astral shell go and draw your attention to another type of the same class."

As he spoke he made a swift upward motion with his hands over it and uttered some words in an unknown language, whereupon the astral--which had hitherto floated on beside us--stopped and seemed to waver about for a few seconds until an advancing current of magnetism caught it, and it was swept away from us like a piece of driftwood upon the waves. As I turned from watching it I saw a small cluster of dark, weird, horrible looking forms approaching us. These were astral shells which had never known soul life, but, unlike the pleasant waxy looking astral from which we had just parted, these were in all respects repulsive.

"These," said Hassein, "are the emanations thrown off by men and women of a low intellectual type and evil, sensual lives. They are from the slums of the earth life--not alone the social slums, but also from a higher grade of society where there are moral slums quite as degraded. Such beings as these, when animated by an evil intelligence can be used for the very worst purposes. Being so very material, they can even be used to affect material matter upon earth, and have been so used in the practice of what is known as Black Magic and witchcraft, and they are also (but very rarely) used by higher intelligences to effect physical phenomena at seances. Where wise and good intelligences control them no harm will be done, but under the direction of the evil or ignorant they become a danger beyond my power fully to express. To these astrals, and to those of a similar class in which the soul germ yet lingers as in a prison, are due those rough and dangerous manifestations sometimes seen in spirit circles (seances), where men of bad lives, and others too ignorant to protect themselves, are assembled from motives of curiosity or mere amusement."

"And amongst what class of spirits do you place those ghouls and vampires so firmly believed in, in many parts of the world?"

"Vampire spirits are those who have themselves known earth life, but have so misused it that their souls are still imprisoned in the astral envelope. Their object in sucking away the animal life principle of men and women is in order to retain thereby their hold upon the life of the earth plane, and so save themselves from sinking to far lower spheres. They are anxious to cling to their astral envelope and to prolong its life, just as men of very evil lives upon earth cling to the life of the earthly body because they fear that when they are separated from it they will sink into some unknown depths of darkness and horror. The constant renewal of the animal and astral life often enables these vampire spirits to hang about the earth for centuries."

"Is it possible for a vampire spirit to possess itself of a sufficient amount of materiality to appear in mortal form and mingle with men as described in many of the tales told of such creatures?"

"If you mean to ask if the vampire can make to itself a material body, I say no, but it can and does sometimes take complete possession of one belonging to a mortal, just as other spirits do, and can cause its acquired body to act in accordance with its will. Thus it is quite possible for a vampire spirit clothed in the mortal body of another to so change its expression as to make it bear some resemblance to the vampire's own former earthly appearance, and through the power obtained by the possession of a material body he (or she, for the vampires are of both sexes) might really lead the curious double life ascribed to them in those weird tales current and believed in in many countries. By far the larger number of vampire spirits, however, are not in possession of an earthly body, and they hover about the earth in their own astral envelope, sucking away the earthly life of mediumistic persons whose peculiar organization makes them liable to become the prey of such influences, while they are themselves quite ignorant that such beings as these astrals exist. The poor mortals suffer from a constant sense of exhaustion and languor without suspecting to what it is to be attributed."

"But cannot spirit guardians protect mortals from these beings?"

"Not always. In a great measure they do protect them, but only as one may protect a person from infectious fevers, by showing them the danger and warning them to avoid spots where, owing to the associations with their earthly lives, the vampire spirits are specially attracted. This the guardian spirit does by instilling into the mind of the mortal an instinctive dread of the places where crimes have been committed, or persons of evil lives have lived. But since man is and must be in all respects a free agent, it is not possible to do more. He cannot be directed in all things like a puppet, and must in a great measure gather his own experience for himself, however bitter may prove its fruits. Knowledge, guidance and help will always be given, but only in such a manner as will not interfere with man's free will, and only such knowledge as he himself desires; nothing will ever be forced upon him by the spirit world."

CHAPTER XVIII.--The Approach to Hell.

I would have liked to ask Hassein a great many more questions about the astral plane and its many curious forms of life, but we were now fast leaving it behind, and passing downwards through those lower spheres which I had partly explored before. We were traveling through space at a wonderful velocity, not quite with the rapidity of thought but at a speed difficult for the mind of mortal to conceive. Onward and still onward we swept, sinking ever lower and lower away from the bright spheres, and as we sank a certain sense of awe and expectancy crept over our souls and hushed our talk. We seemed to feel in advance the horrors of that awful land and the sorrows of its inhabitants.

And now I beheld afar off great masses of inky black smoke which seemed to hang like a pall of gloom over the land to which we were approaching. As we still floated on and down, these great black clouds became tinged with lurid sulphurous-looking flames as from myriads of gigantic volcanoes. The air was so oppressive we could scarcely breathe, while a sense of exhaustion, such as I had never experienced before, seemed to paralyze my every limb. At last our leader gave the order for us to halt, and we descended on the top of a great black mountain which seemed to jut out into a lake of ink, and from which we saw on the horizon that awful lurid country.

Here we were to rest for a time, and here, too, we were to part from our friends who had so far escorted us upon our journey. After a simple repast consisting of various sustaining spiritual fruits and food which we had brought with us, our leader on behalf of the whole company offered up a short prayer for protection and strength, and then we all lay down upon that bleak mountain top to rest.

PART III.
The Kingdom of Hell.

CHAPTER XIX

The companion who was assigned to me in this expedition was a spirit who had been in this sphere before, and who was, therefore, well fitted to act as my guide on entering this Land of Horrors. After a short time we were to separate, he told me, and each to follow his own path--but at any time either of us could, if needful, summon the other to his aid in case of extremity.

As we drew near the great bank of smoke and flame I remarked to my companion upon the strangely material appearance they presented. I was accustomed in the spirit world to the realism and solidity of all our surroundings which mortals are apt to imagine must be of some ethereal and intangible nature, since they are not visible to ordinary eyesight,--still these thick clouds of smoke, these leaping tongues of flame, were contrary to what I had pictured Hell as being like. I had seen dark and dreary countries and unhappy spirits in my wanderings, but I had seen no flames, no fire of any sort, and I had totally disbelieved in material flames in a palpable form, and had deemed the fires of Hell to be merely a figure of speech to express a mental state. Many have taught that it is so, and that the torments of Hell are mental and subjective, not objective at all. I said something of this to my companion, and he replied:

"Both ideas are in a sense right. These flames and this smoke are created by the spiritual emanations of the unhappy beings who dwell within that fiery wall, and material as they seem to your eyes, opened to the sight of spiritual things, they would be invisible to a mortal's sight, could one still in the body of flesh by any miracle visit this spot. They have, in fact, no earthly material in them, yet they are none the less material in the sense that all things earthly or spiritual are clothed in matter of some kind. The number and variety of degrees of solidity in matter are infinite, as without a certain covering of etherealized matter even spiritual buildings and spiritual bodies would be invisible to you, and these flames being the coarse emanations of these degraded spirits, possess for your eyes an appearance even more dense and solid than for the inhabitants themselves."

My companion's spirit name was "Faithful Friend," a name given him in memory of his devotion to a friend who abused his friendship and finally betrayed him, and whom he had even then forgiven and helped in the hour when shame and humiliation overtook the betrayer, and when reproach and contempt or even revenge might have seemed amply justifiable to many minds. This truly noble spirit had been a man of by no means perfectly noble character in his earthly life, and had therefore passed at death into the lower spheres near the earth plane, but he had risen rapidly, and at the time I met him he was one of the Brotherhood in the second sphere, to which I had so recently been admitted, and had been once before through the Kingdoms of Hell.

We now drew near what appeared like the crater of a vast volcano--ten thousand Vesuviuses in one! Above us the sky was black as night, and but for the lurid glare of the flames we should have been in total darkness. Now that we have reached the mass of fire I saw that it was like a fiery wall surrounding the country, through which all who sought to enter or leave it must pass.

"See now, Franchezzo," said Faithful Friend, "we are about to pass through this wall of fire, but do not let that alarm you, for so long as your courage and your will do not fail, and you exert all your will-power to repel these fiery particles, they cannot come in actual contact with your body. Like the waters of the Red Sea they will fall apart on either side and we shall pass through unscathed.

"Were any one of weak will and timid soul to attempt this they would fail, and be driven back by the force of these flames which are propelled outwards by a current of strong will-force set in motion by the fierce and powerful beings who reign here, and who thus, as they imagine, protect themselves from intrusions from the higher spheres. To us, however, with our more spiritualized bodies, these flames and the walls and rocks you will find in this land, are no more impenetrable than is the solid material of earthly doors and walls, and as we can pass at will through them, so can we pass through these, which are none the less sufficiently solid to imprison the spirits who dwell in this country. The more ethereal a spirit is the less can it be bound by matter, and at the same time the less direct power can it have in the moving of matter, without the aid of the physical material supplied by the aura of certain mediums. Here, as on earth, we would, in order to move material substances, require to use the aura of some of the mediumistic spirits of this sphere. At the same time we shall find that our higher spiritual powers have become muffled, so to say, because in order to enter this sphere and make ourselves visible to its inhabitants, we have had to clothe ourselves in its conditions, and thus we are more liable to be affected by its temptations. Our lower natures will be appealed to in every form, and we shall have to direct our efforts to prevent them from again dominating us.

My friend now took my hand firmly in his and we "willed" ourselves to pass through the wall of fire. I confess that a momentary sense of fear passed over me as we began to enter it, but I felt we were "in for it," so exerting all my powers and concentrating my thoughts I soon found that we were floating through--the flames forming a fiery arch below and above us through which as through a tunnel we passed. Thinking of it now I should say it must have been about a quarter to half a mile thick, judging as one would by earthly measurements, but at the time I did not take sufficient note to be very exact, all my energies being directed to the repelling of the fiery particles from myself.

As we emerged we found ourselves in a land of night. It might have seemed like the bottomless pit of desolation had we not stood upon solid enough ground, while above us was this canopy of black smoke. How far this country extended it was impossible to form any idea, since the heavy atmosphere like a black fog shut in our vision on every side. I was told that it extended through the whole of this vast and dreadful sphere. In some parts there were great tumbled jagged mountains of black rocks, in others long and dreary wastes of desert plains, while yet others were mighty swamps of black oozing mud, full of the most noisome crawling creatures, slimy monsters, and huge bats. Again there were dense black forests of gigantic, repulsive-looking trees, almost human in their power and tenacity, encircling and imprisoning those who ventured amongst them. Ere I left this awful land I had seen these and other dreadful regions, but truly neither I nor anyone else could ever really describe them in all their loathsomeness and foulness.

As we stood looking at this country my sight, gradually becoming used to the darkness, enabled me to perceive the surrounding objects dimly, and I saw that before us there was a highway marked by the passage of many spirit feet across the black plain on which we stood. A plain covered with dust and ashes, as though all the blighted hopes, the dead ashes of misused earthly lives had been scattered there.

CHAPTER XX.--The Imperial City.

We were now traversing a wide causeway of black marble, on either side of which were deep, dark chasms of which it was impossible to see the bottom from the great clouds of heavy vapor that hung over them. Passing and repassing us upon this highway were a great many dark spirits, some bearing great heavy loads upon their backs, others almost crawling along on all fours like beasts. Great gangs of slaves passed us, wearing heavy iron collars on their necks and linked together by a heavy chain. They were coming from the second or inner gate of what was evidently a large fortified city whose dark buildings loomed through the dense masses of dark fog in front of us. The causeway, the style of buildings, and the appearance of many of the spirits made me feel as though we were entering some ancient fortified city of the old Roman Empire, only here everything gave one the sense of being foul and horrible, in spite of the fine architecture and the magnificent buildings whose outlines we could dimly trace. The second gateway was finer in appearance than the first, and the gates being open we passed in with the stream of spirits hurrying through it, and as before we seemed to pass unseen.

"You will perceive," said Faithful Friend, "that here there is a life in no way different from the earthly life of such a city at the time when the one of which this is the spiritual reflection, was in the full zenith of its power, and when the particles of which this is formed were thrown off from its material life and drawn down by the force of attraction to form this city and these buildings, fit dwellings for its spiritual inhabitants; and you will see in the more modern appearance of many of the buildings and inhabitants how it has been added to from time to time by the same process which is going on continuously. You will notice that most of the spirits here fancy themselves still in the earthly counterpart and wonder why all looks so dark and foul and dingy. In like manner this same city has its spiritual prototype in the higher spheres to which all that was fair and good and noble in its life has been attracted, and where those spirits who were good and true have gone to dwell; for in the lives of cities as of men the spiritual emanations are attracted upwards or downwards according as there is good or evil in the deeds done in them. And as the deeds done in this city have in evil far exceeded those which were good, so this city is far larger, far more thickly peopled in this sphere than in those above. In the ages to come when the spirits who are here now shall have progressed, that heavenly counterpart will be fully finished and fully peopled, and then will this place we gaze at now have crumbled into dust--faded from this sphere."

We were now in a narrow street, such as it must have been in the earthly city, and a short distance farther brought us into a large square surrounded with magnificent palaces, while before us towered one more splendid in design than all the others. A great wide flight of marble steps led up to its massive portico, and looming through

89

the dark cloudy atmosphere we could trace its many wings and buildings. All was truly on a magnificent scale, yet all to my eyes appeared dark, stained with great splashes of blood, and covered with slimy fungus growth which disfigured the magnificence and hung in great repulsive-looking festoons, like twisted snakes, from all the pillars and cope-stones of the buildings. Black slimy mud oozed up through the crevices of the marble pavement, as though the city floated upon a foul swamp, and noisome vapors curled up from the ground and floated above and around us in fantastic and horrible smoke wreaths like the huge phantoms of past crimes. Everywhere were dark spirits crawling across the great square and in and out of the palace doors, driven onward by other stronger dark spirits with lash or spear. Such cries of execration as broke forth from time to time, such fearful oaths, such curses and imprecations, it was truly the pandemonium of the lost souls in the Infernal regions! And over all hung those black night clouds of sorrow and suffering and wrong.

Far away to the earth my thoughts traveled, back to the days of the Roman Empire, and I saw reflected as in a glass this city in all the splendor of her power, in all the iniquities of her tyranny and her crimes, weaving down below, from the loom of fate, this other place of retribution for all those men and women who disgraced her beauties by their sins; I saw this great city of Hell building atom by atom till it should become a great prison for all the evil spirits of that wicked time.

We went up the wide flight of steps through the lofty doorway and found ourselves in the outer court of the Emperor's Palace. No one spoke to us or seemed aware of our presence, and we passed on through several smaller halls till we reached the door of the Presence Chamber. Her my companion stopped and said:

"I cannot enter with you, friend, because I have already visited the dark spirit who reigns here, and therefore my presence would at once excite his suspicions and defeat the object of your visit, which is that you may rescue an unhappy spirit whose repentant prayers have reached the higher spheres, and will be answered by the help you are sent to give him. You will find the person you seek without any difficulty. His desire for help has already drawn us thus near to him and will draw you still closer. I must now for a time part from you because I have my own path of work to follow, but we shall meet again ere long, and if you but keep a stout heart and a strong will and do not forget the warnings given you, no harm can befall you. Adieu, my friend, and know that I also shall need all my powers."

Thus, then, I parted from Faithful Friend and passed out alone into the Council Chamber, which I found thronged with spirits, both men and women, and furnished with all the barbaric splendor of the days of the Emperors; yet to my sight there was over everything the same stamp of foul loathsomeness which had struck me in the exterior of the palace. The men and women, haughty patricians in their lives, no doubt, appeared to be eaten up with a loathsome disease like lepers, only they were even more horrible to look upon. The walls and floors seemed stained with dark pools of blood and hung with evil thoughts for drapery. Worm-eaten and corrupting were the stately robes these haughty spirits wore, and saturated with the disease germs from their corrupted bodies.

On a great throne sat the Emperor himself, the most foul and awful example of degraded intellect and manhood in all that vast crowd of degraded spirits, while stamped upon his features was such a look of cruelty and vice that beside him the others sank into insignificance by comparison. I could not but admire, even while it revolted me, the majestic power of this man's intellect and will. The kingly sense of power over even such a motley crew as these, the feeling that even in Hell he reigned as by a right, seemed to minister to his pride and love of dominion even in the midst of his awful surroundings.

Looking at him I beheld him for one brief moment, not as I saw him and as he saw these disgusting creatures round him, but as he still appeared in his own eyes, which even after all these centuries were not opened to his true state, his real self. I saw him as a haughty handsome man, with cruel clear-cut features, hard expression, and eyes like a wild vulture, yet withal possessing a certain beauty of form, a certain power to charm. All that was repulsive and vile was hidden by the earthly envelope, not revealed as now in all the nakedness of the spirit.

I saw his court and his companions change back to the likeness of their earthly lives, and I knew that to each and all they appeared just the same in their own eyes, all were alike unconscious of the horrible change in themselves, yet perfectly conscious of the change in each of their companions.

Were all unconscious? No! not quite all. There was one man crouching in a corner, his mantle drawn over his disfigured face, whom I perceived to be fully conscious of his own vileness as well as the vileness of all who surrounded him.

And in this man's heart there had sprung up a desire, hopeless, as it seemed to himself, for better things, for a path to open before him which, however hard and thorny, might lead him from this night of Hell and give him even at this eleventh hour the hope of a life removed from the horrors of this place and these associates; and as I looked I knew it was to this man that I was sent, though how I was to help him I knew not, I could not guess. I only felt that the power which had led me so far would open up my path and show me the way.

While I had stood thus gazing around me the dark spirits and their Ruler became conscious of my presence, and a look of anger and ferocity passed over his face, while in a voice thick and hoarse with passion he demanded who I was and how I dared to enter his presence.

I answered: "I am a stranger only lately come to this dark sphere and I am still lost in wonder at finding such a place in the spirit world."

A wild ferocious laugh broke from the spirit, and he cried out that they would soon enlighten me as to many things in the spirit world. "But since you are a stranger," he continued, "and because we always receive strangers right royally here, I pray you to be seated and partake with us of our feast."

He pointed to a vacant seat at the long table in front of him at which many of the spirits were seated, and which was spread with what bore the semblance of a great feast, such as might have been given in the days of his earthly grandeur. Everything looked real enough, but I had been warned that it was all more or less illusionary, that the food never satisfied the awful cravings of hunger which these former gluttons felt, and that the wine was a fiery liquid which scorched the throat and rendered a thousand times worse the thirst which consumed these drunkards. I had been told to neither eat nor drink anything offered me in these regions, nor to accept any invitation to rest myself given by these beings; for to do so would mean the subjugation of my higher powers to the senses once more, and would at once put me more on a level with these dark beings and into their power. I answered: "While I fully appreciate the motives which prompt you to offer me the hospitality of your place, I must still decline it, as I have no desire to either eat or drink anything."

At this rebuff his eyes shot gleams of living fire at me and a deeper shade of anger crossed his brow, but he still maintained a pretense of graciousness and signed to me to approach yet nearer to him. Meanwhile the man whom I had come to help, aroused from his bitter meditations by my arrival and the Emperor's speech with me, had drawn near in wonder at my boldness and alarmed for my safety, for he knew no more of me than that I seemed some unlucky new arrival who had not yet learned the dangers of this horrible place. His anxiety for me and a certain sense of pity created a link between us, which, unknown to either, was to be the means whereby I would be able to draw him away with me.

When I advanced a few steps towards the Emperor's throne, this repentant spirit followed me, and, coming close, whispered:

"Do not be beguiled by him. Turn and fly from this place while there is yet time, and I will draw their attention from you for the moment."

I thanked the spirit but said: "I shall not fly from any man, be he whom he may, and will take care not to fall into any trap."

Our hurried speech had not been unnoticed by the Emperor, for he became most impatient, and striking his sword upon the ground he cried out to me:

"Approach, stranger! Have you no manners that you keep an Emperor waiting? Behold my chair of state, my throne, seat yourself in it and try for a moment how it feels to be in an Emperor's place."

I looked at the throne as he pointed, and saw it was like a great chair with a canopy over it. Two immense winged figures in bronze stood at the back of the seat, each with six long arms extended to form the back and sides, while upon the heads of these figures the canopy rested as upon pillars. I had no thought to sit in such a place; its late occupant was too repulsive to me to desire to go any nearer to him, but had even curiosity made me wish to examine the chair the sight I saw would have effectually prevented me. The chair seemed suddenly to become endowed with life, and before my eyes I beheld a vision of an unhappy spirit struggling in the embraces of those awful arms which encircled it and crushed its body into a mangled writhing mass. And I knew that such was the fate of all those whom the Emperor induced to try the comforts of his chair. Only for one brief instant the vision lasted and then I turned to the Emperor and, bowing, said to him:

"I have no desire to place myself upon your level, and must again decline the honor you would do me."

Then he broke into a tempest of rage, and cried out to his guards to seize me and thrust me into that chair and pour the food and the wine down my throat till they choked me.

Immediately there was a rush made towards me, the man I had come to save throwing himself before me to protect me, and in a moment we were surrounded by a seething, fighting mass of spirits, and for that moment, I confess my heart sank within me and my courage began to fail. They looked so horrible, so fiendish, so like a pack of wild beasts let loose and all setting upon me at once. Only for a moment, however, for the conflict aroused all my combative qualities of which I have been thought to possess my fair share. And I threw out all my will to repel them, calling upon all good powers to aid me while I grasped firm hold of the poor spirit who had sought to help me. Thus I retreated to the door, step by step, the whole crowd of dark spirits following us with wild cries and menacing gestures, yet unable to touch us while I kept firm my determination to keep them off. At last we reached the door and passed through it, whereupon it seemed to close fast and keep in our pursuers. Then strong arms seemed to lift us both up and bear us away into a place of safety on the dark plain.

My rescued companion was by this time in a state of unconsciousness, and as I stood by him I saw four majestic spirits from the higher spheres making magnetic passes over his prostrate form; and then I beheld the most wonderful sight I had ever seen. From the dark disfigured body which lay as in a sleep of death there arose a mist-like vapor which grew more and more dense till it took shape in the form of the spirit himself; the purified soul of that poor spirit released from its dark envelope; and I saw those four angelic spirits lift the still unconscious risen soul in their arms as one would bear a child, and then they all floated away from me up, up, till they vanished from my sight. At my side stood another bright angel who said to me: "Be of good cheer, oh! Son of the Land of Hope, for many shalt thou help in this dark land, and great is the joy of the angels in Heaven over these sinners that have repented."

As he finished speaking he vanished, and I was alone once more on the bleak plains of Hell.

CHAPTER XXI.--The Fires of Hell--A Vengeful Spirit--Pirates--The Sea of Foul Mud--The Mountains of Selfish Oppression--The Forest of Desolation-- Messages of Love.

Away before me stretched a narrow path, and curious to see where it would lead I followed it, sure that it would somehow lead me to those whom I could help. After following it for a short time I came to the foot of a range of black mountains, and before me was the entrance to a huge cavern. Horrible reptiles were hanging on to the walls and crawling at my feet. Great funguses and monstrous air plants of an oozy slimy kind hung in festoons like ragged shrouds from the roof, and a dark pool of stagnant water almost covered the floor. I thought of turning away from this spot, but a voice seemed to bid me go on, so I entered, and skirting round the edge of the dark pool found myself at the entrance to a small dark passage in the rocks. Down this I went, and turning a corner saw before me a red light as from a fire, while dark forms like goblins passed and repassed between it and myself. Another moment and I stood at the end of the passage. Before me was a gigantic dungeon-like vault, its uneven rocky roof half revealed and half hidden by the masses of lurid smoke and flames which arose from an enormous fire blazing in the middle of the cavern, while round it were dancing such a troop of demons as might well typify the Devils of Hell. With shrieks and yells of laughter they were prodding at the fire with long black spears and dancing and flinging themselves about in the wildest fashion, while in a corner were huddled together a dozen or so of miserable dark spirits towards whom they made frantic rushes from time to time as if about to seize and hurl them into the fire, always retreating again with yells and howls of rage.

I soon perceived that I was invisible to these beings, so taking courage from that fact, I drew nearer. To my horror I discovered that the fire was composed of the bodies of living men and women who writhed and twisted in the flames, and were tossed about by the spears of those awful demons. I was so appalled by this discovery that I cried out to know if this was a real scene or only some horrible illusion of this dreadful place, and the same deep mysterious voice that had often spoken to me in my wanderings answered me now.

"Son! they are living souls who in their earthly lives doomed hundreds of their fellow men to die this dreadful death, and knew no pity, no remorse, in doing so. Their own cruelties have kindled these fierce flames of passion and hate in the breast of their many victims, and in the spirit world these fiery germs have grown till they are now a fierce flame to consume the oppressors. These fires are fed solely by the fierce cruelties of those they now consume; there is not here one pang of anguish which has not been suffered a hundred fold more in the persons of these spirits' many helpless victims. From this fire these spirits will come forth touched by a pity, born of their own sufferings, for those they wronged in the past, and then will be extended to them the hand of help and the means of progression through deeds of mercy as many and as great as have been their merciless deeds in the past. Do not shudder nor marvel that such retribution as this is allowed to be. The souls of these spirits were so hard, so cruel, that only sufferings felt by themselves could make them pity others. Even since they left the earth life they have only been intent upon making others more helpless suffer, till the bitter hatred they have aroused has become at last a torrent which has engulfed themselves. Furthermore, know that these flames are not truly material, although to your eyes and to theirs they appear so, for in the spirit world that which is mental is likewise objective, and fierce hatred or burning passion does indeed seem a living fire. You shall now follow one of these spirits and see for yourself that what seems to you cruel justice is yet mercy in disguise. Behold these passions are burning themselves out and the souls are about to pass into the darkness of the plain beyond."

As the voice ceased the flames died down and all was darkness save for a faint bluish light like phosphorus that filled the cavern, and by it I saw the forms of the spirits rise from the ashes of the fire and pass out of the cavern. As I followed them one became separated from the others and passing on before me went into the streets of a city that was near. It seemed to me like one of the old Spanish cities of the West Indies or South America. There were Indians passing along its streets and mingling with Spaniards and men of several other nations.

Following the spirit through several streets we came to a large building which seemed to be a monastery of the order of Jesuits--who had helped to colonize the country and force upon the unhappy natives the Roman Catholic religion, in the days when religious persecution was thought by most creeds to be a proof of religious zeal; and then, while I stood watching this spirit, I saw pass before me a panorama of his life.

I saw him first chief of his order, sitting as a judge before whom were brought many poor Indians and heretics, and I saw him condemning them by hundreds to torture and flames because they would not become converts to his teachings. I saw him oppressing all who were not powerful enough to resist him, and extorting jewels and gold in enormous quantities as tribute to him and to his order; and if any sought to resist him and his demands he had them arrested and almost without even the pretense of a trial thrown into dungeons and tortured and burned. I read in his heart a perfect thirst for wealth and power and an actual love for beholding the sufferings of his victims, and I knew (reading as I seemed to do his innermost soul) that his religion was but a cloak, a convenient name, under which to extort the gold he loved and gratify his love of power.

Again I saw the great square or market place of this city with hundreds of great fires blazing all round it till it was like a furnace, and a whole helpless crowd of timid gentle natives were bound hand and foot and thrown into the flames, and their cries of agony went up to Heaven as this cruel man and his vile accomplices chanted their false prayers and held aloft the sacred cross which was desecrated by their unholy hands, their horrible lives of cruelty and vice, and their greed for gold. I saw that this horror was perpetrated in the name of the Church of Christ--of him whose teachings were of love and charity, who came to teach that God was perfect Love. And I saw this man who called himself Christ's minister, and yet had no thought of pity for one of these unhappy victims; he thought alone of how the spectacle would strike terror to the hearts of other Indian tribes, and make them bring him more gold to satisfy his greedy lust. Then I beheld this man returned to his own land of Spain and revelling in his ill-gotten wealth, a powerful wealthy prince of the church, venerated by the poor ignorant populace as a holy man who had gone forth into that Western World beyond the seas to plant the banner of his church and preach the blessed gospel of love and peace, while, instead, his path had been marked in fire and blood, and then my sympathy for him was gone. Then I saw this man upon his deathbed, and I saw monks and priests chanting mass for his soul that it might go to Heaven, and instead I saw it drawn down and down to Hell by the chains woven in his wicked life. I saw the great hordes of his former victims awaiting him there, drawn down in their turn by their thirst for revenge, their hunger for power to avenge their sufferings and the sufferings of those most dear to them.

I saw this man in Hell surrounded by those he had wronged, and haunted by the empty wraiths of such as were too good and pure to come to this place of horror or to wish for vengeance on their murderer, just as I had seen in the Frozen Land with the man in the icy cage; and in Hell the only thought of that spirit was rage because his power on earth was no more--his only idea how he might join with others in Hell as cruel as himself and thus still oppress and torture. If he could have doomed his victims to death a second time he would have done it. In his heart there was neither pity nor remorse, only anger that he was so powerless. Had he possessed one feeling of sorrow or one thought of kindness for another, it would have helped him and created a wall between himself and these vengeful spirits, and his sufferings, though they might be great, would not have at last assumed the physical aspect in which I had beheld them. As it was, his passion of cruelty was so great it fed and fanned into fresh life the spiritual flames which theirs created, till at last when I saw him first they were dying out exhausted by their own violence. Those demons I had beheld were the last and most fierce of his victims in whom the desire for revenge was even then not fully satisfied, while those I had beheld crouching in the corner were some who, no longer desirous of tormenting him themselves, had yet been unable to withdraw themselves from beholding his sufferings and those of his accomplices.

And now I beheld that spirit with the newly awakened thought of repentence, returning to the city to warn others of his Jesuit fraternity, and to try to turn them from the path of his own errors. He did not yet realize the length of time that had elapsed since he had left the earth life, nor that this city was the spiritual counterpart of the one he had lived in on earth. In time, I was told, he would be sent back to earth to work as a spirit in helping to teach mortals the pity and mercy he had not shown in his own life, but first he would have to work here in this dark place, striving to release the souls of those whom his crimes had dragged down with him. Thus I left this man at the door of that building which was the counterpart of his earthly house, and passed on by myself through the city.

Like the Roman city this one was disfigured and its beauties blotted out by the crimes of which it had been the silent witness; and to me the air seemed full of dark phantom forms wailing and weeping and dragging after them their heavy chains. The whole place seemed built upon living graves and shrouded in a dark red mist of blood and tears. It was like one vast prison house whose walls were built of deeds of violence and robbery and oppression.

And as I wandered on I had a waking dream, and saw the city as it had been on earth ere the white man had set his foot upon its soil. I saw a peaceful primitive people living upon fruits and grains and leading their simple lives in an innocence akin to that of childhood, worshiping the Great Supreme under a name of their own, yet none the less worshiping him in spirit and in truth--their simple faith and their patient virtues the outcome of the inspiration given them from that Great Spirit who is universal and belongs to no creeds, no churches. Then I saw white men come thirsting for gold and greedy to grasp the goods of others, and these simple people welcomed them like brothers, and in their innocence showed them the treasures they had gathered from the earth--gold and silver and jewels. Then I saw the treachery which marked the path of the white man; how they plundered and killed the simple natives; how they tortured and made slaves of them, forcing them to labor in the mines till they died by thousands; how all faith, all promises, were broken by the white man till the peaceful happy country was filled with tears and blood.

Then I beheld afar, away in Spain, a few good, true, kindly men whose souls were pure and who believed that they alone had the true faith by which only man can be saved and live eternally, who thought that God had given this light to but one small spot of his earth, and had left all the rest in darkness and error--had left countless thousands to perish because this light had been denied to them but given exclusively to that one small spot of earth, that small section of his people.

I thought that these good and pure men were so sorry for those who, they thought, were in the darkness and error of a false religion, that they set forth and crossed that unknown ocean to that strange far-away land to carry with them their system of religion, and to give it to those poor simple people whose lives had been so good and gentle and spiritual under their own faith, their own beliefs.

I saw these good but ignorant priests land on this strange shore and beheld them working everywhere amongst the natives, spreading their own belief and crushing out and destroying all traces of a primitive faith as worthy of respect as their own. These priests were kind good men who sought to alleviate the physical lot of the poor oppressed natives even while they labored for their spiritual welfare also, and on every side there sprang up missions, churches and schools.

Then I beheld great numbers of men, priests as well as many others, come over from Spain, eager, not for the good of the church nor to spread the truths of their religion, but only greedy for the gold of this new land, and for all that could minister to their own gratification; men whose lives had disgraced them in their own country till they were obliged to fly to this strange one to escape the consequences of their misdeeds. I saw these men arrive in hordes and mingle with those whose motives were pure and good, till they had outnumbered them, and then thrust the good aside everywhere, and made of themselves tyrannical masters over the unhappy natives, in the name of the Holy Church of Christ.

And then I saw the Inquisition brought to the unhappy land and established as the last link in the chain of slavery and oppression thus riveted round this unhappy people, till it swept almost all of them from the face of the earth; and everywhere I beheld the wild thirst, the greed for gold that consumed as with a fire of hell all who sought that land. Blind were most of them to all its beauties but its gold, deaf to all thought but how they might enrich themselves with it; and in the madness of that time and that awful craving for wealth was this city of Hell, this spiritual counterpart of the earthly city built, stone upon stone, particle by particle, forming between itself and the city of earth chains of attraction which should draw down one by one each of its wicked inhabitants, for truly the earthly lives are building for each man and woman their spiritual habitations. Thus all these monks and priests, all these fine ladies, all these soldiers and merchants, yea, and even these unhappy natives had been drawn down to Hell by the deeds of their earthly lives, by the passions and hatreds, the greed of gold, the bitter sense of wrongs unrequited and the thirst for revenge which those deeds had created.

At the door of a large square building, whose small grated windows looked like a prison, I stopped, arrested by the cries and shouts which came from it; then guided by the mysterious voice of my unseen guide I entered, and following the sounds soon came to a dungeon cell. Here I found a great number of spirits surrounding a man who was chained to the wall by an iron girdle round his waist. His wild glaring eyes, disheveled hair and tattered clothing suggested that he had been there for many years, while the hollow sunken cheeks and the bones sticking through his skin told that he was to all appearance dying of starvation; yet I knew that here there was no death, no such relief from suffering. Near him stood another man with folded arms and bowed head, whose wasted features and skeleton form scarred with many wounds made him an even more pitiable object than the other, though he was free while the other was chained to the wall. Around them both danced and yelled other spirits, all wild and savage and degraded. Some of them were Indians, a few Spanish, and one or two looked, I thought, like Englishmen. All were at the same work--throwing sharp knives at the chained man that never seemed to hit him, shaking their fists in his face, cursing and reviling him, yet, strange to say, never able to actually touch him, and all the time there he stood chained to the wall, unable to move or get away from them. And there stood the other man silently watching him.

As I stood looking at this scene I became conscious of the past history of those two men. I saw the one who was chained to the wall in a handsome house like a palace, and knew he had been one of the judges sent out from Spain to preside over the so-called courts of justice, which had but proved additional means for extorting money from the natives and oppressing all who sought to interfere with the rich and powerful. I saw the other man who had been a merchant, living in a pretty villa with a beautiful, a very beautiful, wife and one little child. This woman had attracted the notice of the judge, who conceived an unholy passion for her, and on her persistently repulsing all his advances he made an excuse to have the husband arrested on suspicion by the Inquisition and thrown into prison. Then he carried off the poor wife and so insulted her that she died, and the poor little child was strangled by order of the cruel judge.

Meantime the unfortunate husband lay in prison, ignorant of the fate of his wife and child and of the charge under which he had been arrested, growing more and more exhausted from the scanty food and the horrors of the dungeon, and more and more desperate from the suspense. At last he was brought before the council of the Inquisition, charged with heretical practices and conspiracy against the crown, and on denial of these charges was tortured to make him confess and give up the names of certain of his friends who were accused of being his accomplices. As the poor man, bewildered and indignant, still protested his innocence he was sent back to his dungeon and there slowly starved to death, the cruel judge not daring to set him at liberty, well knowing that he would make the city ring with the story of his wrongs and his wife's fate when he should learn it.

As so this poor man had died, but he did not join his wife, who, poor injured soul, had passed at once with her little innocent child into the higher spheres. She was so good and pure and gentle that she had even forgiven her murderer--for such he was, though he had not intended to kill her--and between her and the husband she so dearly loved there was a wall created by his bitter revengeful feelings against the man who had destroyed them both.

When this poor wronged husband died, his soul could not leave the earth. It was tied there by his hatred of his enemy and his thirst for revenge. His own wrongs he might have forgiven, but the fate of his wife and child had been too dreadful. He could not forgive that. Before even his love for his wife came this hate, and day and night his spirit clung fast to the judge, seeking for the chance of vengeance; and at last it came. Devils from Hell--such as had once tempted me--clustered round the wronged spirit and taught it how through the hand of a mortal it could strike the assassin's dagger to the judge's heart, and then when death severed the body and the spirit he could drag that down with him to Hell. So terrible had been this craving for revenge, nursed through the waiting years of solitude in prison and in the spirit land, that the poor wife had tried and tried in vain to draw near her husband and soften his heart with better thoughts. Her gentle soul was shut out by the wall of evil drawn round the unhappy man, and he also had no hope of ever seeing her again. He deemed that she had gone to Heaven and was lost to him for evermore. A Roman Catholic of the narrow views held nearly two hundred years ago when this man had lived, he believed that being under the ban of its priests and denied the ministrations of the church when he died, was the reason he was one of the eternally lost, while his wife and child must be with the angels of Heaven. Is it wonderful, then, that all this poor spirit's thoughts should center in the desire for vengeance, and that he should plan only how to make his enemy suffer as he had been made to suffer? Thus, then, it was he who inspired a man on earth to kill the judge; his hand guided the mortal's with so unerring an aim that the judge fell pierced to his false, cruel heart. The earthly body died but the immortal soul lived, and awakened to find itself in Hell, chained to a dungeon wall as he had chained his victim, and face to face with him at last.

There were others whom the judge had wronged and sent to a death of suffering to gratify his anger or to enrich himself at their expense, and these all gathered round him and made his awakening a Hell indeed. Yet such was the indomitable strength of will of this man that none of the blows aimed at him could touch him, none of the missiles strike, and thus through all the years had those two deadly enemies faced each other, pouring out their hatred and defiance while those other spirits, like the chorus of a Greek tragedy, came and went and amused themselves devising fresh means to torment the chained man whose strong will kept them at bay.

And away in the bright spheres mourned the poor wife, striving and hoping till the time should come when her influence would be felt even in this awful place, when her love and her unceasing prayers should reach the soul of her husband and soften it, that he might relent in his bitter purpose and turn from his revenge. It was her prayers which had drawn me to this dungeon, and it was her soul which spoke to mine, telling me all the sad cruel story, and pleading with me to carry to her unhappy husband the knowledge that she lived only in thoughts of him, only in the hope that he would be drawn by her love to the upper spheres to join her in peace and happiness at last. With this vision strong upon me, I drew near the sullen man who was growing tired of his revenge, and whose heart was full of longing for the wife he loved so passionately.

I touched him upon the shoulder and said: "Friend, I know why you are here, and all the cruel story of your wrongs, and I am sent from her you love to tell you that in the bright land above she awaits you, wearying that you do not come and marveling that you can find revenge more sweet than her caresses. She bids me tell you that you chain yourself here when you might be free."

The spirit started as I spoke, then turning to me grasped my arm and gazed long and ernestly into my face as though to read there whether I spoke truly or falsely. Then he sighed as he drew back, saying: "Who are you and why do you come here? You are like none of those who belong to this awful place, and your words are words of hope, yet how can there be hope for the soul in Hell?"

"There is hope even here; for hope is eternal and God in his mercy shuts none out from it, whatever man in his earth-distorted image of the divine teachings may do. I am sent to give hope to you and to others who are, like you, in sorrow for the past, and if you will but come with me, I can show you how to reach the Better Land."

I saw that he hesitated, and a bitter struggle went on in his heart, for he knew that it was his presence which kept his enemy a prisoner, that were he to go the other would be free to wander through this Dark Land, and even yet he could hardly let him go. Then I spoke again of his wife; his child; would he not rather go to them? The strong passionate man broke down as he thought of those loved ones, and burying his face in his hands wept bitter tears. I put my arm through his and led him, unresisting, out of the prison and out of the city. Here we found kind spirit friends were awaiting the poor man, and with them I left him that they might bear him to a bright land where he would see his wife from time to time, till he worked himself up to the level of her sphere, where they would be united forever in a happiness more perfect than could ever have been their lot on earth.

I did not return to the city, for I felt my work there was done, and so wandered on in search of fresh fields of usefulness. In the middle of a dark lonely plain I came upon a solitary hut, in which I found a man lying on some wisps of dirty straw, unable to move and to all appearance dying.

He told me that in his earth life he had thus abandoned and left to die a sick comrade, whom he had robbed of the gold for which they had both risked their lives, and that now he also was dead he found himself lying in the same helpless deserted way.

I asked him if he would not wish to get up and go and do something to help others and thus atone for the murder of his friend, because if so I thought I could help him.

He thought he would like to get up certainly. He was sick of this hole, but he did not see why he should work at anything or bother about other people. He would rather look for the money he had buried, and spend that. Here his cunning eyes glanced furtively at me to see what I thought of his money and if I was likely to try to find it.

I suggested to him that he ought rather to think of trying to find the friend he had murdered and make reparation to him. But he wouldn't hear of that, and got quite angry, said he was not sorry he had killed his friend, and only sorry he was here. He thought I would have helped him to get away. I tried to talk to this man and make him see how he really might better his position and undo the wrong he had done, but it was no use, his only idea was that once given the use of his limbs again he could go and rob or kill some one else. So at last I left him where he lay, and as I went out his feeble hand picked up a stone and flung it after me.

"What," I asked mentally, "will become of this man?"

I was answered: "He has just come from earth after dying a violent death, and his spirit is weak, but ere long he will grow strong, and then he will go forth and join other marauders like himself who go about in bands, and add another horror to this place. After the lapse of many years--it may even be centuries--the desire for better things will awake, and he will begin to progress, but very slowly, for the soul which has been in chains so long and is so poorly developed, so degraded as in this man, often takes cycles of time to develop its dormant powers."

After I had wandered for some time over this dreary desolate plain I felt so tired, weary of heart, that I sat down, and began musing upon what I had seen in this awful sphere. The sight of so much evil and suffering had depressed me, the awful darkness and heavy murky clouds oppressed my soul that ever had loved the sunshine and the light as I fancy only we of the Southern nations love it. And then I wearied. Ah! how I wearied and longed for news from her whom I had left on earth. No word had reached me as yet from my friends--no news of my beloved. I knew not how long I had been in this place where there was no day to mark the time, nothing but eternal night that brooded and reigned in silence over everything. My thoughts were full of my beloved, and I prayed earnestly, that she might be kept safe on earth to gladden my eyes when the time of probation in this place should be over. While I prayed I became conscious of a soft pale light suffused around me, as from a glowing star, that grew and grew till it expanded and opened out into a most glorious picture framed in rays of light, and in the centre I saw my darling, her eyes looking into mine and smiling at me, her sweet lips parted as though speaking my name; then she seemed to raise her hand and touching her lips with her finger tips, threw me a kiss. So shyly, so prettily, was it done that I was in raptures, and rose to return her that kiss, to look more closely at her, and lo! the vision had vanished and I was alone on the dark plain once more. But no longer sad, that bright vision had cheered me, and given me hope and courage to go on once more and bring to others such hope as cheered myself.

I arose and went on again, and in a short time was overtaken by a number of dark and most repulsive-looking spirits; they wore ragged black cloaks and seemed to have their faces concealed by black masks like spectral highwaymen. They did not see me, and I had found that as a rule the dwellers of this sphere were too low in intelligence and spiritual sight to be able to see anyone from the spheres above unless brought into direct contact with them. Curious to see what they were about, I drew back and followed them at a little distance. Presently another party of dark spirits approached, carrying what looked like bags with some sort of treasure. Immediately they were attacked by the first-comers. They had no weapons in their hands, but they fought like wild beasts with teeth and claws, their finger nails being like the claws of a wild animal or a vulture. They fastened upon each other's throats and tore them. They scratched and bit like tigers or wolves, till one-half at least were left lying helpless upon the ground, while the rest rushed off with the treasure (which to me seemed only lumps of hard stone).

When all who were able to move had gone, I drew near the poor spirits lying moaning on the ground to see if I could help any of them. But it seemed to be no use doing so; they only tried to turn upon me and tear me in pieces. They were more like savage beasts than men, even their bodies were bent like a beast's, the arms long like an ape's, the hands hard, and the fingers and nails like claws, and they half walked and half crawled on all-fours. The faces could scarcely be called human; the very features had become bestial, while they lay snarling and showing their teeth like wolves. I thought of the strange wild tales I had read of men changing into animals, and I felt I could almost have believed these were such creatures. In their horrible glaring eyes there was an expression of calculation and cunning which was certainly human, and the motions of their hands were not like those of an animal; moreover they had speech and were mingling their howls and groans with oaths and curses and foul language unknown to animals.

"Are there souls even here?" I asked.

Again came the answer: "Yes, even here. Lost, degraded, dragged down and smothered, till almost all trace is lost, yet even here there are the germs of souls. These men were pirates of the Spanish main, highwaymen, freebooters, slave dealers, and kidnappers of men. They have so brutalized themselves that almost all trace of the human is merged in the wild animal. Their instincts were those of savage beasts; now they live like beasts and fight like them."

"And for them is there still hope, and can anyone help them?" I asked.

"Even for these there is hope, though many will not avail themselves of it for ages yet to come. Yet here and there are others who even now can be helped."

I turned, and at my feet lay a man who had dragged himself to me with great difficulty and was now too exhausted for further effort. He was less horrible to look upon than the others, and in his distorted face there were yet traces of better things. I bent over him and heard his lips murmur: "Water! Water for any sake! Give me water for I am consumed with a living fire."

I had no water to give him and knew not where to get any in this land, but I gave him a few drops of the essence I had brought from the Land of Dawn for myself. The effect upon him was like magic. It was an elixir. He sat up and stared at me and said:

"You must be a magician. That has cooled me and put out the fire that has burned within me for years. I have been filled with a living fire of thirst ever since I came to this Hell."

I had now drawn him away from the others, and began to make passes over his body, and as I did so his sufferings ceased and he grew quiet and restful. I was standing by him wondering what to do next, whether to speak or to go away and leave him to himself, when he caught my hand and kissed it passionately.

"Oh! friend, how am I to thank you? What shall I call you who have come to give me relief after all these years of suffering?"

"If you are thus grateful to me, would you not wish to earn the gratitude of others by helping them? Shall I show you how you could?"

"Yes! Oh! yes, most gladly, if only you will take me with you, good friend."

"Well, then, let me help you up, and if you are able we had bettr leave this spot as soon as we can," said I, and together we set forth to see what we could do.

My companion told me he had been a pirate and in the slave trade. He had been mate of a ship and was killed in a fight, and had awakened to find himself and others of the crew in this dark place. How long he had been there he had no idea, but it seemed like eternity. He and other spirits like him went about in bands and were always fighting. When they did not meet another party to fight they fought amongst themselves; the thirst for fighting was the only excitement they could get in this horrible place where there was never any drink to be got which could quench the awful burning thirst which consumed them all; what they drank only seemed to make them a thousand times worse, and was like pouring living fire down their throats. Then he said: "You never could die, no matter what you suffered, that was the awful curse of the thing, you had got beyond death, and it was no use trying to kill yourself or get others to kill you, there was no such escape from suffering.

"We are like a lot of hungry wolves," he said, "for want of anyone to attack us we used to fall upon each other and fight till we were exhausted, and then we would lie moaning and suffering till we recovered enough to go forth again and attack someone else. I have been longing for any means of escape. I have almost got to praying for it at last. I felt I would do anything if God would only forgive me and let me have another chance; and when I saw you standing near me I thought perhaps you were an angel sent down to me after all. Only you've got no wings nor anything of that sort, as they paint 'em in pictures. But then pictures don't give you much idea of this place, and if they are wrong about one place why not about the other?"

I laughed at him; yes, even in that place of sorrow I laughed, my heart felt so much lightened to find myself of so much use. And then I told him who I was and how I came to be there, and he said if I wanted to help people there were some dismal swamps near where a great many unhappy spirits were imprisoned, and he could take me to them and help a bit himself he thought. He seemed afraid to let me go out of his sight lest I should disappear and leave him alone again. I felt quite attracted to this man because he seemed so very grateful and I was also glad of companionship of any sort (except that of those most repulsive beings who seemed the majority of the dwellers here) for I felt lonely and somewhat desolate in this far-off dismal country.

The intense darkness, the horrible atmosphere of thick fog, made it almost impossible to see far in any direction, so that we reached the land of swamps before I was aware of it except for feeling a cold, damp, offensive air which blew in our faces. Then I saw looming before me a great sea of liquid mud, black, fetid and stagnant, a thick slime of oily blackness floating on the top. Here and there monstrous reptiles, with huge inflated bodies and projecting eyes were wallowing. Great bats, with almost human faces like vampires, hovered over it, while black and grey smoke wreaths of noisome vapor rose from its decaying surface, and hung over it in weird fantastic phantom shapes that shifted and changed ever and anon into fresh forms of ugliness--now waving aloft wild arms and shaking, nodding, gibbering heads, which seemed almost endowed with sense and speech--then melting into mist again to form into some new creature of repulsive horror.

On the shores of this great foul sea were innumerable crawling slimy creatures of

106

hideous shape and gigantic size that lay sprawling on their backs or plunged into that horrid sea. I shuddered as I looked upon it and was about to ask if there could indeed be lost souls struggling in that filthy slime, when my ears heard a chorus of wailing cries and calls for help coming from the darkness before me, that touched my heart with their mournful hopelessness, and my eyes, growing more accustomed to the mist, distinguished here and there struggling human forms wading up to their armpits in the mud. I called to them and told them to try and walk towards me, for I was on the shore, but they either could not see or could not hear me for they took no notice, and my companion said he believed they were both deaf and blind to everything but their immediate surroundings. He had been in the sea of foul mud himself for a time, but had managed to struggle out, though he had understood that most were unable to do so without help from another, and that some went on stumbling about in it for years. Again we heard those pitiful cries, and one sounded so near us that I thought of plunging in myself and trying to drag the wretched spirit out, but faugh! it was too horrible, too disgusting. I recoiled in horror at the thought. And then again that despairing cry smote upon my ears and made me feel I must venture it. So in I went, trying my best to stifle my sense of disgust, and, guided by the cries, soon reached the man, the great phantoms of the mist wavering and swooping and rushing overhead as I did so. He was up to his neck in the mud and seemed sinking lower when I found him, and it seemed impossible for me alone to draw him out, so I called to the pirate spirit to come and help me, but he was nowhere to be seen. Thinking he had only led me into a trap and deserted me, I was about to turn and struggle out again, when the unfortunate spirit besought me so pitifully not to abandon him that I made another great effort and succeeded in dragging him a few yards and drawing his feet out of a trap of weeds at the bottom in which they appeared to be caught. Then, somehow, I half dragged, half supported him till we reached the shore where the unfortunate spirit sank down in unconsciousness. I was a good deal exhausted also and sat down beside him to rest. I looked round for my pirate friend, and beheld him wallowing about in the sea at some distance and evidently bringing out someone along with him. Even in the midst of my awful surroundings I could not help feeling a certain sense of amusement in looking at him, he made such frantic and exaggerated efforts to haul along the unlucky spirit, and was so shouting and going on that it was calculated to alarm anyone who was timid, and I did not wonder to hear the poor spirit almost imploring not to be so energetic, to take it a little slower, and to give him time to follow. I went over to them, and the poor rescued one being now near the shore I helped to get him out and to let him rest beside the other one.

The pirate spirit seemed greatly delighted with his successful efforts and very proud of himself, and was quite ready to set off again, so I sent him after someone else whom we heard calling, and was attending to the other two when I again heard most pitiful wailings not far from me, though I could see no one at first, then a faint, tiny speck of light like a will-o'-the-wisp glimmered in the darkness of that disgusting swamp, and by its light I saw someone moving about and calling for aid, so, not very willingly, I confess, I went into the mud again. When I reached the man I found he had a woman with him whom he was supporting and trying to encourage, and with considerable trouble I got them both out and found the pirate spirit had also arrived with his rescued one.

Truly a strange group we must have made on the shores of that slimy sea, which I learned afterwards was the spiritual creation of all the disgusting thoughts, all the impure desires of the lives of men on earth, attracted and collected into this great swamp of foulness. Those spirits who were thus wallowing in it had reveled in such low abominations in their earth lives and had continued to enjoy such pleasures after death through the mediumship of mortal men and women, till at last even the earth plane had become too high for them by reason of their own exceeding vileness, and they had been drawn down by the force of attraction into this horrible sink of corruption to wander in it till the very disgust of themselves should work a cure.

One man I had rescued had been one of the celebrated wits of Charles the Second's court, and after his death had long haunted the earth plane, sinking, however, lower and lower till he had sunk into this sea at last, the weeds of his pride and arrogance forming chains in which his feet were so entangled that he could not move till I released him. Another man had been a celebrated dramatist of the reign of the early Georges. While the man and woman had belonged to the court of Louis the Fifteenth and had been drawn together to this place. Those rescued by the pirate were somewhat similar in their histories.

I had been somewhat troubled at first as to how I was going to free myself from the mud of that horrible sea, but I now suddenly saw a small clear fountain of pure water spring up near to us as if by magic, and in its fresh stream we soon washed all traces of the mud away.

I now advised those whom we had rescued to try what they could do to help others in this land of darkness as a return for the help given to themselves, and having given them what advice and help I could I started once more upon my pilgrimage. The pirate, however, seemed so very unwilling to part from me that we two set forth together once more.

I shall not attempt to describe all whom we sought to help in our wanderings. Were I to do so this narrative would fill volumes and probably only weary my readers, so I shall pass over what seemed to me like weeks of earthly time, as nearly as I am able to reckon it, and will describe our arrival at a vast range of mountains whose bleak summits towered into the night sky overhead. We were both somewhat discouraged with the results of our efforts to help people. Here and there we had found a few who were willing to listen and to be helped, but as a rule our attempts had been met with scorn and derision, while not a few had even attacked us for interfering with them, and we had some trouble to save ourselves from injury.

Our last attempt had been with a man and woman of most repulsive appearance who were fighting at the door of a wretched hovel. The man was beating her so terribly I could not but interfere to stop him. Whereupon they both set on me at once, the woman spirit doing her best to scratch my eyes out, and I was glad to have the pirate come to my assistance, for, truth to tell, the combined attack had made me lose my temper, and by doing so I put myself for the moment on their level, and so was deprived of the protection afforded me by my superior spiritual development.

These two had been guilty of a most cruel and brutal murder of an old man (the husband of the woman) for the sake of his money; and they had been hanged for the crime, their mutual guilt forming a bond between them so strong that they had been drawn down together and were unable to separate in spite of the bitter hatred they now felt for each other. Each felt the other to be the cause of their being in this place, and each felt the other more guilty than themselves, and it had been their eagerness each to betray the other which had helped to hang both. Now they seemed simply to exist in order to fight together, and I can fancy no punishment more awful than theirs must have been, thus linked together in hate.

In their present state of mind it was not possible to help them in any way.

Shortly after leaving this interesting couple we found ourselves at the foot of the great dark mountains, and by the aid of a curious pale phosphorescent glow which hung in patches over them we were able to explore them a little. There were no regular pathways, and the rocks were very steep, so we stumbled up as best we might--for I should explain that by taking on a certain proportion of the conditions of this low sphere I had lost the power to rise at will and float, which was a privilege of those who had reached the Land of Dawn. After a toilsome ascent of one of the lower ranges of the mountains we began to tramp along the crest of one, faintly lighted by the strange gleaming patches of phosphorescent light, and beheld on either side of us vast deep chasms in the rocks, gloomy precipices, and awful looking black pits. From some of these came wailing cries and moans and occasionally prayers for help. I was much shocked to think there were spirits down in such depths of misery, and felt quite at a loss how to help them, when my companion, who had shown a most remarkable eagerness to second all my efforts to rescue people, suggested that we should make a rope from some of the great rank, withered-looking weeds and grass that grew in small crevices of these otherwise barren rocks, and with such a rope I could lower him down, as he was more used to climbing in that fashion than I, and thus we might be able to draw up some of these spirits out of their dreadful position.

This was a good idea, so we set to work and soon had a rope strong enough to bear the weight of my friend, for you should know that in spiritual, as well as in material things, weight is a matter of comparison, and the materiality of those low spheres will give them a much greater solidity and weight than belongs to a spirit sphere more advanced, and though to your material eyes of earth life my pirate friend would have shown neither distinct material form nor weight, yet a very small development of your spiritual faculties would have enabled you to both see and feel his presence, though a spirit the next degree higher would still remain invisible to you. Thus I am not in error, nor do I even say what is improbable, when I thus speak of my friend's weight, which for a rope made of spiritual grass and weeds was as great a strain as would have been the case with an earthly man and earth materials. Having made one end of the rope fast to a rock, the spirit descended with the speed and sureness acquired by long practice as a sailor. Once there he soon made it fast round the body of the poor helpless one whom he found lying moaning at the bottom. Then I drew up the rope and the spirit, and when he had been made safe I lowered it to my friend and drew him up, and having done what we could for the rescued one we went on and helped a few more in like fashion.

When we had pulled out as many as we could find, a most strange thing happened. The phosphorescent light died out and left us in utter darkness, while a mysterious voice floating, as it seemed, in the air, said, "Go on now, your work here is done. Those whom you have rescued were caught in their own traps, and the pitfalls that they made for others had received themselves, till that time when repentance and a desire to atone should draw rescuers to help them and free them from the prisons they had themselves made. In these mountains are many spirits imprisoned who may not yet be helped out by any, for they would only be a danger to others were they free, and the ruin and evil they would shed around make their longer imprisonment a necessity. Yet are their prisons of their own creating, for these great mountains of misery are the outcome and product of men's earthly lives, and these precipices are but the spiritual counterparts of those precipices of despair over which they have in earthly life driven their unhappy victims. Not till their hearts soften, not till they have learned to long for liberty that they may do good instead of evil, will their prisons be opened and they be drawn forth from the living death in which their own frightful cruelties to others have entombed them."

The voice ceased, and alone and in darkness we groped our way down the mountain side till we reached the level ground once more. Those awful mysterious dark valleys of eternal night--those towering mountains of selfishness and oppression--had struck such a chill to my heart that I was glad indeed to know there was no call of duty for me to linger longer there.

Our wandering now brought us to an immense forest, whose weird fantastic trees were like what one sees in some awful nightmare. The leafless branches seemed like living arms held out to grasp and hold the hapless wanderer. The long snake-like roots stretched out like twisting ropes to trip him up. The trunks were bare and blackened as though scorched by the blasting breath of fire. From the bark a thick foul slime oozed and like powerful wax held fast any hand that touched it. Great waving shrouds of some strange dark air plant clothed the branches like a pall, and helped to enfold and bewilder any who tried to penetrate through this ghostly forest. Faint muffled cries as of those who are exhausted and half smothered came from this awful wood, and here and there we could see the imprisoned souls held captive in the embrace of these extraordinary prisons, struggling to get free, yet unable to move one single step.

"How," I wondered, "shall we help these?" Some were caught by the foot--a twisted root holding them as in a vice. Another's hand was glued to the trunk of a tree. Another was enveloped in a shroud of the black moss, while yet another's head and shoulders were held fast by a couple of branches which had closed upon them. Wild ferocious looking beasts prowled round them, and huge vultures flapped their wings overhead, yet seemed unable to touch any of the prisoners, though they came so near.

"Who are those men and women?" I asked.

"They are those," was the reply, "who viewed with delight the sufferings of others, those who gave their fellow men to be torn in pieces by wild beasts that they might enjoy the excitement of their sufferings. They are all those who for no reason but the lust of cruelty have, in many different ways and in many different ages, tortured and entrapped and killed those who were more helpless than themselves, and for all now here release will only come when they have learned the lesson of mercy and pity for others and the desire to save some one else from suffering, even at the expense of suffering to themselves. Then will these bands and fetters which hold them be loosed, then they will be free to go forth and work out their atonement. Till then no one else can help them--none can release them. Their release must be effected by themselves through their own more merciful desires and aspirations. If you will but recall the history of your earth and think how men in all ages have enslaved, oppressed and tortured their fellow men in every country of that globe, you will not wonder that this vast forest should be well peopled. It was deemed right that for your own instruction you should see this fearful place, but as none of those you see and pity have so far changed their hearts that you can give them aid, you will now pass on to another region where you can do more good."

After leaving the Forest of Desolation we had not gone far upon our road when to my joy I saw my friend Hassein approaching. Mindful, however, of Ahrinziman's warning I gave him the sign agreed upon and received the countersign in return. He had come, he said, with a message from my father and from my beloved who had sent me what were indeed sweet words of love and encouragement. Hassein told me that my mission would now lie amongst those great masses of spirits whose evil propensities were equalled only by their intellectual powers, and their ingenuity in works of evil. "They are those," said he, "who were rulers of men and kings of intellect in all branches, but who have perverted and abused the powers with which they were endowed till they have made of them a curse and not a blessing. With most of them you will have to guard yourself at all points against the allurements they will hold out to tempt you, and the treachery of every kind they will practice on yourself. Yet amongst them are a few whom you are sent to succor and whom your own instinct and events will point out as those to whom your words will be welcome and your aid valuable. I shall not in all probability bring you messages again, but some other may be sent to do so, and you must, above all things and before all things, remember to distrust any who come to you and cannot give the sign and symbol I have given. You are now in reality about to invade the enemies' camp, and you will find that your errand is known to them and resented, whatever it may suit them to pretend. Beware, then, of all their false promises, and when they seem most friendly distrust them most."

I promised to remember and heed his warning, and he added that it was necessary I should part for a time from my faithful companion, the pirate, as he could not safely accompany me in those scenes to which my path would now lead, but he promised he would place him under the care of one who could and would help him to leave that dark country soon.

After giving him loving and helpful messages to my beloved and my father, which he promised to deliver to them, we parted, and I set forth in the direction pointed out, greatly cheered and comforted by the good news and loving messages I had received.

I had proceeded but a short distance when I saw Faithful Friend sitting by the wayside, evidently waiting for me. I was truly glad to see him again and to have further guidance from him. We greeted one another with much cordiality. He was now, he said, appointed to accompany me during a part of my present journey, and he told me of many strange circumstances which had befallen him and which I am sure would prove very interesting, but as they do not properly belong to my own Wanderings I will not give any account of them here.

Faithful Friend took me to a tall tower, from the top of which we could see all over the city we were about to visit--this view of it beforehand being, he said, likely to prove both useful and interesting to me. We were, as I have said, surrounded always by this dark midnight sky and heavy smoky atmosphere somewhat like a black fog yet different and not quite so dense, since it was possible to see through it. Here and there this darkness was lighted up in some places by the strange phosphorescent light I have described, and elsewhere by the lurid flames kindled from the fierce passions of the spiritual inhabitants.

When we had climbed to the top of the tall tower, which appeared to be built of black rocks, we saw lying below us a wide stretch of dark country. Heavy night clouds hung upon the horizon, and near to us lay the great city, a strange mixture of magnificence and ruin, such as characterized all the cities I saw in this dark land. A treeless blackened waste surrounded it and great masses of dark blood-tinged vapor hung brooding over this great city of sorrow and crime. Mighty castles, lofty palaces, handsome buildings, all stamped with ruin and decay--all bleared and blotched with the stains of the sinful lives lived within them. Crumbling into decay, yet held together by the magnetism of their spiritual inhabitants--buildings that would last while the links woven by their spiritual occupants' earthly lives held them in this place, and would crumble into the dust of decay whenever the soul's repentance should sever those links and suffer it to wander free; crumble into decay, however, only to be reconstructed by another sinful soul in the shape into which his earthly life of pleasure should form it. Here there was a palace--there beside it a hovel. Even as the lives and ambitions of the indwelling spirits had been interwoven and blended on earth, so were their dwellings constructed here side by side.

Have you ever thought, ye who dwell yet on earth, how the associates of your earthly lives may become those of your spiritual? How the ties of magnetism which are formed on earth may link your spirits and your fates together in the spirit land so that you can only with great difficulty and much suffering sever them? Thus I saw in these buildings before me the proud patrician's palace, built of his ambitions and disfigured by his crimes, joined to the humble abodes of his slaves and his parasites and

113

panderers of earth which had been as surely formed by their desires and disfigured by their crimes, and between which and his palace there were the same links of spiritual magnetism as between himself and those who had been the sharers and instruments of his evil ambitions. He was no more able to free himself from them and their importunities than they were able to free themselves from his tyranny, till a higher and purer desire should awaken in the souls of one set or the other of them and thus raise them above their present level. So it was that they still repeated over again their lives of earth in hideous mockery of the past, impelled thereto by that past itself, their memories presenting to them over and over again as in a moving panorama their past acts and the actors, so that by no plunge into wild excess in that dark land could they escape the grinding of memory's millstones, till at length the last lust of sin and wickedness should be ground out of their souls.

Over this great spiritual city of past earth lives hung, as I have said, patches of light of a dim misty appearance like faintly luminous smoke, steel grey in color. This, I was told, was the light thrown off from the powerful intellects of the inhabitants whose souls were degraded but not undeveloped, and whose intellects were of a high order but devoted to base things, so that the true soul light was wanting and this strange reflection of its intellectual powers alone remained. In other parts of the city the atmosphere itself seemed on fire. Flames hung in the air and flickered from place to place, like ghostly fires whose fuel has turned to ashes ere the flames have burned out, and as the floating phantom flames were swept to and fro by the currents of the air I saw groups of dark spirits passing up and down the streets heedless, or perhaps unconscious, of these spectral flames that were thrown into the atmosphere by themselves, and were created by their own fierce passions which hung around them as spiritual flames.

As I looked and gazed upon this strange city of dead and ruined souls, a strange wave of feeling swept over me, for in its crumbling walls, its disused buildings, I could trace a resemblance to the one city on earth with which I was most familiar and which was dear to my heart since I had been one of her sons, and I called aloud to my companion to ask what this meant--what was this vision I beheld before me. Was it the past or the future or the present of my beloved city?

He answered, "It is all three. There before you now are the buildings and the spirits of its past--such, that is, as have been evil--and there among them are buildings half finished, which those who are dwelling there now are forming for themselves; and as these dwellings of the past are, so shall these half finished buildings be in the days to come when each who builds now shall have completed his or her lifework of sin and oppression. Behold and look upon it well, and then go back to earth a messenger of warning to sound in the ears of your countrymen the doom that awaits so many. If thy voice shall echo in even one heart and arrest the building of but one of these unfinished houses, you shall have done well and your visit here would be worth all that it may cost you. Yet that is not the only reason for your coming. For you and me, oh! my friend, there is work even in this city; there are souls whom we can save from their darkened lives, who will go back to earth and with trumpet tongues proclaim in the ears of men the horrors of the retribution they have known, and from which they would save others.

"Bethink you how many ages have passed since the world was young and how much improvement there has been in the lives and thoughts of the men who dwell upon it, and shall we not suppose that even ordinary reason might admit it must naturally be due to the influence of those who have returned to earth to warn others from the precipice over which themselves had fallen in all the pride and glory and lust of sin. Is it not a far nobler ideal to place before men--the idea that God sends these his children (sinful and disobedient once if you will, but repentant now), back to earth as ministering spirits to war and help and strengthen others who struggle yet in the unregenerated sinfulness of their lower natures rather than believe that he would doom any to the hopeless, helpless misery of eternal punishment? You and I have both been sinners--beyond pardon, some of the good of earth might have said--yet we have found mercy in our God even after the eleventh hour, and shall not even these also know hope? If they have sunk lower than we, shall we therefore in our little minds set limits to the heights to which they may yet climb? No! perish the thought that such horrors as we have looked upon in these Hells could be eternal. God is good and his mercy is beyond any man's power to limit."

We descended now from the tower and entered the city. In one of the large squares-- with whose earthly counterpart I was very familiar--we found quite a large crowd of dark spirits assembled, listening to some sort of proclamation. Evidently it was one which excited their derision and anger for there were yells, and hoots, and cries resounding on all sides, and as I drew yet more near I perceived it was one which had been read recently in the earthly counterpart, and had for its object the further liberation and advancement of the people--an object which, down here in this stronghold of oppression and tyranny, only provoked a desire for its suppression and these dark beings around me were vowing themselves to thwart the good purpose as far as lay in their power. The more men were oppressed and the more that they quarreled and fought against the oppression with violence, the stronger were these beings here below to interfere in their affairs and to stir up strife and fightings among them. The more men became free and enlightened and improved, the less chance was there that these dark spirits would be drawn to earth by the kindling of kindred passions there and thus be enabled to mingle with and control men for their own evil purposes. These dark beings delight in war, misery and bloodshed, and are ever eager to return to earth to kindle men's fierce cruel passions afresh. In times of great national oppression and revolt when the heated passions of men are inflamed to fever heat, these dwellers of the depths are drawn up to earth's surface by the force of kindred desires, and excite and urge on revolutions, which, begun at first from motives that are high and pure and noble, will under the stress of passion and the instigation of these dark beings from the lower sphere become at last mere excuses for wild butcheries and excesses of every kind. By these very excesses a reaction is created, and these dark demons and those whom they control are in their turn swept away by the higher powers, leaving a wide track of ruin and suffering to mark where they have been. Thus in these lowest Hells a rich harvest is reaped of unhappy souls who have been drawn along with the evil spirits that tempted them.

As I stood watching the crowd, Faithful Friend drew my attention to a group of spirits who were pointing over at us and evidently mediated addressing us.

"I shall go," said he, "for a few moments and leave you to speak with them alone. It will be better to do so, for they may recognize me as having been here before, and I would wish you to see them by yourself. I shall not, however, be far away, and will meet you again later when I see that I can help you by doing so. At this moment something tells me to leave you for a little."

As he spoke he moved away, and the dark spirits drew near to me with every gesture of friendliness. I thought it as well to respond with politeness, though in my heart I felt the most violent repugnance to their company, they were so repulsive looking, so horrible in their wicked, leering ugliness.

One touched me on the shoulder, and as I turned to him with a dim sense of having seen him before, he laughed--a wild horrid laugh--and cried out: "I hail thee, friend--who I see dost not so well remember me as I do thee, though it was upon the earth plane we met before. I, as well as others, then sought hard to be of service to thee, only thou wouldst have none of our help, and played us, methinks, but a scurvy trick instead. None the less for this, we, who are as lambs, didst thou but know us, have forgiven thee."

Another also drew near, leering in my face with a smile perfectly diabolical, and said: "So ho! You are here after all, friend, in this nice land with us. Then surely you must have done something to merit the distinction? Say whom you have killed or caused to be killed, for none are here who cannot claim at least one slain by them, while many of us can boast of a procession as long as the ghosts that appeared to Macbeth, and others again--our most distinguished citizens--count their slain by hundreds. Did you kill that one after all?--ha! ha! ha!" and he broke into such a wild horrible peal of laughter that I turned to fly from them--for like a flash had come across my mind the memory of that time when I, too, could have been almost a murderer, and I recognized in these horrible beings those who had surrounded me and counseled me how to fulfill my desire--how to wreak my vengeance even though no earthly form was still mine. I recoiled from them but they had no thought to let me go. I was here--drawn down, as they hoped, at last--and they sought to keep me with them that I might afford them some sport and they might avenge themselves upon me for their former defeat.

I read in their minds this thought, though outwardly they were crowding around me with every protestation of hearty friendliness. For a moment I was at a loss what to do. Then I resolved to go with them and see what they intended, watching at the same time for the first opportunity to free myself from them. I therefore suffered them to take me by an arm each, and we proceeded towards a large house on one side of the square which they said was theirs, and where they would have the pleasure of introducing me to their friends. Faithful Friend passed close to us and looking at me impressed the warning,

"Consent to go, but beware of entering into any of their enjoyments or allowing your mind to be dragged down to the level of theirs."

We entered and passed up a wide staircase of greyish stone, which like all things here bore the marks and stains of shame and crime. The broad steps were broken and imperfect, with holes here and there large enough, some of them, to let a man through into the black dungeon-like depths beneath. As we passed up I felt one of them give me a sly push just as we were stepping over one of these, and had I not been watching for some such trick I might have been tripped up and pushed in. As it was I simply drew aside and my too officious companion narrowly escaped tumbling in himself, whereat the rest all laughed and he scowled savagely at me. I recognized him just then as the one whose hand had been shriveled in the silver ring of fire drawn around my darling on the occasion when her love had drawn me to her and saved me from yielding to these dark fiends. This spirit held his hand carefully hidden under his black cloak, yet I could see through it, and I beheld the shriveled hand and arm, and knew then that I might indeed beware of its owner.

At the top of the staircase we passed into a large magnificent room, lighted up by a glare of fire and hung around with dark draperies which were in perfect rags and tatters and all splashed with crimson stains of wet blood, as though this had been the scene of not one but many, murders. Around the rooms were placed ghostly phantoms of ancient furniture--ragged, dirty, and defaced, yet retaining in them a semblance to an earthly apartment of great pretensions to splendor. This room was filled with the spirits of men and women. Such men! and alas! such women! They had lost all that could ever have given them any claim to the charms and privileges of their sex. They were worse to look upon than the most degraded bedraggled specimens to be seen in any earthly slum at night. Only in Hell could women sink to such an awful degradation as these. The men were to the full as bad or even if possible worse, and words utterly fail me to describe them, were it indeed advisable to do so. They were eating, drinking, shouting, dancing, playing cards and quarreling over them--in short, going on in such a way as the worst and lowest scenes of earthly dissipation can but faintly picture.

I could see a faint reflection of the earthly lives of each, and knew that each and all of them, men and women alike, had been guilty, not only of shameless lives, but also of murder from one motive or another. On my left was one who had been a Duchess in the days of the sixteenth century, and I beheld that in her history she had from jealousy and cupidity poisoned no less than six persons. Beside her was a man who had belonged to the same era, and had caused several persons obnoxious to him to be assassinated by his bravoes, and had moreover slain another with his own hand in a most treacherous manner during a quarrel.

Another woman had killed her illegitimate child because it stood between her and wealth and position. She had not been many years in this place and seemed more overcome by shame and remorse than any of the others, so I resolved if possible to get near to and speak to her.

My entrance was greeted with great shouts of laughter and wild applause, while half a dozen or so of eager hands took hold of me and dragged me to the table, whereupon there were cries: "Let us drink to the damnation of this our new Brother! Let us baptize him with a draught of this our new Brother! Let us baptize him with a draught of this fine cooling wine?" And before I well realized their intentions, they were all waving their glasses aloft amidst yells and shouts and horrible laughter, whilst one, seizing a full glass of the fiery liquid, tried to throw it over me. I had just presence of mind enough to step lightly aside, so that the liquor was nearly all spilt upon the floor and only a small portion fell upon my robe which it scorched and burned like vitrol, while the wine itself turned into a bluish flame--such as one sees with lighted whiskey--and disappeared at last with an explosion as of gunpowder. Then they put before me a tray full of dishes which at first sight resembled earthly delicacies, but on closer inspection I saw they were full of the most horrible corrupting and loathsome maggots. As I turned away from them one hag of a woman (for she was much more old and ugly and horrible to look upon than the most degraded specimen you can imagine) whose bleared eyes and fiendish expression made me recoil from her, seized me round the neck and tried, with many grimaces which she intended for coquettish smiles (she had been, oh ye powers! a great beauty on earth) to induce me to join her and her party in a little game of cards. She said: "The stakes for which we would play consist of the liberty of the loser. We have invented this pleasing mode of passing our time here since it revives for us the divertissements of the past; and because there is no money here which one can win, or use if you win, seeing it all turns to dross in your hands, we have adopted this mode of paying our debts, and we agree to be the slave of anyone who beats us at our games of chance and skill till we can turn the tables on them by ourselves winning and making them in turn our slaves. 'Tis a charming arrangement, as you would find did you join our party for a little. These others here," she added, with a strange mixture of insolent arrogance and animosity in her tone--"these others here are but the canaille, the scum of the place, and you do well to turn from them and their amusements. But for me, I am a Royal Duchess, and these my friends are all noble also--and we would adopt you, who are also, I perceive, one of the elite, among ourselves."

With the air of a queen she signed me to be seated beside herself, and had she been a few degrees less horrible I might have been tempted to do so if only from my curiosity to see what their game would be like. But disgust was too strong in me and I shook myself free of her as well as I could, saying, which was true, that cards had never possessed any attraction for me. I was bent on getting near the woman I wished to speak to, and very soon an opening in the crowd allowed me to do so.

As soon as I got beside her I addressed her in a low voice and asked if she was sorry for the murder of her child, and would she wish to leave this place even though it would be a long and sad and suffering road that would take her from it? How her face brightened as I spoke! How eagerly she faltered out: "What do you mean?"

"Be assured," I said, "I mean well to you, and if you will watch and follow me, I shall doubtless find some means for us both to leave this dreadful place." She pressed my hand in assent, for she did not venture to speak for the other spirits were again crowding around us in a way that was rapidly growing more and more threatening, although the guise of friendliness was still kept up.

The Duchess and her party had returned to their cards with a frightful avidity; they were quarreling over them and accusing each other of cheating, which I have no doubt was the case, and it seemed as though a fight was about to begin in that corner of the room to vary the monotony of their existence. I noticed also that the others were collecting in groups round the doors so as to keep me from leaving in case I desired to do so, and I saw my enemy with the withered hand whispering with some others of very low degraded type, such as might have been slaves in their past lives. Half a dozen men and women came up and urged me to join in a dance they were indulging in, which was like some of those abominations we read of in descriptions of the Witches' Sabbaths of the old days of witchcraft, and which I shall certainly not attempt further to describe. Can it be, I thought to myself as I looked at them, that there was truth in these old tales after all? and can the explanation be that these unfortunate beings, who were accused as witches, did really allow themselves to be so dominated by evil spirits that their souls were for a time drawn down to one of these spheres, and took part in some of its frightful orgies? I know not, but there seems truly a marvelous resemblance between these things I was now witnessing and what was related by the so-called witches, most of them poor half-witted mortals more to be pitied than condemned.

As these creatures, whose gestures it were an insult to call dancing, approached, I saw they were trying to get behind us in a ring and surround us, and some instinct seemed to tell me not to allow them. I drew back close to the wall, holding the woman's hand in mine and whispering to her not to leave go of me on any account. The whole crowd of spirits were now gathering towards my end of the room, the dull ferocity of their faces and wild savage glitter of their eyes in terrible contrast to their affectation of light-hearted gaiety. Closer and closer they gathered--a moving mass of evil personified.

For once their quarrels and jealousies merged in their common desire to do me harm, to get me down and trample me and rend me to pieces. As the muttering of a storm came here and there broken disjointed words of hate and menace, while those dancing demons kept up their wild antics in front of us. All at once a great cry--a yell--of fury broke from them. "A spy! a traitor! An enemy has got amongst us! It is one of the accursed brothers from above come here to spy upon us and carry away our victims. Down upon him! Stamp upon him! Crush him to death! Tear him to pieces! Hurl him into the vaults below! Away with him! Away! Away!"

Like as an avalanche sweeps down the mountain side they rushed upon us--those raging fiends--and I for one thought we were done for and could not but regret that I had been drawn into entering the place at all. I thought I was lost, when lo! just as the nearest of them were actually upon us the wall behind opened and Faithful Friend and another spirit drew us through, the wall closing again so suddenly that the yelling crowd scarce realized how we had disappeared.

CHAPTER XXIII.--The Palace of My Ancestors--False Brothers Baffled.

On the outskirts of the town we came to a magnificent palace, also most strangely familiar and yet unfamiliar to my eyes. In wandering through this city I was so reminded of its earthly double that I felt as one who sees some familiar beloved spot in a nightmare vision which has distorted and rendered hideous all that he demed so fair. I had oftentimes in my youth gazed up at this beautiful palace and taken pride to myself that I came of the race who had once owned it and all its broad lands, and now, here, to behold it thus, with all its beauties tarnished, its marble stained and mildewed, its terraces and statues broken and defaced, its fair front marred with the black cobwebs of past crimes and wrongs done within its walls, and its lovely gardens a dreary blackened waste as though the breath of a pestilence had swept over it--sent through me a thrill of sorrow and dismay, and it was with a saddened heart I followed my friend into the interior.

Up its great broad stairways we passed, and through the handsome doors which opened of themselves to admit us. Around us were many dark spirits flitting to and fro. Each and all seemed to expect and welcome us as guests whose coming was awaited. At the last door Faithful Friend once again left me, saying he would rejoin me in another place.

A great blaze of ruddy light greeted my eyes as this last door opened, and seemed as though someone had opened the door of a furnace, so hot and stifling was the atmosphere. At first I almost deemed the place on fire, then by degrees the blaze of light died down to a dull red glow and a wave of steel grey mist swept through the hall instead, while a wind as of ice froze the blood at my heart and seemed to impart its icy chill. These strange waves of heat and cold were caused by the intense fire of passion and the cold selfish chill of the dual nature of the man who reigned here as Prince. To the most fierce insatiable passions he united an intense selfishness and an intellect of the highest order. As these swayed him in turn in his earthly life, causing strange alternations of fiery passion and cool calculation in his conduct, so did these as waves thrown off by his spirit cause in this his spiritual mansion these extraordinary variations of intense heat and extreme cold that knew no medium of temperature between. As he had dominated all men on earth who came within the range of his power, so did he dominate the spiritual beings around him now, and rule as absolutely over them as he had ruled over his earthly subjects.

At the top of this great hall I beheld him seated in his chair of state which had around it all but imperial insignia. His walls were hung with the semblance of ancient tapestry, but, ah! how more than merely faded and ragged it looked. It was as though the thoughts and the life and the magnetism of the man had become woven into those ghostly hangings and had corrupted them with his own corruption. Instead of pictures of the chase, of floating nymphs, and crowned sea-gods there was a constantly shifting panorama of this man's past life in all its hideousness and nakedness, thrown like pictures from a magic lantern upon the stately mouldering ragged Arras drapery behind and around him. The great windows, through which the light of day never shone, were hung with the semblance of what had on earth been handsome velvet curtains, but which now appeared as some funeral pall shrouding the skeleton shapes that lurked like avenging spectres within them--spectral forms of those victims whom this man had sacrificed to his lust and ambition. Great drinking cups of silver, that seemed of a white heat when you touched them, and huge costly vases adorned the tables, and here as elsewhere there was the same hideous phantom of a feast--the same bitter mockery of earthly pleasure.

At my entrance the Lord of this horrid place rose from his throne to greet me with welcoming words, and I recognized with a thrill of horror that he was the spiritual counterpart of that ancestor of my family from whom we had all been so proud to think we were descended, and whose portraits I had often been told I much resembled. The same man, the same haughty handsome features, without doubt, but, ah! how subtle, how awful was the change upon them, the brand of shame and dishonor stamped on every line, the corruption showing through the mask with which he still strove to cover it. Here in Hell all men are seen as they are, and no power can avail to hide one atom of their vileness--and this man was vile indeed. Even in an age of sensuality he had been distinguished for his sins, and in an age when men thought but little of cruelty he had shown as one without pity or remorse. I saw it all now mirrored in those pictures around him, and I felt overwhelmed to think that there could have been points of resemblance of any sort between us. I shuddered at the false empty pride of those who had gloried in saying they were allied to such a man, simply because he had in his day wielded almost regal power. And this man spoke to me now as one in whom he had an interest, since I was of his race.

He told me he welcomed me here and would that I should dwell with him. By the mysterious link that earthly relationship gave he had attached himself to my earth-life and had from time to time been able to influence it. When I had felt most of ambition and a proud desire to rise and be again one with the great ones of earth as had been my ancestors in the past, then had he been drawn up to me and had fed and fostered my pride and my haughty spirit, that was in a sense akin to his own. And he it was, he told me, who had prompted those acts of my life of which I felt now the most ashamed--acts that I would have given all my life to undo, after I had done them. And it was he, he said, who had from time to time sought to raise me in the world till I should be able to grasp power of some kind and reign a king in the field of intellect if I could not reign king of a country as he had done. Through me, he had hoped himself again to wield power over men, which should be some compensation for his banishment to this place of darkness and decay.

"Faugh!" he cried. "This is as a charnel-house of mouldering bones and dead skeletons, but now you are come to join me we shall see if we cannot, combined, do something to make ourselves feared, if not obeyed, by the dwellers of the earth. I have had many a disappointment in you, oh! son of our noble race, and I feared you would escape me at last. I have tried for years to draw you down, but was ever baffled by some unseen power. Once and again when I deemed I had beyond doubt made all things sure, you would shake me off and break away from all control, till I had well nigh abandoned the struggle. But I do not yield readily to anyone, and when I could not be with you myself I sent some of my henchmen to do you service--ho! ho! service--yes, service--and so here you are at last, and by my faith you shall not again leave me. Behold how fair are the pleasures I have prepared for you."

He took my hand--his seemed as though burning with more than the fire of fever--and led me to a seat beside himself. I hesitated, then resolved to sit down and see this adventure out, but prayed in my heart to be kept safe from temptation. I noticed he did not offer me wine or food--(his instinct and knowledge told him I should only despise them)--but he caused a most lovely strain of music to sound in my ears that had so long been deprived of the solace of that heavenly art which ever appealed most strongly to my senses. A wild weird sensuous strain, such as a siren might have sung when she sought to lure her victims, swelled, died away, and rose again. No music of the earth could have been at once so beautiful and so horrible--could at the same time intoxicate and inflame the brain and heart, and yet fill my soul with so intense a feeling of fear and repugnance.

And then before us rose a great black mirror in which I saw reflected the earth and its life, and myself swaying the minds and the thoughts of thousands through the fevered fascinations of such music which I could make mine, and through its spell waken the lowest yet the most refined of passions, till those who heard should lose themselves and their souls under its potent witchery.

Then he showed me armies and nations dominated to ambitious ends by himself and his influence, so that he should reign again as a despot through the organism of an earthly tyrant. Here, too, he said, I should share his power.

Again, I saw the power in intellect and in literature which I could control and influence through the imaginative descriptive faculties of mortals who, under my prompting, would write such books as appealed to the reason, the intellect, and the sensual passions of mankind, until the false glamour thrown over them should cause men to view with indulgence and even approval the most revolting ideas and the most abominable teachings.

He showed me picture after picture, illustrating how man on earth could be used by spirits, who possessed sufficient will power and knowledge, as mere tools through which to satisfy their lust for power and sensual enjoyments of every sort. Much of this I had known before but had never fully realized the vast extent of the mischief possible to such a being as the one before me, were it not for the checks imposed upon him by those higher powers whose wills are as strong as his. Them he only knows as an unseen force opposed to him, which baffles his efforts at every turn, unless he can find in man a medium of so congenial a nature that they can truly work together as one. Then indeed do sorrow and devastation follow in their train and then do we see such monsters of triumphant wickedness as have disgraced the annals of all times. Now, thank Heaven, these are growing fewer and farther between, as the human race and the spirit spheres become purified through the teachings of the angels of the celestial spheres.

Last of all there appeared before us a woman's form, of such surpassing loveliness, such seductive charm, that for one instant I arose to look more closely at her and see if she could be real, and at that moment there came between me and the black magic mirror the mist-like form of an angel with the face of my beloved. And beside her this woman seemed so coarse and material and revolting to me that the momentary illusion of the senses was gone and I knew her for what she was, what all her kind are in truth--sirens that betray and ruin and drag men's souls to Hell while they themselves are all but soulless.

This revulsion of feeling in myself caused the waves of magnetic ether on which the music and these images were borne to us, to waver and break and vanish, leaving me alone with my tempter once more, with his voice sounding in my ears, pointing out to me how all these delights might still be enjoyed by me if I would but join him and be his pupil. But his words fell upon deaf ears, his promises allured me not. In my heart was only a horror of all these things, only a wild longing to free myself from his presence.

I rose and turned from him, and sought to go forth, but found I could not move one step. An invisible chain held me fast, and with a derisive laugh of rage and triumph, he called out to me ironically: "Go, since thou wilt have none of my favors or my promises. Go forth now and see what awaits you." I could not move one step, and began to feel a strange alarm creeping over me and a strange numbness of limbs and brain. A mist seemed to gather round and enfold me in its chill embrace, while phantom forms of awful shape and giant size drew near and yet more near. Oh, horror! they were my own past misdeeds, my own evil thoughts and desires, which had been prompted by this very man beside me and which nestling in my heart had formed those links between us that held me to him now.

A wild, fierce, cruel laugh broke from him at my discomfiture. He pointed to these weird shapes, and bid me see what I was who thought myself too good for his company. Darker and darker grew the hall, and wave on wave the grim phantoms crowded round us, growing each more black and fearful as they gathered, hemming me in on every side, while below our feet opened a great vault or pit in which I saw, or seemed to see, a seething mass of struggling human forms. My fearful ancestor shook in wild paroxysms of rage and fiendish laughter, and, pointing to the gathering phantoms bid them hurl me into the black pit. But suddenly above me in the darkness gleamed a star and from it fell a ray of light like a rope, which I grasped with both my hands and as the folds of light diffused themselves around me I was drawn up, out of that dark place, away from that fearful palace.

Faithful Friend now proposed to me that we should visit one more city in this strange land, in order that I might see the man whose fate might have been my own but for the constancy and love which has so helped and sustained me. Our earthly histories were in some respects different, but there were some points of resemblance both in that and in our dispositions which would make the sight of this man and the knowledge of his history useful to me, while at a future time I might be able to help him.

"It is now more than ten years," he said, "since this man passed from earth, and it is only lately that he has begun to wish to progress. I found him here on my former visit to this place and was able to assist him a little and finally to enroll him as one of our Brotherhood, and I am now told that he is shortly to leave this sphere for a higher one."

I assented to the proposed journey, and after a short but very rapid flight we found ourselves hovering over a wide lagoon upon whose dark bosom there floated a great city, its towers and palaces rising from the waters, and reflected in them as in a mirror of black marble veined with dark red lines that somehow made me feel they were streams of blood flowing through it. Overhead there hung the same dark pall of cloud lighted by the patches of steel grey and fiery red floating vapor which I had noticed in the other city. The appearance of this place suggested to me that we must be about to enter the Venice of these lower spheres, and on my saying so to Faithful Friend he answered: "Yes, and you will here find many celebrated men whose names were written on the history of their times in letters of fire and blood."

We now found ourselves in the town, and proceeded to pass through its principal canals and squares in order that I might see them.

Yes, there they were, these degraded counterparts of all those beautiful places made familiar by the brush of the artist and the fame of those who have carved for themselves a niche in the Temple of History. There flowed the canals, seeming like dark crimson streams of blood flowing from some vast shambles, washing and rippling up the marble steps of the palaces to leave there a thick foul stain. The very stones of the buildings and pavements seemed to me to ooze and drip blood. The air was thick with its red shade. Deep down below the crimson waters I saw the skeleton forms of the countless thousands who had met their deaths by assassination or more legalized forms of murder, and whose bodies had found sepulture beneath the dark waves. Below in the dungeons which honeycombed the city I beheld many spirits crowded together and like caged wild beasts--the ferocity of the cruel tiger in their gleaming eyes and the vindictive malice of the chained human tyrant in every attitude of their crouching figures. Spirits whom it was needful to thus confine since they were more ferocious than savage animals. Processions of city magistrates and their attendants, haughty nobles with their motley following of soldiers and seamen and slaves, merchants and priests, humble citizens and fishermen, men and women of all ranks and all times, passed to and fro, and nearly all were alike degraded and repulsive-looking. And as they came and went it seemed to me as if skeleton hands, phantom arms, rose through the stones of the pavements from the dungeons beneath, striving to draw these others down to share their own misery. There was a haunted, hunted look on many of their faces, and black care seemed to sit behind them continually.

Far out in the waters of the lagoon spectral galleys floated, filled with slaves chained to their oars, but amongst them there were no longer the helpless victims of political intrigue or private revenge. These beings were the spirits of those who had been the hard taskmasters, the skillful plotters who had consigned many to this living death. Yet farther out at sea, I could behold the great ships, and nearer at hand in the ruined harbor there were more spiritual counterparts of those piratical craft of the Adriatic, filled with the spirits of their piratical crews who had made plunder and rapine and war their delight, and who now spent their time battling with one another and making forays upon others like themselves. Spectral-looking gondolas floated upon the water-ways of the city, filled with spirits bent upon following still the occupations and pleasures of their former lives. In short, in this Venice, as in the other cities I had seen, there existed a life akin to that of earth save that from this place all the good and pure and true, all the real patriots and unselfish citizens were gone, and only the evil left to prey upon each other and act as avenging spirits to their companions in crime.

Seated upon the parapet of one of the smaller bridges we found a man, wearing the dress of the Brothers of Hope--a dark grey robe such as I had myself worn in the earlier stages of my wanderings. His arms were folded upon his breast and his face was so far concealed by the hood that we could not see his features, but I knew at once that this was the man we had come to see, and I likewise recognized his identity as that of a celebrated Venetian painter whom I had known in my youth, though not very intimately. We had not met again and I was ignorant that he had passed from earth, till I saw him sitting thus upon the bridge in this city of Hell. I confess the recognition gave me somewhat of a shock, recalling as it did those days of my youth when I also was a student of art with all the fairest prospects in life, as it would seem, before us, and now to see him and to think what his life must have been to bring him to this pass. He did not see us, so Faithful Friend proposed that we should turn aside for a little, while he told me this spirit's history, and then we could approach together and speak to him. It seemed that this man (whom I shall call by his spirit name of Benedetto, since his earthly life is better to be forgotten) had risen rapidly into fame after I knew him, and had been fairly successful in selling his pictures. But Italy is not now a rich country, and Benedetto's most wealthy patrons were the English and Americans who came to visit Venice, and at the house of one of them Benedetto met the woman who was to overshadow his whole life with her baneful influence. He was young, handsome, talented, highly educated, and of an ancient though poor family, and therefore naturally received by all the best society in Venice. It was to a lady who belonged to the higher ranks of this social sphere that Benedetto lost his heart, and dreamed in his youthful and romantic foolishness that she would be content to become the wife of a struggling artist with nothing but his brains and a growing reputation. The lady was scarce twenty when they first met, very beautiful, perfect alike in face and form, and endowed with all the charms which can enslave the heart of man--and she encouraged Benedetto in every way, so that, poor youth, he believed her love to be as sincere as his. But with all the passionate thirst of her nature for admiration and love she was cold, calculating, ambitious, and worldly; incapable of either understanding or returning such a love as she inspired in a nature like Benedetto's, which knows love or hate only in extremes. She was flattered by his attentions, charmed by his passionate devotion, and proud of having made conquest of one so handsome and so gifted, but she had no idea of sacrificing anything for his sake, and even when she was most tender, most alluring to him, she was striving with all her arts to become the wife of a middle-aged Venetian nobleman, whose wealth and position she coveted even while she despised the man himself.

The end of Benedetto's dream came all to soon. He ventured to lay his heart and all his prospects at the feet of his inamorata, pouring into hear ears all the love and devotion of his soul.

"And she?"

"Well, she received it all very coolly, told him not to be a fool, explained to him how impossible it was that she could do without money and position, and, in fine, dismissed him with a calm indifference to his sufferings which nearly drove him mad. He fled from Venice, went to Paris, and there plunged into all the dissipations of that gay capital, striving to bury the recollection of his unfortunate passion. They did not meet for some years, and then Benedetto's fate took him back to Venice once more, cured, as he hoped, and prepared to despise himself for his folly. He had now become famous as a painter, and could almost command his own price for his pictures. He found that the lady had duly married the Marchese and was reigning as a society beauty and a queen of fashion, surrounded by a crowd of admirers whom she did not always feel it necessary to introduce to her husband. Benedetto had resolved to treat the lady with cool indifference should they meet, but this was not her intention. Once her slave, always so--no lover should dare to break her chain till she chose to dismiss him. She devoted herself once more to the subjugation of Benedetto's heart, and, alas! that heart was only too ready to surrender when she told him, with every accent of feeling in her voice, how she regretted now the path she had chosen. Thus Benedetto became her unacknowledged lover, and for a time he lived in a state of intoxication of happiness. But only for a time. The lady tired of everyone after a little, she liked fresh conquests, new slaves to do her homage. She liked excitement, and Benedetto with his jealousy, his eternal devotion, grew tiresome, his presence wearisome. Moreover there was another admirer, young, rich, handsome also, and the Marchesa preferred him, and told Benedetto so, gave him, in fact, his conge for the second time. His passionate reproaches, his violent protestations, his vehement anger all annoyed the lady greatly; as she grew colder, more insolent towards him, he grew more excited. He threatened, he implored, he vowed he would shoot himself if she proved false to him, and finally after a violent scene they parted and Benedetto went home. When he called next day he was told by the servant that the Marchesa declined to see him again. The insolence of a message thus given him, the heartlessness of the Marchesa, the bitter shame of being a second time trifled with and flung aside like an old glove, were too much for his passionate fiery nature, and he went back to his studio and blew out his brains.

"When his spirit awoke to consciousness it was to all the horrors of finding himself a prisoner in his coffin in the grave. He had destroyed his material body but he could not free his spirit from it, till the decaying of that body should liberate the soul. Those loathsome particles of that corrupting body still clothed the spirit, the link between them was not severed.

"Oh, the horror of such a fate! can anyone hear of it and not shudder to think what the bitter weariness and discontent of life, and a reckless desire to be free of it at any cost, may plunge the soul into. If those on earth would be truly merciful to the suicide they would cremate his body, not bury it, that the soul may, by the speedy dispersal of the particles, be the sooner freed from such a prison. The soul of a suicide is not ready to leave the body, it is like an unripe fruit and does not fall readily from the material tree which is nourishing it. A great shock has cast it forth, but it still remains attached, till the sustaining link shall wither away.

"From time to time Benedetto would lapse into unconsciousness and lose for a little the sense of his terrible position, and from these states of merciful oblivion he would awaken to find that little by little the earthly body was losing its hold upon the spirit and crumbling into dust, but while it did so he had to suffer in all his nerves the pangs of this gradual dissolution. The sudden destruction of the earthly body, while it would have given his spirit a more violent, more painful shock, would at least have spared him the slow torture of this lingering decay. At last the material body ceased to hold the spirit, and he rose from the grave but still hung over it, tied, though he was no longer imprisoned; then the last link snapped and he was free to wander forth into the earth plane. And first his powers of hearing and seeing and feeling were most feebly developed, then gradually they unfolded and he became conscious of his surroundings. With these powers came again the passions and desires of his earthly life and also the knowledge of how he could yet gratify them. And again as in his earthly life he sought oblivion for his sorrow and bitterness in the pleasures of the senses. But he sought in vain. Memory was ever present with him torturing him with the past. In his soul there was a wild hunger, a fierce thirst for revenge, for power to make her suffer as he had done, and the very intensity of his thoughts at last carried him to where she was. He found her as of old, surrounded by her little court of gay admirers. A little older but still the same, still as heartless, still untroubled by his fate and indifferent to it. And it maddened him to think of the sufferings he had brought upon himself for the love of this woman. At last all thoughts became merged in the one thought of how he could find means to drag her down from her positon, how strip her of all those things which she prized more than love or honor or even the lives of those who might be called her victims.

"And he succeeded, for spirits have more powers than mortals dream of. Step by step he saw her come down from her proud position, losing first wealth, then honor, stripped of every disguise she had worn, and known for what she was, a vile temptress who played with men's souls as one plays with dice, careless how many hearts she broke, how many lives she ruined, careless alike of her husband's honor and her own fair fame, so long as she could hide her intrigues from the eyes of the world and rise a step higher in wealth and power upon the body of each new victim.

"And even in his darkness and misery Benedetto hugged himself and was comforted to think it was his hands that were dragging her down and tearing the mask from her beauty and worldliness. She wondered how it was that so many events all tended to one end--her ruin. How it was that her most carefully laid schemes were thwarted, her most jealously guarded secrets found out and held up to the light of day. She began at last to tremble at what each day might bring forth. It was as though some unseen agency, whose toils she could not escape, was at work to crush her, and then she thought of Benedetto and his last threats that if she drove him to despair he would send himself to Hell and drag her with him. She had thought he meant to murder her perhaps, and when she heard he had shot himself and was dead, she felt relieved and soon forgot him, save when some event would recall him to her mind for a moment. And now she was always thinking of him, she could not get away from the obtrusive thought, and she began to shudder with fear lest he should rise from his grave and haunt her.

"And all the time there stood Benedetto's spirit beside her, whispering in her ears and telling her that this was his revenge come to him at last. He whispered to her of the past and of that love that had seemed so sweet and that had turned to bitterest burning hate, consuming him as with the fire of Hell whose flames should scorch her soul also and drive her to a despair as great as his.

"And her mind felt this haunting presence even while her bodily eyes could see nothing. In vain she fled to society, to all places where there were crowds of men and women, in order to escape; the haunting presence was with her everywhere. Day by day it grew more distinct, more real, a something from which there was no escape.

"At last one evening in the dim grey of twilight she saw him, with his wild menacing eyes, his fierce, passionate hate, expressing itself in every line of his face, in every gesture of his form. The shock was too much for her overwrought nerves and she fell dead upon the floor. And then Benedetto knew that he had succeeded and had killed her, and that from henceforth the brand of Cain was stamped upon his brow.

"Then a horror of himself seized upon him, he loathed the deed he had done. He had intended to kill her and then when the spirit left the body to drag it down with him and to haunt and torment it forever, so that on neither side of the grave should she know rest. But now his only thought was to escape from himself and the horror of his success, for all good was not dead in this man, and the shock which had killed the Marchesa had awakened him to the true nature of his revengeful feelings. Then he fled from the earth, down and down even to this city of Hell, the fit dwelling-place for such as he.

"It was in this place that I found him," said Faithful Friend, "and was able to help the now repentant man and to show him how he might best undo the wrong he had done. He awaits now the coming of this woman he so loved and hated, in order that he may ask her to forgive him and that he may forgive her himself. She has also been drawn to this sphere, for her own life was very guilty, and it is in this counterpart of that city which saw the history of their earthly love that they will meet again, and that is why he awaits her upon this bridge where in the past she has so often met him."

And will she meet him soon?"

"Yes! very soon, and then will the sojourn of this man in this sphere be over, and he will be free to pass to a higher one, where his troubled spirit shall at last know a season of rest ere it mounts by slow and painful steps the stony pathway of progression."

"Will she, too, leave here with him?"

"No, oh no! she will be also helped to progress, but their paths will lie widely asunder. There was no true affinity between them, only passion, and pride, and wounded self-love. They will part here to meet no more."

We now drew near Benedetto, and as I touched him on the shoulder he started and turned round but at first did not recognize me. Then I made myself known and said how I should rejoice to renew our early friendship in those higher spheres in which I hoped we would both soon meet again. I told him briefly that I, too, had sinned and suffered, and was working my way upwards now. He seemed glad to see me and wrung my hand with much emotion when we said good-bye, and then Faithful Friend and I went away, leaving him still seated upon the bridge waiting for his last interview with her who had been once so dear to him and who was now but a painful memory.

As we were on our road from Venice to those plains which I now understood to be the spiritual replica of the plains of Lombardy, my attention was suddenly attracted by a voice calling to me in a pitiful tone for help. Turning back a little way to my right hand I saw a couple of spirits lying apparently helpless upon the ground, and one was making gestures to cause me to come to him. So thinking it was some one in need of my help I let my companion go on and went to see what he wanted. The spirit holding out his hand to me and murmuring something about helping him to rise, I bent down to lift him up, when to my surprise he made a clutch at my legs with his hands and contrived to fasten his teeth in my arm. While the other one, suddenly jumping up, tried to fasten upon my throat like a wolf.

With some trouble and a good deal of anger on my part, I confess, I shook myself free of them and was stepping back, when I half stumbled, and turning my head saw what a great pit had suddenly opened behind me into which with another step backwards I must have fallen.

Then I remembered the warnings given me not to allow my lower passions to be aroused and thus place myself on a level with these beings, and I regretted my momentary burst of anger and resolved to keep calm and cool. I turned towards the two dark spirits again and saw that the one who I fancied had been hurt was crawling along the ground to reach me, while the other was gathering himself together like a wild beast about to spring. I fixed my eyes steadily upon the pair, whom I now recognized as the man with the withered hand and his friend, who had tried to deceive me with the false message a short time before. Steadily I looked at them, throwing all the power of my will into the determination that they should not advance nearer to me. As I did so they faltered and stopped, and finally rolled over on the ground snarling and showing their teeth like a couple of wolves, but unable to approach a step nearer. Leaving them thus I hurried after Faithful Friend--whom I soon overtook--and narrated to him what had occurred.

He laughed and said, "I could have told you who those were, Franchezzo, but I felt it would be no harm to let you find out for yourself, and likewise learn how valuable a protection your own force of character and determination could be. You are naturally strong willed, and so long as you do not use it to domineer over the just rights of others it is a most useful and valuable quality, and in your work in the spirit world you will have found that it is the great lever by which you can act, not alone upon those round you but even upon apparently inanimate matter, and I thought as those two are very likely to come across you from time to time you might as well settle now which should be master, which should be the dominant personality. They will be shy of directly meddling with you again, but so long as you work about the earth plane you will find them ready at any chance to thwart your plans if the opportunity comes."

CHAPTER XXV.--A Pitched Battle in Hell.

We now saw before us a vast slightly undulating plain upon which great masses of dark spirits were moving. At Faithful Friend's suggestion we ascended a small hillock that we might observe their movements.

"We are now," said Faithful Friend, "about to witness one of the great battles that take place here between the opposing forces of dark spirits whose delight was in war and its rapine and bloodshed, and who, here in the dark state which is the result of their earthly cruelty and ambition, carry on yet their warlike operations against each other and contend for the supremacy of these kingdoms of Hell. Behold how they are massing their forces for an attack upon those others on our right, and observe the skill they will display in their maneuvres. The powerful minds of men who swayed armies on earth sway such unhappy beings here as are not strong enough to resist their spell, and thus they force these less powerful spirits to fight under their banners whether they will nor not, just as they did with mortals on earth. You will see these powerful leaders engage in a struggle worse than deadly since no death can come to end the contest, which they renew over and over again, as it would almost seem eternally--or until, as is to be hoped, the satiety of mind of one or other of these powerful leaders will at last make him long for some nobler form of contest, some higher triumph of the soul than is won over these miserable beings in battles where victory gives only a fresh right to torture and oppress the vanquished. The same instincts and natural gifts which are now perverted to personal ambition and the lust for cruelty and dominion as their only aim, will, when purified, make these spirits mighty helpers, where now they are destroyers, and the same powers of Will will help forward the progress they now retard. When this progress shall take place depends, for each, upon the latent nobility of the soul itself--the awakening of the dormant love of goodness and justice and truth to be found in all. Though like seeds in the earth these germs of better things may lie long hidden beneath the mass of evil that overloads them, there must and does come a time for each when the better soul awakens and these germs of good send out shoots that lead to repentance and bring forth an abounding harvest of virtue and good works."

We looked over the vast plain and now beheld the two mighty hosts of spirits drawn up to confront one another in the array of battle. Here and there I beheld powerful spirits, leading each his band or regiment as in an earthly army. In the van of the opposing forces were two majestic beings who might have been models for Milton's Lucifer, so strong was the sense of power and high intellect with which they impressed me. In each there was a certain beauty and grandeur of form and feature--a regal majesty even in the degradation of Hell--but alas! the beauty was that of a wild fierce tiger or lion that watches how he may rend his army in pieces and drag his prey into his den. Dark and forbidding were their countenances, cruel and ferocious their gleaming eyes, the false smile, showing their sharp teeth like those animals of prey. The cunning of the serpent was in their looks, and the pitiless hunger of the vulture in their smile. Each rode in his chariot of war drawn, not by horses, but by the spirits of degraded men, whom they lashed forward as beasts of burden and drove furiously on to be trampled down in the melee as cattle. Wild strains of music that sounded like the shrieks of the souls of the damned and the thunders of a mighty storm broke from the assembled armies, and with one fell swoop they rushed forward and bore down upon each other--flying and hurrying through the air, or dragging themselves along the ground. Pushing, hustling, jostling, and trampling like a herd of wild animals--on they came, and as they met, their fierce cries and shouts and imprecations rent the air and made even Hell more hideous. They charged and re-charged, they maneuvered, marched, and counter-marched, these phantom spirit armies of the dead, even as they had done in the battles of earth life. They fought and wrestled like demons, not men, for they had no weapons save those of wild beasts--their teeth and claws. If a battle with mortal weapons is horrible, this was doubly so, where they fought as wolves and tigers might--the two powerful leaders directing the mass, urging them on and guiding the fight as the tide of battle swept back one side or the other.

Over all had towered these two dark regal spirits, and now no longer content to let their soldiers fight, but bent each upon the destruction of the other, they rose from the fighting mass, and, soaring high above them, turned their looks upon each other with deadliest hate--then flying through the air with their dark robes extended behind and above them like wings, they grappled and wrestled together in a fierce struggle for supremacy. It was as though two eagles fought in mid-air while a mass of carrion crows grubbed and fought for worms beneath them. I turned from the crows to watch the eagles and to mark how, with no weapons but their hands and their powerful wills they fought as wild beasts do in a forest.

They uttered no sound, no cry, but gripped each other with a death-grip that neither would relax, and swayed to and fro in the air before us. Now one upward, now the other, their fierce eyes stabbing each other with fiery darts--their hot breath scorching each other's faces--their fingers clutching at each other's throats, and both seeking for a chance to fasten on their enemy with their teeth. Backwards and forwards, up and down they swayed and writhed in what seemed to me a death struggle for both. At last one seemed to fail. He sank below the other, who was bearing him to the ground to dash him, as I saw, over a deep precipice into a chasm in the rocks that skirted the field of battle--a deep and dark and awful pit into which he meant to hurl the vanquished one, and keep him prisoner. Fierce and long was the struggle, for the one below would not give in and clung to the other to drag him down with him if possible. But in vain. His powers were failing fast and as they reached the black chasm and hung poised over it, I saw the uppermost one wrench himself free by a mighty effort and fling the other from him, down into those awful depths.

With a shudder I turned away and saw that the battle had been raging as fiercely on the plain. Those spectral hosts had fought and the army of the victorious general had beaten back the forces of his vanquished foe till they were broken and dispersed in all directions, leaving their disabled comrades on the field lying as wounded men do in an earthly battle, while the victors were dragging away with them their captives, to what fate I could only too well guess.

Sickened and disgusted with their brutishness I would fain have left this place, but Faithful Friend, touching my shoulder, said: "Now has come the time for our work, my friend. Let us descend yonder and see if there are none whom we can help. Amongst the fallen and vanquished we may find those who are as sick of war and its horrors as you, and who will be but too glad of our help." So we went down to the plain.

It was as might have been a battle-field when night has fallen upon it and there are but the wounded and the slain left behind. All the other spirits had gone like a flock of evil birds to seek fresh carrion. I stood among a writhing, moaning mass of beings and knew not where to begin my help--there were so many. It was worse--a thousand times worse--than any mortal battle-field. I have seen the dead and dying lying in the streets of my native town thick as fallen leaves, and my heart has ached and bled for them and burned with shame and anger that such things could be; but even there was at least the peace and sleep of death to soften the anguish, and there was the hope of helping those who yet lived. But here--in this awful Hell--there seemed no hope and no death that could relieve these suffering ones, no morning that should dawn upon the night of their miseries. If they revived would it not be to live again this awful life, to find themselves surrounded ever by this awful night, and these fierce wild beasts of men?

I stooped down and tried to raise the head of one poor wretch who lay moaning at my feet--crushed till his spirit-body seemed but a shapeless mass--and as I did so the mysterious Voice spoke in my ears and said:

"Even in Hell there is Hope or why else are you come? The darkest hour is ever before the dawn, and for these--the vanquished and the fallen--has come the hour of their change. The very cause that has made them to be thus borne down and trampled under is that which shall now raise them. The desire for higher and better things, the shrinking from the evil around them has rendered them weak in the wickedness which is the strength of Hell and its inhabitants, and has made them waver and hesitate to thrust at and harm another with the ruthless force of these other wild and worthless beings, and thus they have been borne down and vanquished, but their fall from power here will open to them the doors of a higher state and thus shall there dawn for them the grey glimmer of a Higher Hope. Mourn not for them but seek to ease their sufferings that they may sink into a sleep of Death to this sphere and waken to a new life in the sphere next above."

"And what," I asked, "of that powerful spirit whom I saw thrown into the dark chasm?"

"He too will be helped in time, but his soul is not yet ripe for help, and it is of no use to try till then."

The Voice ceased and Faithful Friend, who was beside me, made signs to show me how to soothe these weary ones to sleep, and pointed out to me numerous stars of light which had gathered on that field of pain, and said they were carried by those of our Brotherhood who were, like ourselves, drawn here on their mission of Love and Mercy.

Ere long the writhing, moaning forms had sunk into unconsciousness and a short time after I saw a sight that was strange and wonderful indeed. Over each silent form there arose a faint misty floating vapor, such as I had seen once before in the case of a spirit we had rescued, as I have already told. Gradually these vapors took shape and solidity and assumed the form of the released spirit or soul, then each was borne away by bands of bright ethereal spirits--who had gathered above our heads--till the last was gone and our work and theirs was done.

CHAPTER XXVI.--Farewell to the Dark Land.

I now perceived that those Brothers of Hope, who like myself had been assisting the poor wounded spirits, all belonged to the same company as myself, and they were all collecting together, the little starry lights we each carried looking indeed like emblems of hope in darkness. Faithful Friend and I joined the others and were soon interchanging greetings and congratulations, like a brigade of soldiers about to return home after a successful campaign.

Before we again passed through the fiery ring that encompassed this region, the leader of our band conducted us to the top of a high pinnacle of rock from which we beheld the cities and plains and mountains of that Land of Darkness, through which each of us had passed in our pilgrimage. And standing on that mountain peak we could survey the mighty panorama of Hell stretched out at our feet. He then addressed us in grave, solemn tones:

"This scene upon which we look is but a small, a very small, fractional portion of the great sphere which men have been wont to speak of as 'Hell.' There are dark spheres above this which may seem to many to deserve the name until they have seen this place and learned in it how low a soul can sink and how much more terrible in this sphere can be both the crimes and the sufferings. The great belt of dark matter of which is composed this, the lowest of the earth spheres, extends for many million miles around us, and has received within its borders all those multitudes of sinful souls whose material lives have been passed on earth, and whose existences date back to the remote far-off ages in which the planet Earth first began to bear its harvest of conscious immortals, destined to sin and suffer and work out each their own salvation till they should be purified from all earthly stain--all taint of their lower nature. The multitudes of such lives have been, and shall yet be, as the stars of the sky and the sands of the sea in number, and as each builds for himself his own habitation in the higher or in the lower spheres, so are the vast spheres peopled and their many dwelling places and cities formed.

"Far beyond the power of any mortal to carry even his thoughts, lie the myriad dwelling places of the spheres, each spot or locality bearing upon it the individual stamp of the spirit whose life has created it, and as there are no two faces, no two minds, exactly similar in all the countless beings that have peopled the earth--so there are no two places in the spirit world exactly alike. Each place--yea, even each sphere-- is the separate creation of the particular class of minds that have created it, and those whose minds are in affinity being drawn to each other in the spirit world every place will bear more or less the peculiar stamp of its inhabitants.

"Thus in giving a description of this or any other sphere you will naturally be able to tell only what you have seen, and to describe those places to which you were attracted, while another spirit who has beheld a different portion of the same sphere may describe it so very differently that men on earth, who limit all things too much, and measure them by their own standards of probability, will say that since you differ in describing the same sphere you must both be wrong. They forget that Rome is not Genoa, Milan, or Venice, yet these are all in Italy. Lyons is not Paris, yet both are in France--and both will bear certain characteristic features, certain national traits of resemblance. Or to extend the simile still further, New York and Constantinople are both cities upon the planet Earth, yet there is between them and their population so great a difference, so wide a gulf, that it requires that we should look no longer for national characteristics but only for the broad fact that both are inhabited by the human race, differing, however widely, in manners and appearance.

"And now I would have you each observe that in all your wanderings--in all the sad sights you have seen--all the unhappy beings you have known groveling in this sink of their own iniquities, there were yet the germs of human souls inextinguishable and undestroyable, and you have each learned, I trust, that long as may be the probation of the soul--greatly as it may retard the hour of its release by the perversion of its powers--yet to all is given the inalienable birthright of hope, and to each will come at last the hour of awakening, and those who have sunk to the lowest depths will arise even as a pendulum swung to its farthest limit will arise and swing back again as high as it has sunk low.

"Bitter and awful is the reckoning the sinful soul must pay for its wild indulgence in evil, but once paid there is not again that reckoning to be met, there is no inexorable creditor whose ears are deaf to the voice of prayer or who will say to the repentant prodigal, "Begone, for your doom is sealed and the hour of your redemption past. Oh, Brethren of Hope! Can man in his littleness measure the power of the Almighty whose ways are past his finding out? Can man put a limit to his mercy and say it shall be denied to any sorrowful sinner however deep has been his sin? God alone can condemn, and he alone can pardon and his voice cries out to us in everything, in every blade of grass that grows, in every ray of light that shines: 'how great is the goodness and mercy of our God--how long-suffering and how slow to anger.' And his voice calls with trumpet tongue, through his many angels and ministering spirits, to all who repent and seek for mercy that mercy is ever given--pardon, full and free, is granted unto all who earnestly seek it and would truly labor that they may win it. Even beyond the grave, even within the gates of Hell itself, there is yet mercy and pardon, yet hope and love held out to all. Not one atom of the immortal soul essence which has been breathed into man and become a living conscious individuality is ever again truly lost, wholly doomed either to annihilation or eternal misery. They err, I had almost said they sin, who teach man otherwise, for by so doing they shut a door upon his hopes and render the erring soul yet more desperate because more hopeless, when, as he deems, Death has put the final seal of damnation upon his fate. I would when each of you returns to the earth plane that you proclaim to all this truth which you have learned in these your wanderings, and strive ever that each and all may feel the sense of hope and the need there is to take heed to their ways while there is yet time. Far easier were it for man in his earth life to undo his misdeeds than if he wait till Death has placed his barrier between him and those to whom he would atone.

"In those Hells which you have seen all has been the outcome of men's own evil lives--the works of their own past--either upon earth or in its spheres. There is nothing but what has been the creation of the soul itself, however horrible to you may appear its surroundings. However shocked you may have felt at the spiritual appearance of these beings, yet must you ever remember that such as they are, have they made themselves. God has not added one grain's weight to the burden of any, and equally must it be the work of each to undo what he has done, to build up again what he has destroyed, to purify what he has debased. And then will these wretched dwellings, these degraded forms--these fearful surroundings--be exchanged for brighter and happier scenes--purer bodies--more peaceful homes, and when at last in the fullness of time the good on earth and in its spheres shall overcome the bad, the evil sights and evil places will be swept away as the froth upon the sea is swept on by the advancing tide, and the pure Water of Life shall flow over these spots and purify them till these solid black mountains, this dense heavy atmosphere, and these foul dwelling-places shall melt in the strong purifying fire of repentance, even as the hard granite rock is melted in the crucible of the chemist till it is dissipated into the atmosphere and floated away to form other rocks elsewhere. Nothing is ever lost, nothing ever destroyed. All things are imperishable. Those atoms which your body has attracted to it to-day are thrown off again tomorrow, and pass on to form other bodies eternally, as these emanations of men's spiritual natures are formed into the earth spheres, and when there is no longer magnetism sufficiently gross to hold together these gross particles which form the lower spheres, these atoms will become detached from following the earth and its sphere in their rushing journey through the limitless ether of space, and will float in suspension in the ether till drawn to another planet whose spheres are congenial and whose spiritual inhabitants are on an equally gross plane. Thus these same rocks and this country have all formed in the past the lower spheres of other planets which have now grown too highly developed to attract them and they will, when this, our earth, has ceased to attract them, be drawn off and form the spheres of some other planet.

"So too are our higher spheres formed of matter more etherealized, yet still matter, which has been cast off from planet spheres much in advance of ours, and in like manner these atoms will be left by us and reabsorbed in turn by our successor. Nothing is lost, nothing wasted, nothing is really new. The things called new are but new combinations of that which exists already, and is in its nature eternal. To what ultimate height of development we shall reach, I know not--none can know since there can be no limit to our knowledge or our progress. But I believe that could we foresee the ultimate destiny of our own small planet, as we can in part judge of it from seeing the more advanced ones around us, we should learn to look upon even the longest earthly life and the longest, saddest probation of these dark spheres as but stepping stones on which man shall mount to the thrones of angels at last.

"What we can see--what we do know and may grasp--is the great and ever present truth that hope is truly eternal and progression is ever possible even to the lowest and most degraded and sin-stained soul. It is this great truth we would have each of you to preach both to mortal and immortal man, when you return to the earth planes and to your work there, and as you have been helped and strengthened and taught, so do you feel bound by the obligations of gratitude and the ties of Universal Brotherhood to help others.

"Let us now bid farewell to this Dark Land, not in sorrow over its sadness and its sins, but in hope and with earnest prayer for the future of all who are yet in the bonds of suffering and sin."

As our great leader concluded his speech we took our last look at the Dark Country, and, descending the mountain, we passed once more through the Ring of Fire, which, as before, was by our will power driven back on either side of us that we might pass through in safety.

Thus ended my wanderings in the Kingdoms of Hell.

PART IV.
"Through the Gates of Gold."

CHAPTER XXVII.--Welcome on Our Return--A Magic Mirror--Work in the Cities of Earth--The Land of Remorse--The Valley of Phantom Mists--A Home of Rest.

On our return to the Land of Dawn, we met with a right royal welcome from our Brotherhood, and a festival was given in our honor.

On entering our own little rooms each of us found a new robe awaiting him. It was of a very light grey, almost white color, and the border, girdle, and device of our order-- an anchor and a star upon the left sleeve--were in deep golden yellow.

I greatly prized this new dress because in the spirit world the dress symbolizes the state of advancement of the spirit, and is esteemed as showing what each one has attained. What I prized even more than this new dress, however, was a most beautiful wreath of pure white spirit roses which I found had clustered around and framed the magic picture of my beloved--a frame that never withered, never faded, and whose fragrance was wafted to me as I reposed on the snow white couch and gazed out upon those peaceful hills behind which there shone the dawning day.

I was aroused from my reverie by a friend who came to summon me to the festival, and on entering the great hall I found my father and some friends of my wanderings awaiting me. We greeted one another with much emotion, and after we had enjoyed a banquet similar to the one I have described on my first entrance to this sphere, we all assembled at the lower end of the hall before a large curtain of grey and gold which completely covered the walls.

While we waited in expectation of what we were to see, a soft strain of music floated towards us as though borne upon some passing breeze. This grew stronger, fuller, more distinct, till a solemn majestic measure like the march of an army fell upon our ears. Not a march of triumph or rejoicing but one such as might be played by an army of giants mourning over a dead comrade, so grand, so full of pathos was this strain.

Then the curtains glided apart and showed us a huge mirror of black polished marble. And then the music changed to another measure, still solemn, still grand, but with somewhat of discordance in its tones. It wavered too and became uneven in the measure of its time, as though halting with uncertain step, stumbling and hesitating.

Then the air around us darkened till we could scarce see each other's faces; slowly the light faded, and at last all we could see was the black polished surface of the gigantic mirror, and in it I saw reflected the figures of two of the members of our expedition. They moved and spoke and the scenery around them grew distinct and such as I had seen in the Inferno we had left. The weird music stirred my soul to its inmost core, and looking upon the drama being enacted before my eyes I forgot where I was--I forgot everything--and seemed to be wandering once more in the dark depths of Hell.

Picture melted into picture, till we had been shown the varied experiences of each of our bank, from the lowest member to our leader himself--the last scene showing the whole company assembled upon the hill listening to the farewell discourse of our commander; and like the chorus in a Greek Tragedy, the wild music seemed to accompany and explain it all, varying with every variation in the dramas, now sad and sorrowful, now full of repose or triumph, and again wailing, sobbing, shrieking or changing into a murmuring lullaby as some poor rescued soul sank to rest at last--then again rising into wild notes of clamor, fierce cries of battle, hoarse curses and imprecations; now surging in wild waves of tumultous melody, then dying away amidst discordant broken notes. At last as the final scene was enacted it sank into a soft plaintive air of most exquisite sweetness, and died away note by note. As it ceased the darkness vanished, the curtains glided over the black mirror and we all turned with a sigh of relief and thankfulness to congratulate each other that our wanderings in that dark land were past.

I asked my father how this effect had been produced, was it an illusion or what?

"My son," he answered, "what you have seen is an application of scientific knowledge, nothing more. This mirror has been so prepared that it receives and reflects the images thrown upon it from a series of sheets of thin metal, or rather what is the spiritual counterpart of earthly metal. These sheets of metal have been so highly sensitized that they are able to receive and retain these pictures somewhat in the fashion of a phonograph (such as you saw in earth life) receives and retains the sound waves.

"When you were wandering in those dark spheres, you were put in magnetic communication with this instrument and the adventures of each were transferred to one of these sensitive sheets, while the emotions of every one of you caused the sound waves in the spheres of music and literature to vibrate in corresponding tones of sympathy.

"You belong to the spheres of Art, Music and Literature, and therefore you are able to see and feel and understand the vibrations of those spheres. In the spirit world all emotions, speeches, or events reproduce themselves in objective forms and become for those in harmony with them either pictures, melodies, or spoken narratives. The spirit world is created by the thoughts and actions of the soul, and therefore every act or thought forms its spiritually material counterpart. In this sphere you will find many things not yet known to men on earth, many curious inventions which will in time be transmitted to earth and clothed there in material form. But see! you are about to receive the Palm branch which is given to each of you as a reward of your victory."

At this moment the large doors of the hall were once more thrown open and our grand master entered, followed by the same train of handsome youths I had seen before, only this time each carried a branch of palm instead of a wreath of laurel. When the grand master had seated himself under his canopy of state we were each summoned to his presence to receive our branch of palm, and when we had all done so and returned to our places again a most joyous hymn of victory was sung by everyone, our palm branches waving in time to the music and our glad voices filling the air with triumphant harmony.

I now enjoyed a long quiet season of rest which much resembled that half-waking, half-sleeping state, when the mind is too much in repose to think and yet retains full consciousness of all its surroundings. From this state, which lasted some weeks, I arose completely recovered from the effects of my wanderings in the dark spheres.

And my first thought was to visit my beloved, and see if she could see me and be conscious of my improved appearance. I shall not, however, dwell upon our interview; its joy was for ourselves alone--I only seek to show that death does not of necessity either end our affection for those we have left or shut us out from sharing with them our joys or sorrows.

I found that I was now much more able to communicate with her through her own mediumistic powers, so that we did not need any third person to intervene and help us, and thus were my labors lightened and cheered by her sweet affection and her conscious recognition of my presence and of my continued existence.

My work at this time was once more upon the earth plane and in those cities whose counterparts I had seen in Hell. I had to labor among those mortals and spirits who thronged them, and impress their minds with a sense of what I had seen in that dark sphere far below. I knew I could only make them dimly conscious of it, only arouse a little their dormant sense of fear of future retribution for their present misdeeds, but even that was something and would help to deter some from a too complete abandonment of themselves to selfish pleasure. Moreover, amongst the spirits who were earth-bound to those cities I found many whom I could assist, with the knowledge and strength which I had gained in my journey.

There ever is and ever must be ample work for those who work upon the earth plane, for multitudinous as are the workers there, more are always being wanted, since men are passing over from earth life every hour and every minute, who need all the help that can be given them.

Thus passed some months for me, and then I began once more to feel the old restless longing to rise higher myself, to attain more than I had yet done, to approach nearer to that sphere to which my beloved one would pass when her earthly life was ended, and by attaining which I could alone hope to be united to her in the spirit world. I used to at this time be tormented with a constant fear lest my darling should pass from earth before I had risen to her spiritual level, and thus I should again be parted from her.

This fear it was which had ever urged me on to fresh efforts, fresh conquests over myself, and now made me dissatisfied even with the progress I had made. I knew that I had overcome much, I had struggled hard to improve, and I had risen wonderfully fast, yet in spite of all I was still tormented by the jealous and suspicious feelings which my disposition and my earthly experience had gathered about me.

There were even times when I would begin to doubt the constancy of my beloved herself. In spite of all the many proofs of her love which she had given me, I would fear lest while I was away from her someone yet in the flesh should after all win her love from me.

And thus I was in danger of becoming earth-bound by reason of my unworthy desire to watch her continually. Ah! you who think a spirit has changed all his thoughts and desires at the moment of dissolution, how little you understand of the conditions of that other life beyond the grave, and how slowly, how very slowly we change the habits of thought we have cultivated in our earthly lives or how long they cling to us in the spiritual state.

I was then in character much what I had been on earth, only a little better, only learning by degrees wherein my ideas had been wrong and full of prejudice, a lesson we may go on learning through many spheres, higher than any I had attained to.

Even while I doubted and feared, I was ashamed of my doubts and knew how unjust they were, yet could I not free myself from them; the experiences of my earth life had taught me suspicion and distrust, and the ghosts of that earth life were not so easily laid.

It was while I was in this state of self-torment that Ahrinziman came to me and told me how I might free myself from these haunting shadows of the past.

145

"There is," said he, "a land not far from here called the Land of Remorse; were you to visit it, the journey would be of much service to you, for once its hills and valleys were passed and its difficulties overcome, the true nature of your earthly life and its mistakes would be clearly realized and prove a great means of progression for your soul. Such a journey will indeed be full of much bitterness and sorrow, for you will see displayed in all their nakedness, the actions of your past, actions which you have already in part atoned for but do not yet see as the eyes of the higher spiritual intelligences see them.

"Few who come over from earth life really realize the true motives which prompted their actions; many indeed go on for years, some even for centuries, before this knowledge comes to them. They excuse and justify to their own consciences their misdeeds, and such a land as this I speak of is very useful for enlightening them. The journey must, however, be undertaken voluntarily, and it will then shorten by years the pathway of progression.

"In that land men's lives are stored up as pictures which, mirrored in the wondrous spiritual atmosphere, reflect for them the reasons of many failures; and show the subtle causes at work in their own hearts which have shaped the lives of each. It would be a severe and keen self-examination through which you would pass--a bitter experience of your own nature, your own self, but though a bitter it is a salutary medicine, and would go far to heal your soul of those maladies of the earth life which like a miasma hang about it still."

"Show me," I answered, "where this land is, and I will go to it."

Ahrinziman took me to the top of one of those dim and distant hills which I could see from the window of my little room, and leading me to where we looked down across a wide plain bounded by another range of hills far away, said:

"On the other side of those farther hills lies this wondrous land of which I speak, a land through which most spirits pass whose lives have been such as to call for great sorrow and remorse. Those whose errors have been merely trivial, daily weaknesses such as are common to all mankind, do not pass through it; there are other means whereby they may be enlightened as to the source of their mistakes. This land is more particularly useful to such as yourself, of strong powers and strong will, who will recognize readily and admit freely wherein you have done wrong, and in doing so arise to better things. Like a strong tonic this circle of the sphere would be too much for some weak erring spirits who would only be crushed and overwhelmed and disheartened by the too rapid and vivid realization of all their sins; such spirits must be taught slowly, step by step, a little at a time, while you who are strong of heart and full of courage will but rise the more rapidly the sooner you see and recognize the nature of those fetters which have bound your soul."

"And will it take me long to accomplish this journey?"

No, it will last but a short time--two or three weeks of earth time--for behold as I shadow it forth to you I see following it fast the image of your returning spirit, showing that the two events are not separated by a wide interval. In the spirit world where time is not reckoned by days or weeks or counted by hours, we judge of how long an event will take to accomplish or when an occurrence will happen by seeing how near or how far away they appear, and also by observing whether the shadow cast by the coming event touches the earth or is yet distant from it--we then try to judge as nearly as possible of what will be its corresponding time as measured by earthly standards. Even the wisest of us may not always be able to do this with perfect correctness; thus it is as well for those who communicate with friends on earth not to give an exact date for foreseen events, since many things may intervene to delay it and thus make the date incorrect. An event may be shown very near, yet instead of continuing to travel to the mortal at the same speed it may be delayed or held in suspense, and sometimes even turned aside altogether by a stronger power than the one which has set it in motion."

I thanked my guide for his advice and we parted. I was so very eager to progress that a very short time after this conversation saw me setting forth upon my new journey.

I found my progress not so rapid as had been the case in my previous travels through the spirit land, for now I had taken upon me the full burden of my past sins, and like the load carried by the pilgrim Christian it almost weighed me down to the earth, making my movements very slow and laborious. Like a pilgrim, I was habited in a coarse grey robe, my feet were bare and my head uncovered, for in the spirit world the condition of your mind forms your clothing and surroundings, and my feelings then were as though I wore sackcloth and had put dust and ashes upon my head.

When I had at last crossed those dim far-off hills there lay before me a wide sandy plain--a great desert--in which I saw the barren sands of my earthly life lie scattered. No tree, no shrub, no green thing was there anywhere for the eye to rest upon, no water of refreshment to sparkle before us like hopes of happiness. There was no shade for our weary limbs should we seek for repose. The lives of those who crossed this plain in search of the rest beyond, had been barren of true, pure, unselfish affection and that self-denial which alone can make the desert to blossom like the rose and sweet waters of refreshment to spring up around their paths.

I descended to this dreary waste of sand, and took a narrow path which seemed to lead to the hills on the other side. The load I carried had now become almost intolerable to me and I longed to lay it down--but in vain; I could not for one moment detach it. The hot sand seemed to blister my feet as I walked, and each step was so labored as to be most painful. As I passed slowly on there rose before me pictures of my past and of all those whom I had known. These pictures seemed to be just in front of me and to float in the atmosphere like those mirages seen by earthly travelers through the desert.

Like dissolving views they appeared to melt into one another and give place to fresh scenes. Through them all there moved the friends or strangers whom I had met and known, and the long forgotten unkind thoughts and words which I had spoken to them rose up in an accusing array before me--the tears I had made others shed--the cruel words (sharper and harder to bear than any blow) with which I had wounded the feelings of those around me. A thousand hard unworthy thoughts and selfish actions of my past--long thrust aside and forgotten or excused--all rose up once more before me, picture after picture--till at last I was so overwhelmed to see what an array of them there was, that I broke down, and casting my pride to the winds I bowed myself in the dust and wept bitter tears of shame and sorrow. And where my tears fell on the hot dry sand there sprang up around me little flowers like white stars, each little waxy blossom bearing in its heart a drop of dew, so that the place I had sunk down upon in such sorrow had become a little oasis of beauty in that weary desert.

I plucked a few of those tiny blossoms and placed them in my bosom as a memorial of that spot, and then rose to go on again. To my surprise the pictures were no longer visible, but in front of me I beheld a woman carrying a little child whose weight seemed too much for her strength, and it was wailing with weariness and fear.

I hurried up to them and offered to carry the poor little one, for I was touched by the sight of its poor little frightened face and weary drooping head. The woman stared at me for a moment and then put the little one in my arms, and as I covered him over with a part of my robe the poor tired little creature sank into a quiet sleep. The woman told me the child was hers, but she had not felt much affection for it during its life. "In fact," said she, "I did not want a child at all. I do not care for children, and when this one came I was annoyed and neglected it. Then, as it grew older, and was (as I thought then) naughty and troublesome, I used to beat it and shut it up in dark rooms, and was otherwise hard and unkind. At last when it was five years old it died, and then I died not long afterwards of the same fever. Since I came to the spirit world that child has seemed to haunt me, and at last I was advised to take this journey, carrying him with me since I cannot rid myself of his presence."

"And do you even yet feel no love for the poor little thing?"

"Well, no! I can't say I have come to love it, perhaps I never shall really love it as some mothers do, indeed I am one of those women who should not be mothers at all--

the maternal instinct is, as yet at all events, quite wanting in me. I do not love the child, but I am sorry now that I was not kinder to him, and I can see that what I thought was a sense of duty urging me to bring him up properly and correct his faults, was only an excuse for my own temper and the irritation the care of him caused. I can see I have done wrong and why I did so, but I cannot say I have much love for this child."

"And are you to take him with you through all your journey?" I asked, feeling so sorry for the poor little unloved thing that I bent over him and kissed him, my own eyes growing dim as I did so, for I thought of my beloved on earth and what a treasure she would have deemed such a child, and how tender she would have been to it. And as I kissed him he put his little arms around my neck and smiled up at me in a half-asleep way that should have gone straight to the woman's heart. Even as it was her face relaxed a little, and she said more graciously than she had yet spoken:

"I am only to carry him a little farther I believe, and then he will be taken to a sphere where there are many children like him whose parents do not care about them and who are taken care of by spirits who are fond of children."

"I am glad to think that," I said, and then we trudged on together for a bit farther, till we reached a small group of rocks where there was a little pool of water, beside which we sat down to rest. Presently I fell asleep, and when I awoke the woman and the child had gone.

I arose and resumed my way, and shortly after arrived at the foot of the mountains, which pride and ambition had reared. Hard, rocky, and precipitous was the pathway across them, with scarce foothold to help one on, and ofttimes it seemed as though these rocks reared by selfish pride would prove too difficult to surmount. And as I climbed I recognized what share I had had in building them, what atoms my pride had sent to swell these difficulties I now encountered.

Few of us know the secrets of our own hearts. We so often deem that it is a far nobler ambition than mere self-aggrandisement which inspires our efforts to place ourselves on a higher level than our fellow men who are not so well equipped for the battle of life.

I looked back upon my past with shame as I recognized one great rock after another to be the spiritual emblems of the stumbling blocks which I had placed in the path of my feebler brothers, whose poor crude efforts had once seemed to me only worthy of prompt extinction in the interests of all true art, and I longed to have my life to live over again that I might do better with it and encourage where I had once condemned, help where I had crushed.

149

I had been so hard to myself, so eager ever to attain to the highest possible excellence, that I had never been satisfied with any of my own efforts--even when the applause of my fellows was ringing in my ears, even when I had carried off the highest prizes from all competitors--and so I had thought myself entitled to exact as high a standard from all who sought to study my beautiful art. I could see no merit in the efforts of the poor strugglers who were as infants beside the great master minds. Talent, genius, I could cordially admire, frankly appreciate, but with complacent mediocrity I had no sympathy; such I had had no desire to help. I was ignorant then that those feeble powers were like tiny seeds which though they would never develop into anything of value on earth, would yet blossom into the perfect flower in the great Hereafter. In my early days, when success first was mine, and before I had made shipwreck of my life, I had been full of the wildest, most ambitious dreams, and though in later years when sorrow and disappointments had taught me somewhat of pity for the struggles of others, yet I could not learn to feel true cordial sympathy with mediocrity and its struggles, and now I recognized that it was the want of such sympathy which had piled up high these rocks so typical of my arrogance.

In my sorrow and remorse at this discovery I looked around to see if there might be anyone near me weaker than myself, whom it may not be too late to assist upon his path, and as I looked I saw above me on this hard road a young man almost spent and much exhausted with his effort to climb these rocks, which family pride and an ambition to rank with the noble and wealthy had piled up for him--a pride to which he had sacrificed all those who should have been most dear. He was clinging to a jutting-out portion of rock, and was so spent and exhausted he seemed almost ready to let go and fall.

I shouted to him to hold on, and soon climbed up to where he was, and there with some difficulty succeeded in dragging him up to the summit of these rocks. My strength being evidently double his, I was only too ready to help him as some relief to the remorse I now felt at thinking how many feeble minds I had crushed in the past.

When we reached the top and sat down to rest, I found myself to be much bruised and torn by the sharp stones over which we had stumbled. But I also found that in my struggles to ascend, my burden of selfish pride had fallen from me and was gone, and as I looked back over the path by which I had climbed I clothed myself anew in the sackcloth and ashes of humility, and resolved I would go back to earth and seek to help some of those feebler ones to a fuller understanding of my art. I would seek as far as I could to give them the help of my higher knowledge. Where I had crushed the timid aspiring soul I would now encourage; where my sharp tongue and keen wit had wounded I would strive to heal. I knew now that none should dare to despise his weaker brother or crush out his hopes because to a more advanced mind they seem small and trivial.

I sat long upon that mountain thinking of these things--the young man whom I had helped going on without me. At last I rose and wended my way slowly through a deep ravine spanned by a broken bridge and approached by a high gate, at which many spirits were waiting, and trying by various means to open it in order that they might pass through. Some tried force, others tried to climb over, others again sought to find some secret spring, and when one after another tried and failed some of the others again would seek to console the disappointed ones. As I drew near six or seven spirits who still hovered about the gate drew back, curious to see what I would do. It was a great gate of what looked to me like sheets of iron, though its real nature I do not even now know. It was so high and so smooth, no one could climb it, so solid it was vain to dream of forcing it, so fast shut there appeared no chance of opening it. I stood in front of it in despair, wondering what I should do now, when I saw a poor woman near me weeping most bitterly with disappointment; she had been there some time and had tried in vain to open the gate. I did my best to comfort her and give her all the hope I could, and while I was doing so the solid gate before us melted away and we passed through. Then as suddenly I saw it rise again behind me, while the woman had vanished, and beside the bridge stood a feeble old man bent nearly double. As I was still wondering about the gate a voice said to me, "That is the gate of kind deeds and kind thoughts. Those who are on the other side must wait till their kind thoughts and acts for others are heavy enough to weigh the gate down, when it will open for them as it did for you who have tried so hard to help your fellows."

I now advanced to the bridge where the old man was standing, poking about with his stick as if feeling his way, and groaning over his helplessness. I was so afraid he would fall through the broken part without seeing it, that I rushed impulsively forward and offered to help him over. But he shook his head, "No! no! young man, the bridge is so rotten it will never bear your weight and mine. Go on yourself, and leave me here to do the best I can."

"Not so, you are feeble, and old enough to be my grandfather, and if I leave you you will most likely drop through the broken place. Now, I am active and strong, and it will go hard with us if I do not contrive somehow to get us both across."

Without waiting for his reply I took hold of him and hoisted him on to my back, and telling him to hold tight by my shoulders I started to cross the bridge.

Sapristi! what a weight that old man seemed! Sinbad's old man of the sea was a joke to him. That bridge, too, how it creaked, groaned and bent under our weight. I thought we must both be tumbled into the chasm below, and all the time the old man kept imploring me not to drop him. On I struggled, holding with my hands as well as I could, and crawling on all-fours when we reached the worst part. When we got to the middle there was a great ragged hole and only the broken ends of the two great beams to catch hold of. Here I did feel it a difficulty. I could have swung myself across I felt certain, but it was a different thing with that heavy old man clinging to me and half choking me, and a thought did cross my mind that I might have done better to leave him alone, but that seemed so cruel to the poor old soul that I made up my mind to risk it. The poor old man gave a great sigh when he saw how matters stood, and said:

"You had better abandon me after all. I am too helpless to get across and you will only spoil your own chance by trying it. Leave me here and go on alone."

His tone was so dejected, so miserable, I could never have so left him, and I thought to make a desperate effort for us both, so telling him to hold on tight I grasped the broken beam with one hand and, making a great spring, I swung myself over the chasm with such a will we seemed to fly across, and alighted upon the other side unharmed.

As I looked back to see what we had escaped, I cried out in astonishment, for there was no break in the bridge at all, but it was as sound a bridge as ever I saw, and by my side there stood not a feeble old man but Ahrinziman himself, laughing at my astonishment. He put his hand on my shoulder and said:

"Franchezzo, my son, that was but a little trial to test if you would be unselfish enough to burden yourself with a heavy old man when your own chance seemed so small. I leave you now to encounter the last of your trials and to judge for yourself the nature of those doubts and suspicions you have cherished. Adieu, and may success attend you."

He turned away from me and immediately vanished, leaving me to go on alone through another deep valley which was before me.

It lay between two precipitous hills, and was called "The valley of the phantom mists." Great wreaths of grey vapor floated to and fro and crept up the hill sides, shaping themselves into mysterious phantom forms and hovering around me as I walked.

The farther I advanced through the ravine the thicker grew these shapes, growing more distinct and like living things. I knew them to be no more than the thought creations of my earthly life, yet seen in this lifelike palpable form they were like haunting ghosts of my past, rising up in accusing array against me. The suspicions I had nursed, the doubts I had fostered, the unkind, unholy thoughts I had cherished, all seemed to gather round me, menacing and terrible, mocking me and taunting me with the past, whispering in my ears and closing over my head like great waves of darkness. As my life had grown more full of such thoughts, so did my path become blocked with them till they hemmed me in on every side. Such fearful, distorted, hateful-looking things! And these had been my own thoughts, these mirrored the state of my own mind towards others. These brooding spirits of the mist--dark, suspicious, and bewildering--contronted me now and showed me what my heart had been. I had had so little faith in goodness--so little trust in my fellow man. Because I had been cruelly deceived I had said in my haste all men, and women too, are liars, and I had sneered at the weakness and the folly around me, and thought it was always the same thing everywhere, all bitterness and disappointment.

So these thought-creations had grown up, mass upon mass, till now that I sought to battle with them they seemed to overwhelm and stifle me, wrapping me up in the great vaporous folds of their phantom forms. In vain I sought to beat them off, to shake myself free of them. They gathered round and closed me in even as my doubts and suspicions had done. I was seized with horror, and fought as if they had been living things that were sweeping me to destruction. And then I saw a deep dark crevasse open in the ground before me, to which these phantoms were driving me, a gulf into which it seemed I must sink unless I could free myself from these awful ghosts. Like a madman I strove and wrestled with them, fighting as for dear life, and still they closed me in and forced me back and back towards that gloomy chasm. Then in my anguish of soul I called aloud for help to be free from them, and throwing out my arms before me with all my force I seemed to grasp the foremost phantom and hurl it from me. Then did the mighty cloud of doubts waver and break as though a wind had scattered them, and I sank overcome and exhausted upon the ground; and as I sank into unconsciousness I had a dream, a brief but lovely dream, in which I thought my beloved had come to me and scattered those foul thoughts, and that she knelt down beside me and drew my head to rest upon her bosom as a mother with her child. I thought I felt her arms encircle me and hold me safe, and then the dream was over and I fell asleep.

When I recovered consciousness I was resting still in that valley, but the mists had rolled away and my time of bitter doubt and suspicion was past. I lay upon a bank of soft green turf at the end of the ravine, and before me there was a meadow watered by a smooth peaceful river of clear crystal water. I arose and followed the windings of the stream for a short distance, and arrived at a beautiful grove of trees. Through the trunks I could see a clear pool on whose surface floated water-lilies. There was a fairy-like fountain in the middle, from which the spray fell like a shower of diamonds into the transparent water. The trees arched their branches overhead and through them I could see the blue sky. I drew near to rest and refresh myself at the fountain, and as I did so a fair nymph in a robe of green gossamer and with a crown of water-lilies on her head drew near to help me. She was the guardian spirit of the fountain, and her work was to help and refresh all weary wanderers like myself. "In earth life," said she,

"I lived in a forest, and here in the spirit land I find a home surrounded by the woods I love so well."

She gave me food and drink, and after I had rested a while showed me a broad pathway through the trees, which led to a Home of Rest where I might repose for a time. With a grateful heart I thanked this bright spirit, and following the path soon found myself before a large building covered with honeysuckle and ivy. It had many windows and wide open doors as though to invite all to enter. It was approached by a great gateway of what looked like wrought iron, only that the birds and flowers on it were so life-like they seemed to have clustered there to rest. While I stood looking at the gate it opened as by magic, and I passed on to the house. Here several spirits in white robes came to welcome me, and I was conducted to a pretty room whose windows looked out upon a grassy lawn and soft fairy-like trees, and here I was bidden to repose myself.

On awakening I found my pilgrim dress was gone, and in its stead there lay my light grey robe, only now it had a triple border of pure white. I was greatly pleased, and arrayed myself with pleasure, for I felt the white to be a sign of my progression--white in the spirit world symbolizing purity and happiness, while black is the reverse.

Presently I was conducted to a large pleasant room in which were a number of spirits dressed like myself, among whom I was pleased to recognize the woman with the child whom I had helped across the Plains of Repentance and Tears. She smiled much more kindly on the child, and greeted me with pleasure, thanking me for my help, while the little one climbed upon my knees and established himself there as an earthly child might have done.

An ample repast of fruits and cakes and the pure wine of the spirit land was set before us, and when we were all refreshed and had returned our thanks to God for all his mercies, the Brother who presided wished us all God's speed, and then with grateful hearts we bade each other adieu and set forth to return to our own homes.

154

CHAPTER XXVIII.--My Home and Work in the Morning Land.

I was not, however, destined to remain in the Land of Dawn. My home was now to be in the circle of the Morning Land, and I was therefore escorted thither by my friends.

It lay beyond the peaceful lake and those hills behind which I used to watch the light of that dawning day which never seemed to grow brighter or advance in the Land of Dawn, but whose beauties belonged to this Morning Land. This land lay in an opposite direction from that range of hills beyond which lay the Plain of Remorse.

Here in the Morning Land I found that I was to have a little house of my own, a something earned by myself. I have always loved a place of my own, and this little cottage, simple as it was, was very dear to me. It was indeed a peaceful place. The green hills shut it in on every side save in front, where they opened out and the ground stretched away in undulating slopes of green and golden meadow land. There were no trees, no shrubs, around my new home, no flowers to gladden my eyes, because my efforts had not yet blossomed into flower. But there was one sweet trailing honeysuckle that clustered around the little porch and shed the fragrance of its love into my rooms. This was the gift of my beloved to me, the spiritual growth of her sweet pure loving thoughts which twined around my dwelling to whisper to me ever of her constant love and truth.

There were only two little rooms, the one for me to receive my friends and to study in, and the other my chamber of repose, where I could rest when weary with my work on the earth plane. And in this room there was my picture framed in roses, and all my little treasures. The blue sky outside shed down on me so pure a light, my eyes, long wearied to see it, gazed on it again and yet again. The soft green grass and the fragrant honeysuckle were all so sweet, so delicious to me, wearied as I was with my long dark wanderings, that I was overcome with the emotions of my gratitude. I was aroused by a kindly hand, a loving voice, and looking up, beheld my father. Ah! what a joy, what a happiness I felt, and still more when he bade me come to earth with him and show this home in a vision to her who was its guiding star!

What happy hours I can recall when I look back to that, my first home in the spirit land. I was so proud to think I had won it. My present home is far finer, my present sphere far more beautiful in every way, but I have never felt a greater happiness than I felt when that first home of my own was given to me.

I should but weary my readers were I to attempt to describe all the work on the earth plane I did at this time, all the sad ones I helped to cheer and direct upon the better way. There is a sameness in such work that makes one example serve for many.

Time passes on for spirits as well as mortals and brings ever new changes--fresh progression. And thus while I was working to help others I was gradually myself learning the lesson which had proved most hard for me to learn. The lesson of that entire forgiveness of our enemies which will enable us to feel that we not only desire them no harm but that we even wish to do them good--to return good for evil cordially. It had been a hard struggle to overcome my desire for revenge, or wish that at all events some punishment should overtake the one who had so deeply wronged me, and it was as hard, or harder even, to desire now to benefit that person. Time and again while I was working on the earth plane I went and stood beside that one, unseen and unfelt save for the thoughts of me that would be awakened, and each time I perceived that my enemy's thoughts were to the full as bitter as my own. There was no love lost between us. Standing there I beheld time after time the events of our lives blended together in one picture, the dark shadows of our passionate hate dimming and blurring these pictures as storm clouds sweep over a summer sky. And in the clearer light of my spiritual knowledge I beheld where my faults had lain, as strongly or more so than I beheld those of my enemy. And from such visits I would return to my little cottage in the spirit land overwhelmed with the bitterest regrets, the keenest anguish, yet always unable to feel aught but bitterness and anger towards the one whose life seemed only to have been linked by sorrow and wrong to my own.

At last one day while standing beside this mortal I became conscious of a new feeling, almost of pity, for this person was also oppressed in soul--also conscious of regret in thinking of our past. A wish had arisen that a different course towards me had been followed. Thus was there created between us a kinder thought, which though faint and feeble was yet the first fruits of my efforts to overcome my own anger--the first softening and melting of the hard wall of hatred between us. Then was there given to me a chance to assist and benefit this person even as the chance had before come to me of doing harm, and now I was able to overcome my bitterness and to take advantage of this opportunity, so that it was my hand--the hand which had been raised to curse and blight--which was now the one to help instead.

My enemy was not conscious of my presence nor of my interference for good, but felt in a dim fashion that somehow the hatred between us was dead, and that, as I was dead, it were perhaps better to let our quarrels die also. Thus came at last a mutual pardon which severed the links which had so long bound our earthly lives together. I know that during the earthly life of that one we shall never cross each other's path again, but even as I had seen in the case of my friend Benedetto, when death shall sever the thread of that earthly life, our spirits will meet once again, in order that each may ask pardon from the other. Not until then will all links be finally severed between us and each pass on to our appointed sphere. Great and lasting are the effects upon the soul of our loves and our hates; long, long after the life of earth is past do they cling to us, and many are the spirits whom I have seen tied to each other, not by mutual love but mutual hate.

When I had at last learned the lesson of self conquest my mind seemed to be free from a great oppressive weight, and I turned to the study of the spirit land and its conditions with renewed interest. At this period of my wanderings I used to see my friend Hassein very often, and he helped me to an understanding of many things which had perplexed me in my earthly life.

On one occasion when we were seated in my little home enjoying one of our many conversations, I asked him to tell me more of the spheres and their relation to the earth.

"The term spheres," said he, "is, as you have seen, applied to those great belts of spiritual matter which encircle the earth and other planets. It is likewise applied to those still vaster, more extended, thought waves which circle throughout all the universe. Thus we may say there are two classes of spheres--those which are in a measure material and encircle each their own planet or their own solar system and form the dwelling places of the spiritual inhabitants of each planet. These spheres are divided into circles indicating, like steps upon the ladder of progress, the moral advancement of the spirits.

"The other class of spheres are mental, not material, in their constituents and do not belong to any planetary or solar system, but are as limitless as the universe, circling in ever widening currents of thought emanations from the central point, around which all the universe is held to be revolving, and which point is said to be the immediate environment of the Supreme Being, from whom these thought waves are held to proceed. It may perhaps make my meaning still clearer to say there is one great sphere of the intellectual faculties or attributes belonging essentially to the soul, and then to divide this sphere into circles such as the circles of Philosophy, of Art, of Music, of Literature, etc.

It is a common mode of expression to call them spheres, but to my mind it is more correct to describe them as circles. These Intellectual Circles, like great wheels, inclose all those lesser wheels, those spiral rings, which surround each their own solar system, or parent planet, wheels within wheels, revolving around the one great centre continually. In the spirit world only those who are in sympathy ever remain together, and though the ties of relationship or the links of kind remembrance may at times draw together those who have no common bonds of union, these will be but flying visits, and each will return to their own circle and sphere, drawn back by the strong magnetic attraction which holds each sphere and each circle of a sphere in unison. A spirit belonging to the sphere of Music or Philosophy, will be drawn to others of a like disposition who are in the same stage of moral advancement as himself, but his development of a higher degree of music or philosophy will not enable him to ascend into a higher circle of the Moral Spheres, or planetary spheres, than his moral development entitles him to occupy. The central suns of each of the vast intellectual circles of the mental sphere shine as burnished magnets. They are as great prisms glowing with the celestial fires of purity and truth, and darting on all sides their glorious rays of knowledge, and in these rays cluster the multitudes of spirits who are seeking to light their lamps at these glowing shrines. In those rays which reach the earth pure and unbroken, are found those gems of truth which have illuminated the minds of men in all ages of the world's history, and shattered into a thousand fragments the great rocks of error and darkness, even as the lightning's flash shivers a granite rock, letting into the depths below the clear light of God's sun, and those spirits who are most highly advanced are those who are nearest to the central force, to the dazzling light of these starlike centres. These great spheres of the intellectual and moral faculties may, then, be termed the "universal" spheres; those around each planet, "planetary" spheres; and those surrounding the sun centres, "solar" spheres; the first being understood to consist of thought or sound essence, the others of various degrees of spiritualized matter."

"And how, then, would you describe the creation of a planet and its spheres?"

"The creation of a planet may be said to begin from the time when it is cast off from the parent sun in the form of a nebulous mass of fiery vapor. In this stage it is a most powerful magnet, attracting to itself the minute particles of matter which float through all the ether of space. This ether has been supposed to be void of all material atoms such as float in the atmosphere of planets, but that is an incorrect supposition, the fact being that the atoms of matter are simply subdivided into even more minute particles compared to which a grain of sand is as the bulk of the sun to the earth. These atoms being thus subdivided and dispersed through space (instead of being clustered by the forces of magnetic attraction in the planet into atoms the size of those which float as motes in the earth's atmosphere), have become not only invisible to man's material sight but are also incapable of being detected by the ordinary chemical means at his disposal. They are, in fact, etherealized, and have become of the first degree of spirit matter in consequence of the amount of soul essence which has become amalgamated with their grosser elements. In becoming attracted to the glowing mass of an embryo planet, these atoms become so thickly clustered together that the more ethereal elements are pressed out and escape back into space, leaving the solid gross portion to form into rock, etc., through the constant attracting of fresh atoms and the necessarily vast increase of pressure thus caused. These atoms exist eternally, and are as indestructible as all the other elements which constitute the universe, and they are absorbed and cast off again by planet after planet as each passes through the various stages of its existence and development.

"The atoms of matter may be broadly classed under three heads, and again each of the three heads may be subdivided into an infinite number of degrees of density, in order to express the various stages of sublimation to which they have attained. The three principal classes may be termed, material or planetary matter--spiritual or soul enveloping matter, which is no longer visible to material sight--and soul essence, this last being so sublimated that it is not possible for me yet to describe its nature to you. Of the material matter the lowest, most gross form, is that of which mineral substances, such as rocks, earth, etc., are formed; these are thrown off into the atmosphere as dust and reabsorbed continually to be changed, by the process continually going on in nature everywhere, into plants, etc. The intermediate degree between the rocks and the plants is the fluidic, in which the more solid particles are held in solution by the various gases or vaporized form of the chemical elements which constitute them. The second degree of material matter is that of plant or vegetable life which is nourished by the blending of the most gross matter with the fluidic. Thus through infinite gradations of earthly matter we reach the highest, namely, flesh and bones and muscles which, whether it clothes the soul of man or one of the lower animals, is still the highest degree of material matter, containing in this highest degree of earthly material development all those elements of which the lower degrees are composed.

"The second or spiritual form of matter is, as I have said, merely the etherealized development of the first or earthly form of matter, while the soul essence is the animating principle of both, the Divine germ, without which the two first forms of matter could not exist. It is a part of the law of the two first classes of matter that they should clothe the higher soul principle, or they lose their power of cohesion and are diffused into their elemental parts again. Soul matter is the only one which possesses any permanent identity. It is the true Ego, since by no power can it be disintegrated or lose its individuality. It is the true life of whatever lower forms of matter it may animate, and as such changes and shapes that lower matter into its own identity. Soul essence is in and of every type of life, from the mineral and vegetable to man, the highest type of animal, and each of these types is capable of development into the highest or celestial form, in which state it is found in the Heavenly Sphere of each planet and each solar system.

"Since, then, we maintain that everything has its soul of a higher or lower type, it need not create surprise in the mind of any mortal to be told that there are plants and flowers, rocks and deserts, beasts and birds, in the spirit world. They exist there in their spiritualized or developed state, and are more etherealized as they advance higher, in accordance with the same law which governs alike the development of man, the highest type, and that of the lowest form of soul matter. When a plant dies or the solid rock is dispersed into dust or fused into gas, its soul essence passes with the spiritual matter pertaining to it, into the spirit world, and to that sphere to which its development is most akin--the most material portion being absorbed by the earth, the more sublimated particles of matter feeling less of the earth attraction and therefore floating farther from it. Thus in the early stages of a planet's life, when it possesses but a small portion of the soul essence and a large amount of gross matter, its spheres are thrown out first in the direction farthest from its sun and are very material, and the development of its spiritual inhabitants is very low.

"At this early stage the vegetable as well as the animal and human types of soul life are coarse and gross, wanting in the refinement and beauty which may be observed as the evolution of the planet advances. Gradually the vegetation changes, the animals change, the races of men who appear become each higher, more perfect, and as a consequence the spiritual emanations thrown off become correspondingly higher. In the first stages of a planet's life the spheres scarcely exist. They may be likened to a cone in shape, the small end being represented by the planet itself, the earth plane being the highest sphere which has developed, and the lower spheres--by reason of the degraded tastes and low intellectual development of the planet's inhabitants--being like the wide end of the cone. As the planet develops the spheres increase in size and number, and the higher ones begin to form, the point of the cone receding from the planet towards the sun as each of the higher spheres begins its existence.

"Thus are the spheres formed below and above the planet by the constant influx of the atmoms thrown off from the parent planet. At a certain stage of their formation, when the intellectual and selfish propensities of man are more highly developed than his moral and unselfish faculties, these lower spheres in extent greatly exceed the higher ones, and these may be termed the Dark Ages of the World's History, when oppression and cruelty and greed spread their dark wings over mankind.

"After a time the eternal law of the higher evolution of all things causes the higher and lower spheres to become equal in extent and number. Then may we see the forces of good and evil equally balanced, and this period may be termed the meridian of the planet's life. Next follows the period when by the gradual improvement of mankind the figure of the cone becomes gradually reversed, the earth plane becoming again the narrow end by reason of the shrinking and disappearance of the lower spheres, while the higher ones expand towards the highest of all, till at last only this highest sphere exists at all and the planet itself shrinks gradually away till all the material gross particles have been thrown off from it, and it vanishes from existence, all its gross atoms floating away imperceptibly, to be reabsorbed by other planets yet in process of formation.

"Then will the sphere of that planet together with its inhabitants become absorbed into the great spheres of its solar system, and its inhabitants will exist there as do already many communities of spirits whose planets have passed out of existence. Each planetary community, however, will retain the characteristics and individuality of their planet--just as different nationalities on earth do--till they become gradually merged in the larger nationality of their solar system. So gradual, so imperceptible, are these processes of development, so vast the periods of time they take to accomplish, that the mind of mortal man may be forgiven for failing to grasp the immensity of the changes which take place. The lives of all planets are not similar in their duration, because size and position in the solar system, as well as other causes, contribute to modify and slightly alter their development, but the broad features will in all cases be found the same, just as the matter of which each planet is composed shows no chemical substance which does not exist in a greater or less degree in every other. Thus we are able to judge from the condition of the planets around us what has been the history of our earth in the past and what will be its ultimate destiny."

"If, as you say, our spheres are to become absorbed into those of our sun centre, will our individuality as spirits become merged in that of the solar system?"

"No! most certainly not. The individuality of each soul germ is indestructible; it is but a minute unit in the vast ocean of soul life, but still it is a distinct unit, the personality of each being in fact its Ego. It is this very individuality, this very impossibility of dispersing or destroying the soul which constitutes its immortality, which distinguishes it from all other matter, and makes its nature so difficult of explanation or analysis. You have become a member of our Brotherhood of Hope, yet you retain your individuality, and so it is with the soul eternally, no matter through what conditions of existence it may pass. Try to imagine a body so light that the most etherealized vapor is heavy beside it, yet a body possessing such power of cohesion that it is utterly impossible to disintegrate its particles, the power of resistance against all material or spiritual forms of matter which it possesses being equal to that which a bar of steel offers to a cloud of vapor. Imagine this and you will realize how it is that as a spirit you can pass through solid doors and walls of earthly matter, and how a spirit higher than yourself can pass with equal ease through these walls of spiritual matter which surround us here. The more perfectly the soul is freed from gross matter, the less can it be bound by any element, and the greater become its powers, since it is not the soul essence but its dense envelope which can be imprisoned on earth or in the spheres. To you now the walls of earthly houses offer no impediment to free ingress or egress. You pass through them as easily as your earthly body used to pass through the fog. The density of the fog might be disagreeable to you, but it could not arrest your progress. Moreover, when you passed through a fog there was no vacuum left to show where your passage through it had been. This was because the elements of which the fog was composed were attracted together again too quickly for you to perceive where they had been dispersed, and that is exactly what happens when we spirits pass through a material door or wall, the material atoms of which it is composed closing after our progress even more quickly than the fog."

I understand you, and now if, as you say, each type of soul essence has a distinct individuality of its own you will not agree with those who believe in the transmigration of the soul of an animal of the lower type into a man, and vice versa."

"Certainly not. The soul of each type we hold to be capable of the highest degree of development in its own type; but the soul of man being the highest type of all is, therefore, capable of the highest degree of development, namely, into those advanced spirits we call angels. Angels are souls who have passed from the lowest degree of human planetary life through all the planetary spheres till they have attained to the celestial spheres of the solar system, our Heaven of Heavens, which is as far in advance of our Heaven of the planetary spheres as that is in advance of the planet itself. We believe that the soul will go on mounting continually as by ever widening spiral rings, till it has reached what we now term the centre of the universe, but whether when we do attain that summit of our present aspirations we shall not find it to be but a finite point revolving round a still greater centre I cannot say. My own feeling is that we shall attain to centre after centre, ever resting, it may be millions of years, in each, till our aspirations shall again urge us to heights as far again above us. The more one contemplates the subject the more vast and limitless it becomes. How, then, can we hope to see an end to our journeyings through that which has no end, and has had no beginning, and how can we even hope to form any clear idea of the nature and attributes of that Supreme Being whom we hold to be the Omnipotent Ruler of the universe, seeing that we cannot even fully and clearly grasp the magnitude of his creation?"

Another time when we were conversing I asked Hassein for his explanation of the phenomena of the spiritualistic movement which has recently been inaugurated upon earth, and in which I am naturally deeply interested, particularly as relates to materialization, and of which I wished to learn all I could.

Hassein replied: "In order that the mind may grasp the full significance of the Atomic theory, which has of late been advanced by men on earth, and which affords one of the most simple as well as logical explanations of the passage of matter through matter, it may not be out of place to say, for the benefit of those who have not given much thought to the subject and like these questions put before them in the simplest form, that the subdivisions of matter are, as we have said, so minute that even the speck of dust which floats invisible to the eye, unless a sunbeam be let in upon it to illuminate it, is composed of an infinite number of smaller particles, which are attracted and held together by the same laws that govern the attraction and repulsion of larger bodies. The knowledge of these laws gives to spirits the power of adapting these atoms to their own use, while making the manifestations called 'Materializations' now familiar to students of Spiritualism. The atoms suitable for their purpose are collected by the spirits wishing to materialize, from the atmosphere, which is full of them and also from the emanations proceeding from the men and women who form the spirit circle. These atoms are shaped by the spirits' will into the form of their earthly bodies, and held in combination by a chemical substance found, in a greater or less degree, in the bodies of all living things. Were the chemists of earth life sufficiently advanced in knowledge, they could extract this chemical from every living thing in nature and store it up to be used at will.

"This substance or essence is in fact the mysterious Elixir of Life, the secret of extracting and retaining which in tangible form has been sought by the sages of all times and countries. So subtle, so ethereal, however, is it that as yet there is no process known to earthly chemists which can bring this essence into a state to be analyzed by them, although it has been recognized and classed by some under the head of 'Magnetic Aura.' Of this, however, it is but one--and that the most ethereal--element. The life-giving rays of the sun contain it, but who is there as yet among chemists who can separate and bottle up in different portions the sunbeams? And of all portions this especially, which is the most delicate, the most subtle. Yet this knowledge is possessed by advanced spirits, and some day when the world has progressed far enough in the science of chemistry, the knowledge of this process will be given to men just as the discoveries in electricity and kindred sciences have been given-- discoveries which in an earlier age would have been styled miraculous.

"Here let me remark as to 'Auras,' that the constituent elements of the auras of the different sitters at a seance have quite as much effect upon the materialization as has that of the medium. Sometimes the chemical elements in the aura of one sitter do not amalgamate or blend thoroughly with those of some other sitter present, and this want of harmony prevents any materialization taking place at all. In extreme cases these antagonistic elements act so strongly in opposition to each other and are so repellent in their effects upon the atoms collected, that they act as a spiritual explosive which scatters the atoms as dynamite shatters a solid wall.

"This antagonism has nothing whatever to do with the moral or mental conditions of such persons. They may both be in all respects most estimable, earnest people, but they should never sit in the same circle and never be brought into magnetic contact, since their auras could never blend, and only general disappointment can result from any atempt to harmonize them. Although, apart, they might each attain satisfactory enough results, they never could do so in any attempt in combination.

"In those known as simply physical mediums, that is mediums with whose assistance purely physical phenomena alone are produced, such as the moving of tables or carrying in the air of musical boxes, and similar feats, this peculiar essence exists, but in a form too coarse to be suitable for materialization, which requires a certain degree of refinement in the essence. In them it is like a coarse raw alcoholic spirit, but in the true materializing medium it is like the same spirit redistilled, refined, and purified, and the purer this essence the more perfect will be the materialization.

"In many mediums there is a combination of the physical and materializing powers, but in exact proportion as the coarse physical manifestations are cultivated so will the higher and finer forms of materialization be lost.

"It is erroneous to imagine that in true materialization you are getting merely the double of the medium transformed for the moment into a likeness of your departed friends, or that the emanations from the sitters must always affect the appearance of the resulting spirit forms. They can only do so when from some cause there is a deficiency of the special essence, or an inability on the spirit's part to use it. In that case the atoms retain the personality of those from whom they are taken, because the spirit is unable to stamp his identity upon them, as a wax image, and until it be melted into a new mold, it will retain the impress of the old. The possession of a sufficient amount of the special essence, on the one hand, enables the spirit to clothe himself in the atoms he has collected and to hold them long enough to melt them, as it were, into a state in which they will take on his identity or the stamp of his individuality. The absence of the essence, on the other hand, causes him to lose his hold before the process has become perfect, and thus he has either hastily to show himself with the imperfect resemblance he has obtained, or else not show himself at all.

"A familiar simile may explain my meaning. When in the earthly body, you took flesh, vegetable, and fluid substances ready formed, containing in a prepared state the elements your earthly body required for its renewal, and by the process of digestion you changed these substances into a part of your soul's earthly envelope. Well, in the same way a spirit takes the ready prepared atoms given off by the medium and members of a materializing seance, and by a process as rapid as lightning artificially digests or arranges them into a material covering or envelope for himself, bearing his own identity more or less completely impressed on it according to his power.

"Every atom of the body of a mortal is drawn, directly or indirectly, from the atmosphere around him, and absorbed in one form or another, and after it has served as clothing for his spirit, it is cast off to be again absorbed in another form by some other living thing. Everyone knows that the material of the human body is continually changing, and yet many think to establish a prescriptive right to those atoms thrown off during a seance, and say that when a spirit makes use of them and adapts them to himself, therefore he must have taken their own mental characteristics along with the material atoms, and thus they try to persuade themselves that the spirit appearing clothed with these material atoms is no more than the thought emanation of their own bodies and brains, ignoring, or more probably not knowing, that the grossest material, not the mental atoms, were all the spirit wanted to clothe himself with and make him visible to material sight.

"The best proof of the fallacy of this supposition is the constant appearance at seances of spirits whom no one present was thinking of at the time, and in some cases even of people whose death was not known to any of the sitters.

"The essence or fluid ether of which I have spoken is that which principally holds the material body together in life. At death, or, more correctly, the withdrawal of the soul and the severance of the connecting link between it and the material atoms of the body, it escapes into the surrounding atmosphere, permitting the particles of that body to decay. Cold retards the dispersal of this fluid ether; heat accelerates it, thus explaining why the body of any animal or plant disintegrates or turns to decay sooner in hot than in cold climates, and thus becomes nourishment fit for those minute parasites which are stimulated and fed by a lower degree of life magnetism which is retained in the discarded envelope. This essence or fluidic ether is akin to the electric fluid known to scientists, but as electricity is the product of mineral and vegetable substances, it is lower in degree and much coarser in quality than this human electricity, and would require the combination of other elements to make it assimilate with the human.

"This higher essence is an important element in what has been termed the Higher Animal Life Principle as distinguished from the Soul-Life Principle and from the

Astral Life Principle. Each of which we make distinct elemental principles.

"In trance, either artificially induced or occurring as part of the spiritual development of certain sensitives or mediums, this life essence remains with the body, but, as life is required for its need in trance, a large portion may be taken away and used by the controlling spirit to clothe himself, care being taken to return it to the medium again. With some mediums this life essence is given off so freely that unless care is taken to replace it continually, the death of the physical body will soon follow. In others it can only be extracted with great difficulty, and in some there is so small a quantity that it would be neither wise nor useful to take any away from them at all.

"The aura of those mediums possessing a large amount of a high and pure quality, will diffuse a most lovely clear silver light, which can be seen by clairvoyants, and it helps even immaterialized spirits to make themselves visible. This silver light can be seen radiating like the rays of a star from the medium, and where it is present in a very high degree no other light is required for the materialized spirits to show themselves, the spirits appearing as though surrounded by a silver halo, and with this beautiful light illuminating their garments, they appear much as you see pictures of saints and angels, whom no doubt the ancient seers beheld through the medium of this species of aura.

"Although the aid of a materializing medium and a good circle of persons still in the material body may simplify the process of building up a body in which a spirit may be able to clothe himself, yet it is quite possible for some spirits of the highest spheres to make for themselves a material body without the aid of any medium or any other person in an earth-body. Their knowledge of the laws of chemistry is sufficient and their will power is adequate to the strain imposed on it in the process, and in the atmosphere of the earth as well as in the plants, minerals, and animals, is to be found every substance of which the body is composed and from which the life essence is extracted. The human body is a combination of all the materials and gases found on and in the earth and its atmosphere, and it only requires a knowledge of the laws governing the combination and adhesion of the various substances to enable a spirit to make a body in all respects similar to that of terrestrial man, and to clothe himself therewith, holding it in combination for a longer or shorter period at will.

"Such knowledge is of necessity unknown as yet except in the higher spheres, because it requires a high degree of development in the mental condition of the spirit before he can duly weigh and understand all the minute points and numerous laws of nature involved in the subject. The ancients were right in saying they could make a man. They could do so, and even animate their manufacture to a certain degree with the astral or lower life-principle, but they could not continue to sustain that life by reason of the extreme difficulty in collecting this lower life-principle, and when they had so animated the artificially made body it would be devoid of intelligence and reason, these attributes belonging exclusively to the soul, and neither man nor spirit can endow such a body with a soul--that which alone can give it intellect and immortality. At the same time an artificially made body could serve as a covering to a spirit (or soul) and enable him to converse with men for a longer or shorter time, according to the power of the spirit to retain this material envelope in the complete state. Thus no doubt those of the ancients who had acquired a knowledge of these things could also renew at will the material covering of their bodies, and make themselves practically live upon the earth forever, or they might disperse these material atoms and walk forth in the spirit freed from the trammels of the flesh, reconstructing the earthly body again when it suited them. Such spirit men are the Mahatmas, who by the knowledge of these and kindred secrets do possess many of the marvellous powers attributed to them.

"But where we differ from them is in the application of the knowledge they have thus gained and the doctrines they deduce from it, and also as to the unadvisability of imparting it freely to men in the flesh, and the duty of withholding it from them as a dangerous thing. We hold there is no knowledge given to any spirit or mortal, which may not be safely possessed by every other, provided they have the mental development to understand and apply this knowledge. Our great teacher of these subjects, the guide Ahrinziman, was a native of the East and has been a student of occult subjects, both in his earth life and in the two thousand and more years that have passed since he left the earth, and this is his decided opinion, and he has seen both the origin and the practice of many of these ideas that are as yet new to the Western mind.

"While thus possessing the power to create a material body from the elemental atoms alone, spirits of advanced knowledge seldom use this power, because for ordinary materializing purposes there is no need to exercise it, the emanations from the members of the materializing circle and the aura of the medium, which are already saturated with the necessary essence for the formation of a body, saving them both time and trouble, and simplifying the process. It is just as the buying a ready made piece of cloth simplifies the making of a garment, instead of the tailor having to proceed first to grow the wool, then to spin it, and finally to weave it into cloth for himself before he can begin to make the garment.

"In some cases so much of the material is taken from the medium's body so as to perceptibly alter its weight. In others nearly the whole of the material covering is used, so that to material sight the medium has vanished, although a clairvoyant may perceive the astral or spirit form still seated in the chair. In such cases it is simply the gross material atoms which have been made use of, while the mental atoms have not been touched. As a rule the spirits who take part in a materializing seance, both those who materialize themselves and those who assist the chief controlling spirit, are ignorant of the means by which the results are obtained, just as many persons who avail themselves of the discoveries of chemistry and the articles manufactured by chemists are ignorant of how those substances are obtained. There is in all materializations an invisible head or director from a sphere greatly in advance of the earth, who may be called the chief chemist, and he passes his directions to a spirit strong in the power of controlling the forces of the astral plane and to others under him, who come in contact with the medium and direct the order of the materializations of personal friends of the sitters, besides sometimes materializing and showing themselves to the circle.

"There is a powerful movement going on now in the spirit world with the object of extending the knowledge of all these subjects, both among spirits and men in the flesh, and the ecclesiasticism, whether of the East or of the West, which would still shut up such knowledge within the precincts of the temple, may fight against this movement, but it will fight in vain. The power is too strong for them. Men are pressing into the avenues of knowledge on all sides and thronging round the doors which, sooner or later, must be opened to them.

"You cannot suppress knowledge. It is the inalienable birthright of every soul. Neither can it be made the property of any class. So soon as the mind begins to think, it will search for knowledge, and feed upon such crumbs as come in its way, and surely it were better to impart the knowledge sought carefully and judiciously so it can be assimilated, than try to suppress the desire for it, or leave the hungry soul to gather it for itself in the garbage heaps of error.

"The human race is advancing eternally, and the tutelage of the child is no longer adapted to the growing youth. He demands freedom, and will break from the leading strings altogether unless their tension is relaxed and he is suffered to wander in the pathways of knowledge to the utmost of his powers. Is it not well, then, that those who are as the sages of the race should respond to this thirst for light and knowledge by giving, through every channel and avenue which can be opened, the wisdom of the ages in such form as may make it the most easily comprehended? This planet is but a speck of the universal knowledge as is adapted to its state, and each hour requires that the expansion of the human mind shall be met by the expansion of its creeds and its resources, by the pouring in of fresh streams of light, not the suppressing of the old lest it should be too strong for the sight."

"And now, Hassein, there is another point I wish to ask you about. I have frequently heard men on earth say they want to know, if the spheres exist around the earth and between them and the sun, why is it that all men cannot see them, and why they cannot even see those spirits who are said to be actually in the room with them. Naturally, men are not all satisfied to be told simply that it is because they are not clairvoyants, and have not the soul-sight. They want a still clearer explanation. I am a spirit myself and I know that I exist, and so does my dwelling-place, but I am unable to give an answer to the question. Can you do so?"

Hassein laughed. "I could give a dozen elaborate explanations, but neither you nor these mortals who are unable to see the spirits would be much wiser after I had done so. I must, therefore, endeavor to make my answer as free from technicalities as I can. First, though, let me ask if you have seen the photographs of unmaterialized spirits which have been obtained by certain mediums in the flesh. You will have noticed that to mortal sight they present a semi-transparent appearance. The material doors and windows, furniture, etc. show through the figures of the spirits.

"Now that gives you a very good idea of the amount of materiality possessed by an astral body (the first degree of spiritualized matter). The material particles are spread so thinly that they are like a fine net-work united by invisible atoms of a more etherealized nature--so sublimated in fact that they cannot be impressed upon the most sensitive plates now used by photographers. Spirits after they leave the earth plane cannot be photographed by the plates now in use--they do not possess gross enough atoms in the composition of their bodies, and have therefore to either materialize a body like an earthly one, or they may use another method which has been found successful and which is the one commonly used in the case of spirit photographs, where the spirits are visible to clairvoyant sight though invisible to material eyes. This is simply described by saying these spirits make use of some of those astral envelopes or bodies that I have already described to you as forming from cloud masses of semi-material human atoms--astral shells which never served as the covering of any soul, and which are so plastic in their nature that spirits can mold them into their own likeness as a sculptor molds the clay. These replicas can be and are photographed, bearing a greater or less resemblance to the spirit, according as his will power and his knowledge enable him to stamp his likeness upon them, and though they are not strictly speaking the photos of the spirits themselves, yet they are none the less evidence of spirit power and of the existence of the spirit who has made use of them, because each spirit must himself stamp his own identity upon the plastic astral form, while more advanced scientific spirits prepare that form to receive the impression.

"In the case of materialized spirits' photographs, the spirits really make a body from the more material atoms and clothe themselves in it.

"A clairvoyant seeing one of these astral forms about to be photographed would probably not be able to distinguish between it and a true spirit man or woman, because the power of distinguishing between them is not yet developed in mediums, neither, as a rule, do they know why a spirit that looks solid enough to them comes out on a photographic plate with a semi-transparent appearance. The see the more spiritualized matter as well as the grosser astral atoms, therefore it appears to them as a solid body with well-rounded, well proportioned limbs, not as a transparent shadow of a spirit whose appearance may well give rise to the idea that returning spirits are mere shades, almost, in fact, empty shells--the real reason of the empty appearance being that, as I have said, the photographic appliances at present in use are not capable of transferring the whole spirit's form but only these grosser particles. In the case of a fully materialized spirit being photographed, this transparent appearance does not exist. The form is so perfect, so life-like and solid, that men turn round and say it, therefore, cannot be a spirit photograph at all--it must be nothing but the medium. Blind seekers, who in trying to grasp a subject so vast, so full of the most subtle difficulties, bring to bear upon it only the knowledge suitable for mundane things, and then conclude that they are able to decide finally so momentous, so scientific a question!

"But to return to your question. Having shown you how a photograph may give a spirit whose appearance is like that of the traditional ghost, I will now show you how mortals may also see them as such, but to illustrate my meaning I will first ask you to imagine yourself back in your earthly body with no more powers of spirit sight than you possessed then. Let us liken the material and spiritual sight to two eyes. The one we will call the left, the other the right eye, and let the left stand for the material sight, the right the spiritual. Suppose you stand with your back to the light and hold your forefinger in front of the right eye where it can be seen by that eye only, the left seeing only the wall before you--shut the right eye and the finger is invisible, yet it is there, only not in the line of vision for the left, or material, sight. Now open both eyes at once and look at your finger and you will now see it certainly, but owing to a curious optical illusion it will appear transparent, a mere shadow of a finger, the wall being seen through it, and it may be likened to a ghost of a finger although you know it to be a solid reality.

"Thus you can imagine how a person whose material sight is alone open cannot see that which requires spiritual sight to discern, and how, when both the material and spiritual sight are open at the same mement a spirit may be visible but with the same transparent appearance as your finger had just now. Hence has arisen the popular idea of a ghost. A clairvoyant, looking at any spiritual object with the spiritual sight, does so with the material sight closed through the power of the controlling intelligence who directs that person's mediumship. Therefore to him or to her the spiritual object does present the appearance of a solid reality such as a material finger appears when seen by the material sight alone.

"Few men know and still fewer consider that even their material sight is dependent upon the material atoms which fill the earth's atmosphere, and without which atoms there would be no light to see anything by.

At night mortals can see the stars--even those which are not themselves suns--distant as they are, because they are material objects from which the light of the sun is reflected. During the day the stars are still there, but the immense mass of material particles in the earth's atmosphere being illuminated by the reflecting of the sun's rays from them, causes so dense an atmosphere of light that the stars are veiled and no longer visible to material eyes. Ascend, however, above this material atmosphere of illuminated atoms, and, behold, the stars are again visible at mid-day and the surrounding ether of space, being free from such material particles, is quite dark. There is nothing to reflect the sun's rays.

Thus, although the mortal would be nearer to the sun, yet its light is no longer visible to his material eyes, which can only see when there is some material object, however small, to reflect the light of the sun for him. How, then, does man know that the light of the sun is traveling through the ether space to earth? Only by reason and analogy, not by sight, for beyond the earth's atmosphere the sun's light is invisible to him. Men know the light of the moon to be only the light of the sun reflected from the moon's surface. Experience and experiment have proved this, and it is now universally admitted. In like manner each little atom of material matter floating in the earth's atmosphere is an infinitesimal moon to reflect the sun's light for man and brighten earth with the splendor of these reflections. So again those minute particles that are continually being thrown off into the atmosphere by the earth itself, are but the larger and grosser atoms enclosing or rather revolving round, minute spiritual germs that form a spiritual atmosphere around the earth and reflect for clairvoyants the spiritual elements of the light of the sun. This spiritual atmosphere forms what is known as the astral plane, and bears the same proportion of density to astral bodies that the material atmosphere does to mortal bodies, and the light from the spiritual elements of the sun striking upon these spiritual particles is the light of the astral plane by which spirits see; the material atmosphere of earth being visible to the material sight of mortals. Is it not, then, easy to imagine that the spirit spheres may exist around the earth, and between man and the material envelope of the sun without his being able to see them, by reason of the fact that his spiritual sight is closed and he can only see what is material? The spiritual spheres and their inhabitants are certainly more transparent and intangible to mortal sight than his finger appeared just now. Yet they exist and are as solid a reality as his finger, and are only invisible by reason of his imperfect sight, which is limited to material things of comparatively great density."

172

I was always fond of watching the clouds float over the sky and shape themselves into pictures suggested by my thoughts. Since I reached the second sphere of the spirit land my skies have always had clouds floating over them, lovely light fleecy clouds which shape themselves into a thousand forms and take on the most lovely shades of color, sometimes becoming rainbow hued and at others of the most dazzling white, and then again vanishing away altogether. I have been told by some spirits that in their skies they never see a cloud, all is serene clear beauty; and no doubt it is so in their lands, for in the spirit world our thoughts and wishes form our surroundings. Thus, because I love to see clouds they are to be seen in my sky, at times veiling and softening its beauties and making cloud-castles for me to enjoy.

Now, some time after I obtained my little home in the Morning Land I began to see between myself and my cloud-pictures a vision which, like the mirage seen in the desert, hovered on the horizon, distinct and lifelike, only to melt away as I gazed. This was a most lovely ethereal gate of wrought gold, such as might be the entrance to some fairy land. A clear stream of water flowed between myself and this gate, while trees so fresh, so green, so aerial, they seemed like fairy trees, arched their branches over it and clustered at the sides. Again and again did I see this vision, and one day while I was gazing at it my father came unnoticed by me and stood by my side. He touched my shoulder and said:

"Franchezzo, that gate is inviting you to go nearer and see it for yourself. It is the entrance to the highest circle of this second sphere, and it is within those gates that your new home is waiting for you. You might have gone some time ago into those circles which lie between you and it, had not your affection for this little cottage made you content to remain in it. Now, however, it would be as well for you to go forth and see if the wonders of that new land will not still more delight you. I am, as you know, in the third sphere, which will, therefore, be still above you, but the nearer you approach to me the more easily can I visit you, and in your new home we shall be much oftener together."

I was so surprised I could not answer for a little time. It seemed incredible that I should be able so soon to pass those gates. Then, taking my father's advice, I bade a regretful adieu to my little home (for I grow much attached to places which I live long in) and set forth to journey to this new country, the gate shining before me all the time, not fading away as it had done before.

In the spirit land where the surface is not that of a round globe as with the planets, you do not see the objects on the horizon vanishing in the same way, and earth and sky meeting at last as one. Instead you see the sky as a vast canopy overhead, and the

174

circles which are above you seem like plateaux resting upon mountain tops on your horizon, and when you reach those mountains and see the new country spread out before you, there are always on its horizon again more mountains and fresh lands lying higher than those you have reached. Thus also you can look down on those you have passed as upon a succession of terraces, each leading to a lower, less beautiful one, till at last you see the earth plane surrounding the earth itself, and then beyond that again (for those spirits whose sight is well developed) lie another succession of terrace-like lands leading down to Hell. Thus circle melts into circle and sphere into sphere, only that between each sphere there exists a barrier of magnetic waves which repels those from a lower sphere who seek to pass it until their condition has become in harmony with the higher sphere.

In my journey to the golden gates I passed through several circles of this second sphere, whose cities and dwelling-places would have tempted me to linger and admire them had I not been so eager to view the fair land which was now the goal of my hopes. I knew, moreover, that I could at any time on my way to earth stop and explore those intermediate lands, because a spirit can always retrace his steps if he desires and visit those below him.

At last I reached the top of the last range of mountains between me and the golden gates, and saw stretched out before my eyes a most lovely country. Trees waved their branches as in welcome to me and flowers blossomed everywhere, while at my feet was the shining river and across it the golden gates. With a great sense of joy in my heart I plunged into that beautiful river to swim across, its refreshing waters closing over my head as I dived and swam. I had taken no heed to my clothing and as I landed on the farther side I looked to see myself dripping with water, but in a moment I found my clothing as dry as could be, and what was still stranger, my grey robe with its triple bordering of white had changed into one of the most dazzling snowy lustre with a golden girdle and golden borderings. At the neck and wrists it was clasped with little plain gold clasps, and seemed to be like the finest muslin in texture. I could scarce believe my senses. I looked and looked again, and then, with a trembling, beating heart I approached those lovely gates. As my hand touched them they glided apart and I passed into a wide road bordered by trees and flowering shrubs and plants of most lovely hues--like flowers of earth, indeed, but ah! how much more lovely, how much more fragrant no words of mine can convey to you.

The waving branches of the trees bent over me in loving welcome as I passed, the flowers seemed to turn to me as greeting one who loved them well, at my feet there was the soft green sward, and overhead a sky so clear, so pure, so beautiful, the light shimmering through the trees as never did the light of earthly sun. Before me were lovely blue and purple hills and the gleam of a fair lake, upon whose bosom tiny islets nestled crowned with the green foliage of groups of trees. Here and there a little boat skimmed over the surface of the lake filled with happy spirits clad in shining robes of many different colors--so like to earth, so like my beloved Southern Land, and yet so changed, so glorified, so free from all taint of wrong and sin!

As I passed up the broad flower-girt road a band of spirits came to meet and welcome me, amongst whom I recognized my father, my mother, my brother and a sister, besides many beloved friends of my youth. They carried gossamer scarfs of red, white and green colors, which they were waving to me, while they strewed my path with masses of the fairest flowers as I approached, and all the time they sang the beautiful songs of our own land in welcome, their voices floating on the soft breeze in the perfection of unison and harmony. I felt almost overcome with emotion; it seemed far too much happiness for one like me.

And then my thoughts even in that bright scene turned to earth, to her who was of all the most dear to me, where all were so dear, and I thought, "Alas that she is not here to share with me the triumphs of this hour; she to whose love more than to any other thing I owe it." As the thought came to me I suddenly beheld her spirit beside me, half asleep, half conscious, freed for a brief moment from the earthly body and borne in the arms of her chief guardian spirit. Her dress was of the spirit world, white as a bride's and shimmering with sparkling gems like dew drops. I turned and clasped her to my heart, and at my touch her soul awoke and she looked smilingly at me. Then I presented her to my friends as my betrothed bride, and while she was still smiling at us all, her guide again drew near and threw over her a large white mantle. He lifted her in his arms once more, and like a tired child she seemed to sink into slumber as he bore her away to her earthly body, which she had left for a time to share and crown this supreme moment of my joy. Ah, me! even in my joy I felt it hard to let her go, to think I could not keep her with me; but the thread of her earthly life was not yet fully spun, and I knew that she like others must travel the path of her earthly pilgrimage to its end.

When my beloved was gone, my friends all clustered round me with tender embraces, my mother whom I had never seen since I was a little child--caressing my hair and covering my face with kisses as though I had been still the little son whom she had left on earth so many, many years ago that his memory of her had been but dim, and that the father had supplied the image of both parents in his thoughts.

Then they led me to a lovely villa almost buried in the roses and jasmine which clustered over its walls and twined around the slender white pillars of the piazza, forming a curtain of flowers upon one side. What a beautiful home it seemed! How much beyond what I deserved! Its rooms were spacious, and there were seven of them, each typical of a phase in my own character or some taste I had cultivated.

My villa was upon the top of a hill overlooking the lake which lay many hundreds of feet below, its calm waters rippled by magnetic currents and the surrounding hills mirrored in its quiet bosom, and beyond the lake there was a wide valley. As one looks down from a mountain top to the low hills and the dark valley and level plains below, so did I now look down from my new dwelling upon a panorama of the lower spheres and circles through which I had passed, to the earth plane and again to the earth itself, which lay like a star far below me. I thought as I looked at it that there dwelt still my beloved, and there yet lay the field of my labors. I have sat many times since gazing out on that lone star, the pictures of my past life floating in a long wave of memory across my day-dream, and with all my thoughts was interwoven the image of her who is my guiding star.

The room from which I could see this view of the distant earth was my music-room, and in it were musical instruments of various kinds. Flowers festooned the walls and soft draperies the windows, which required no glass in their frames to keep out the soft zephyrs of that fair land. A honeysuckle, that was surely the same sweet plant which had so rejoiced my heart in my little cottage in the Morning Land, trailed its fragrant tendrils around the window, and on one of the walls hung my picture of my darling, framed with its pure white roses which always seemed to me an emblem of herself. Here, too, I again found all my little treasures which I had collected in my dark days when hope seemed so far and the shadow of night was ever over me. The room was full of soft masses of lovely spirit flowers, and the furniture was like that of earth only more light in appearance, more graceful and beautiful in every way. There was a couch which I much admired. It was supported by four half-kneeling figures of wood-nymphs, carved as it would seem from a marble of the purest white and even more transparent than alabaster. Their extended arms and clasped hands formed the back and the upper and lower ends; their heads were crowned with leaves and their floating draperies fell around their forms in so graceful, so natural a manner, it was difficult to believe they were not living spirit-maidens. The covering of this couch was of a texture like swan's down, only it was pale gold in color; so soft was it, it seemed to invite one to repose, and often have I lain upon it and looked out at the lovely scene and away to the dim star of earth with its weary pilgrims--its toiling souls.

The next apartment was filled with beautiful pictures, lovely statues, and tropical flowers. It was almost more like a conservatory than a room, the pictures being collected at one end of it and the statues and flowers forming a foreground of beauty that was like another and larger picture. There was a little grotto with a fountain playing, the water sparkling like diamonds and rippling over the sides of the smaller basin into one larger still, with a murmuring sound which suggested a melody to me. Near this grotto was one picture which attracted me at once, for I recognized it as a scene from my earthly life. It was a picture of one calm and peaceful evening in early summer when my beloved and I had floated on the quiet waters of an earthly river. The setting sun glowing in the west was sinking behind a bank of trees, while the grey twilight crept over the hollows through the shade of the trees; and in our hearts there was a sense of peace and rest which raised our souls to Heaven. I looked around and recognized many familiar scenes, which had likewise been full of happiness for me and in whose memories there was no sting.

There were also many pictures of my friends, and of scenes in the spirit world. From the windows I could behold another view than from my music-room. This view showed those lands which were yet far above me, and whose towers and minarets and mountains shone through a dim haze of bright mist, now rainbow hued, now golden, or blue, or white. I loved to change from the one view to the other, from the past which was so clear, to the future that was still dim, still veiled for me.

In this picture salon there was all which could delight the eye or rest the body, for our bodies require repose as well as do yours on earth, and we can enjoy to rest upon a couch of down earned by our labors as much as you can enjoy the possession of fine furniture bought with gold earned by your work on earth.

Another saloon was set apart for the entertainment of my friends, and here again, as in the lower sphere, there were tables set out with a feast of simple but delicious fruits, cakes, and other agreeable foods like earthly foods, only less material, and there was also the delicious sparkling wine of the spirit world which I have before mentioned. Another room again was full of books recording my life and the lives of those whom I admired or loved. There were also books upon many subjects, the peculiarity in them being that instead of being printed they seemed full of pictures, which when one studied them appeared to reflect the thoughts of those who had written the books more eloquently than any words. Here, too, one could sit and receive the inspired thoughts of the great poets and literary men who inhabit the sphere above, and here have I sat, and inscribed upon the blank pages of some book laid open before me, poems to her who filled the larger half of all my thoughts.

From this room we passed out to the garden, my father saying he would show me my chamber of repose, after our friends were gone. Here, as in the house, flowers were everywhere, for I always loved flowers, they spoke to me of so many things and seemed to whisper such bright fancies, such pure thoughts. There was a terrace around the house, and the garden seemed almost to overhang the lake, especially at one secluded corner which was fenced in with a bank of ferns and flowering shrubs and backed by a screen of trees. This nook was a little to the side of the house and soon became my favorite resort; the ground was carpeted with soft green moss as you have not on earth--and flowers grew all around. Here there was a seat whereon I loved to sit and look away to the earth, and fancy where my beloved one's home would be. Across all those millions of miles of space my thoughts could reach her as hers could now reach me, for the magnetic cord of our love stretched between us and no power could ever shut us out from each other again.

When I had seen and admired all, my friends led me back to the house and we all sat down to enjoy the feast of welcome which their love had prepared for me. Ah! what a happy feast that was. How we proposed the progression and happiness of each one, and then drank our toast in wine which left no intoxication behind, no after reckoning of shame to mar its refreshing qualities! How delicious seemed this fruit, these numerous little delicacies which were all the creations of someone's love for me. It seemed too much happiness, I felt as in a delightful dream from which I must surely wake. At last all my friends left except my father and mother, and by them I was conducted to the upper chambers of the house. They were three in number. Two were for such friends as might come to stay with me, and both were most prettily furnished, most peaceful looking; the third room was for myself, my own room, where I would retire when I desired to rest and to have no companion but my own thoughts. As we entered, the thing which attracted me most and filled me with more astonishment that anything I had yet seen, was the couch. It was of snowy white gossamer, bordered with pale lilac and gold, while at the foot were two angels, carved, like the wood-nymphs, out of the dazzlilng white alabaster I have vainly tried to describe. They were much larger than myself or any spirits whom I had seen, and their heads and extended wings seemed almost to touch the roof of my room, and the pose of these two most lovely figures was perfect in its grace. Their feet scarce touched the floor and with their bending forms and half-outstretched wings they appeared to hover over the bed as though they had but just arrived from their celestial sphere.

They were male and female forms, the man wearing on his head a helmet and bearing in his hand a sword, while the other hand held aloft a crown. His figure was the perfection of manly beauty and grace, and his face with its perfect features so firmly moulded, expressing at once strength and gentleness, had to my eyes a look of calm regal majesty that was divine.

The female figure at his side was smaller--more delicate in every way. Her face was full of gentle, tender, womanly purity and beauty. The eyes large and soft even though carved in marble, the long tresses of her hair half-veiling her head and shoulders. One hand held a harp with seven strings, the other rested upon the shoulder of the male angel as though she supported herself with his strength, while the lovely head was half bent forward and rested upon her arm, and on her head she wore a crown of pure white lilies.

The look upon her face was one of such exquisite sweetness, such maternal tenderness, it might well have served for that of the Virgin Mother herself. The attitudes, the expressions of both were the most perfect realization of angelic beauty I have seen, and for some moments I could but gaze at them expecting them to melt away before my eyes.

At last I turned to my father and asked how such lovely figures came to be in my room, and why they were represented with wings, since I had been told that angels had not really wings growing from their bodies at all.

"My son," he answered, "these lovely figures are the gift of your mother and myself to you, and we would fain think of you as reposing under the shadow of their wings, which represent in a material form the protection we would ever give you. They are shown with wings because that is the symbol of the angelic spheres, but if you will look closely at them you will find that these wings are like a part of the drapery of the forms, and are not attached to the bodies at all as though they grew from the shoulder in the fashion earthly artists represent them. The wings, moreover, express the power of angelic beings to soar upon these outstretched pinions into Heaven itself. The shining helmet and the sword represent war, the helmet the war of the Intellect against Error, Darkness and Oppression. The sword, the war man must ever wage against the passions of his lower nature. The crown symbolizes the glory of virtue and self-conquest.

"The harp in the woman's hand shows that she is an angel of the musical sphere, and the crown of lilies expresses purity and love. Her hand resting on the man's shoulder is to show that she derives her strength and power from him and from his stronger nature, while her attitude and looks as she bends over your couch express the tender love and protection of woman's maternal nature. She is smaller than the man, because in you the masculine elements are stronger than the feminine. In some representations of the angels of men's souls they are made of equal size and stature, because in those characters the masculine and feminine elements are both equal, both evenly balanced, but with you it is not so, therefore are they represented with the woman dependent upon the stronger one.

"The male angel typifies power and protection. The female angel purity and love. Together they show the eternal dual nature of the soul and that one-half is not complete without the other. They also are the symbolical representation of the twin guardian angels of your soul whose wings may be said in a spiritual sense to be ever outstretched in protection over you."

Shall I confess that even in that beautiful home there were times when I felt lonely? I had this home, earned by myself, but as yet I had no one to share it with me, and I have always felt a pleasure to be doubly sweet when there was some one whom I could feel enjoyed it also. The one companion of all others for whom I sighed was still on earth, and alas! I knew that not for many years could she join me. Then Faithful Friend was in a circle of the sphere above me in a home of his own, and as for Hassein, he was far above us both, so that though I saw them at times as well as my dear father and mother, there was no one to share my life with me *en bon camarade,* no one to watch for my home-coming, and no one for whom in my turn I could watch. I was often on earth--often with my darling--but I found that with my advanced position in the spirit world I could not remain for so long at a time as I had been wont to do. It had upon my spirit much the effect of trying to live in a foggy atmosphere or down a coal mine, and I had to return more frequently to the spirit land to recover myself.

I used to sit in my lovely rooms and sigh to myself, "Ah, if I had but some one to speak with, some congenial soul to whom I might express all the thoughts which crowd my mind." It was therefore with the greatest pleasure that I received a visit from Faithful Friend, and heard the suggestion he had to make to me.

"I have come," said he, "on behalf of a friend who has just come to this circle of the sphere, but who has not yet earned for himself a home of his own and therefore desires to find one with some friend more richly endowed than himself. He has no relatives here and I thought that you might be glad of his companionship."

"Most truly, I would be delighted to share my home with your friend."

Faithful Friend laughed. "He may be called your friend also, for you know him. It is Benedetto."

"Benedetto!" I cried in astonishment and delight. "Ah! then he will indeed be doubly welcome. Bring him here as soon as possible."

"He is here now--he awaits at your door; he would not come with me till he was sure you would really be glad to welcome him."

"No one could be more so," I said. "Let us go at once and bring him in."

So we went to the door and there he stood, looking very different from when I had last seen him in that awful city of the lower sphere--then so sad, weighed down, so oppressed--now so bright, his robes, like mine, of purest white, and though his face was still sad in expression yet there was peace, and there was hope in the eyes he raised to mine as I clasped his hand and embraced him as we of my Southern Land embrace those we love and honor. It was with much pleasure that we met--we who had both so sinned and so suffered--and we were henceforth to be as brothers.

181

Thus it was that my home became no more solitary, for, when one of us returns from our labors, the other is there to greet him, to share the joy and the care, and to talk over the success or the failure.

CHAPTER XXXIII.--My Vision of the Spheres.

How can I tell of the many friends who came to visit me in this bright home, of the cities I saw in that fair land, the lovely scenes I visited? I cannot. It would take volumes, and already my narrative has reached its limits. I shall only tell of one more vision that I had, because in it I was shown a new path wherein I was to labor, one in which I could apply to the aid of others the lessons I had learned in my wanderings.

I was lying on the couch in my room and had awakened from a long slumber. I was watching, as I often did, those two most beautiful figures of my guardian angels, and seeing fresh beauties, fresh meanings in their faces and their attitudes every time I looked at them, when I became conscious that my Eastern guide, Ahrinziman, in his far-off sphere was seeking to communicate with me. I therefore allowed myself to become perfectly passive and soon felt a great cloud of light of a dazzling white misty substance surrounding me. It seemed to shut out the walls of my room and everything from me. Then my soul seemed to arise from my spirit body and float away, leaving my spirit envelope lying upon the couch.

I appeared to pass upwards and still upwards, as though the will of my powerful guide was summoning me to him, and I floated on and on with a sense of lightness which even as a spirit I had never felt before.

At last I alighted upon the summit of a high mountain, from which I could behold the earth and its lower and higher spheres revolving below me. I also saw that sphere which was my home, but it appeared to lie far below the height upon which I stood.

Beside me was Ahrinziman, and as in a dream I heard his voice speaking to me and saying:

"Behold, son of my adoption, the new path in which I would have you labor. Behold earth and her attendant spheres, and see how important to her welfare is this work in which I would have you to take part. See now the value of the power you have gained in your journey to the Kingdoms of Hell, since it will enable you to become one of the great army who daily and hourly protect mortal men from the assaults of Hell's inhabitants. Behold this panorama of the spheres and learn how you can assist in a work as mighty as the spheres themselves."

I looked to where he pointed, and I beheld the circling belt of the great earth plane, its magnetic currents like the ebb and flow of an ocean tide, bearing on their waves countless millions upon millions of spirits. I saw all those strange elemental astral forms, some grotesque, some hideous, some beautiful. I saw also the earth-bound spirits of men and women still tied by their gross pleasures or their sinful lives, many of them using the organisms of mortals to gratify their degraded cravings. I beheld these and kindred mysteries of the earth plane, and I likewise beheld sweeping up from the dark spheres below waves of dark and awful beings, ten times more deadly unto man in their influence over him than those dark spirits of the earth plane. I saw these darker beings crowd around man and cluster thickly near him, and where they gathered they shut out the brightness of the spiritual sun whose rays shine down upon the earth continually. They shut out this light, with the dark mass of their own cruel evil thoughts, and where this cloud rested there came murder and robbery; and cruelty and lust, and every kind of oppression were in their train, and death and sorrow followed them. Wherever man had cast aside from him the restraints of his conscience and had given way to greed and selfishness, and pride and ambition, there did these dark beings gather, shutting out the light of truth with their dark bodies.

And again I saw many mortals who mourned for the dear ones they had loved and lost, weeping most bitter tears because they could see them no more. And all the time I saw those for whom they mourned standing beside them, seeking with all their power to show that they still lived, still hovered near, and that death had not robbed of one loving thought, one tender wish, those whom death had left behind to mourn. All in vain seemed their efforts. The living could not see or hear them, and the poor sorrowing spirits could not go away to their bright spheres because while those they had left so mourned for them they were tied to the earth plane by the chains of their love, and the light of their spirit lamps grew dim and faded as they thus hung about the atmosphere of earth in helpless sorrow.

And Ahrinziman said to me: "Is there no need here for the means of communication between these two, the living and the so-called dead, that the sorrowful ones on both sides may be comforted? And, again, is there no need for communication that those other sinful selfish men may be told of the dark beings hovering around them who seek to drag their souls to hell?"

Then I beheld a glorious dazzling light as of a sun in splendor, shining as no mortal eye ever saw the sun shine on earth. And its rays dispelled the clouds of darkness and sorrow, and I heard a glorious strain of music from the celestial spheres, and I thought surely now man will hear this music and see this light and be comforted. But they could not--their ears were closed by the false ideas they had gathered, and the dust and dross of earth clogged their spirits and made their eyes blind to the glorious light which shone for them in vain.

Then I beheld other mortals whose spiritual sight was partly unveiled and whose ears were not quite deaf, and they spoke of the spirit world and its wondrous beauties. They felt great thoughts and put them into the language of earth. They heard the wondrous music and tried to give it expression. They saw lovely visions and tried to paint them, as like to those of the spirit as the limits of their earthly environments would allow. And these mortals were termed geniuses, and their words and their music and their pictures all helped to raise men's souls nearer to the God who gave that soul--for all that is highest and purest and best comes from the inspiration of the spirit world.

Yet with all this beauty of art and music and literature--with all these aspirations--with all the fervor of religious feeling, there was still no way opened by which men on earth could hold communion with the loved ones who had gone before them into that land which dwellers upon earth have called the Land of Shades, and from whose bourn, they thought, no traveler could return--a land that was all vague and misty to their thought. And there was likewise no means by which those spirit ones who sought to help man to a higher, purer knowledge of Truth could communicate with him directly. The ideas and the fallacies of ancient theories formulated in the days of the world's infancy continually mixed with the newer, more perfect sight which the spirit world sought to give, and clouded its clearness and refracted its rays so that they reached the minds of mortals broken and imperfect.

Then I beheld that the walls of the material life were pierced with many doors, and at each door stood an angel to guard it, and from each door on earth even to the highest spheres I saw a great chain of spirits, each link being one stage higher than the one below it, and to mortals upon earth were given the keys of these doors that they might keep them open and that between mortals and the spirit world there might be communication.

But, alas! as time passed on I saw that many of those who held these keys were not faithful. They were allured by the joys and the gifts of earth, and turned aside and suffered their doors to close. Others again kept their doors but partly open and where only light and truth should have shown they suffered errors and darkness to creep in, and again the light from the spirit world was sullied and broken as it passed through these darkened doorways. Sill more sad, as time passed on, the light ceased to shine at all and gave place to the thick impure rays from dark deceitful spirits from the lower sphere, and at last the angel would close that door to be opened no more on earth.

Then I turned from this sad sight and beheld many new doors opened where mortals stood, whose hearts were pure and unselfish and unsullied by the desires of earth; and through these doors poured such a flood of light upon the earth that my eyes were dazzled, and I had to turn aside. When I looked again I saw these doorways thronged by spirits, beautiful, bright spirits, and others whose raiment was dark and their hearts sad because their lives had been sinful, but in whose souls there was a desire for good, and there were spirits who were fair and bright, but sorrowful, because they could speak no more with those whom they had left on earth; and I beheld the sorrowful and

185

the sinful spirits alike comforted and helped by means of the communication with the earth, and in the hearts of many mortals there was joy, for death's dark curtain was drawn aside and there was news from those beyond the grave.

Then I saw pass before me great armies of spirits from all the higher spheres, their raiment of purest white and their helmets of silver and gold glittering in the glorious spiritual light. And some among them seemed to be the leaders who directed the others in their work. And I asked, "Who are these? Were they ever mortal men?"

And Ahrinziman answered me: "These were not only mortal men but they were many of them men of evil lives, who by reason thereof descended to those Kingdoms of Hell which you have seen, but who because of their great repentance and the many and great works of atonement which they have done, and the perfect conquest over their own lower natures which they have gained, are now the leaders in the armies of light, the strong warriors who protect men from the evils of those lower spheres."

From time to time I saw dark masses of spirits, like waves washing on a shore and flowing over portions of the earth, drawn thither by man's own evil desires and greedy selfishness, and then I would see them driven back by the armies of light spirits, for between these two there was a constant conflict, and the prize for which they contended was man's soul; and yet these two contending forces had no weapons but their wills. They fought not save with the repelling powers of their magnetism which was so antagonistic that neither could long remain in close contact with the other.

Ahrinziman pointed out to me one door at which stood a mortal woman, and said: "Behold the chain there is incomplete; it wants still one link between her and the spirit chain. Go down and form that link, and then will your strength protect her and make her strong; then will you guard her from those dark spirits who hover near, and help her to keep open her door. Your wanderings in those lower spheres have given you the power of repelling their inhabitants, and where stronger power is required it will be sent to protect her--and those who seek to communicate through her will do so only when you see fit, and when you desire to rest in the spirit world another guide will take your place. And now look again at the earth and the conflict that surrounds it."

I looked as he spoke, and saw black thunder clouds hovering over the earth and gathering dark as night, and a sound as of a rushing storm swept upwards from the dark spheres of hell, and like the waves of a storm-tossed ocean these dark clouds of spirits rolled up against the sea of bright spirits, sweeping them back and rolling over the earth as though to blot out from it the light of truth, and they assailed each door of light and sought to overwhelm it. Then did this war in the spirit world become a war amongst men--nation fighting against nation for supremacy. It seemed as though in the great thirst for wealth and greed for conquest, all nations and all peoples must be

186

engulfed, so universal was this war. And I looked to see were there none to aid, none who would come forth from the realms of light and wrest from the dark spirits their power over the earth. The seething mass of dark spirits were attacking those doors of light and striving to sweep away those poor faithful mortals who stood within them, that man might be driven back to the days of his ignorance again.

Then it was that like a Star in the East I saw a light, glittering and dazzling all by its brightness, and it came down and down, and grew and grew till I saw it was a vast host of radiant angels from the heavenly spheres, and with their coming those other bright spirits whom I had seen driven back by the forces of evil gathered together again and joined those glorious warriors, and this great ocean of light, this mighty host of bright spirits swept down to earth and surrounded it with a great belt of glorious light. Everywhere I saw the rays of light, like spears, darting down and rending the dark mass in a thousand places. Like swords of fire flashed these dazzling rays and cut through the dark wall of spirits on all sides, scattering them to the four winds of heaven. Vainly did their leaders seek to gather their forces together again, vainly seek to drive them on. A stronger power was opposed to them, and they were hurled back by the brightness of these hosts of heaven till, like a dark and evil mist, they sank down, rolling back to those dark spheres from which they had come.

"And who were these bright angels?" I asked again, "these warriors who never drew back yet never slew, who held in check these mighty forces of evil, not with the sword of destruction but by the force of their mighty wills, by the eternal power of good over evil?"

And the answer was: "They are those who are also the redeemed ones of the darkest spheres, who long, long ages ago have washed their sin-stained garments in the pools of repentance, and have, by their own labors, risen from the ashes of their dead selves to higher things, not through a belief in the sacrifice of an innocent life for their sins, but by many years of earnest labors--many acts of atonement--by sorrow and by bitter tears--by many weary hours of striving to conquer first the evil in themselves that they who have overcome may help others who sin to do so likewise. These are the angels of the heavenly spheres of earth, once men like themselves and able to sympathize with all the struggles of sinful men. A might host they are, ever strong to protect, powerful to save."

My vision of the earth and its surroundings faded away, and in its stead I beheld one lone star shining above me with a pure silver light. And its ray fell like a thin thread of silver upon the earth and upon the spot where my beloved dwelt. Ahrinziman said to me:

"Behold the star of her earthly destiny, how clear and pure it shines, and know, oh!

beloved pupil, that for each soul born upon earth there shines in the spiritual heavens such a star whose path is marked out when the soul is born; a path it must follow to the end, unless by an act of suicide it sever the thread of the earthly life and by thus transgressing a law of nature plunge itself into great sorrow and suffering."

"Do you mean that the fate of every soul is fixed, and that we are but straws floating on the stream of our destiny?"

"Not quite. The great events of the earth life are fixed, they will inevitably be encountered at certain periods of the earthly existence, and they are such events as those wise guardians of the angelic spheres deem to be calculated to develop and educate that soul; how these events will affect the life of each soul--whether they shall be the turning point for good or ill, for happiness or for sorrow--rests with the soul itself, and this is the prerogative of our free will, without which we would be but puppets, irresponsible for our acts and worthy of neither reward nor punishment for them. But to return to that star--note that while the mortal follows the destined path with earnest endeavor to do right in all things, while the soul is pure and the thoughts unselfish, then does that star shine out with a clear unsullied ray, and light the pathway of the soul. The light of this star comes from the soul and is the reflection of its purity. If, then, the soul cease to be pure, if it develp its lower instead of its higher attributes, the star of that soul's destiny will grow pale and faint, the light flickering like some will-o'-the-wisp hovering over a dark morass; no longer will it shine as a clear beacon of the soul; and at last, if the soul become very evil, the light of the star will die out and expire, to shine no more upon its earthly path.

"It is by watching these spiritual stars and tracing the path marked out for them in the spiritual heavens, that spirit seers are able to foretell the fate of each soul, and from the light given by the star to say whether the life of the soul is good or evil. Adieu, and may the new field of your labors yield you the fairest fruits."

He ceased speaking and my soul seemed to sink down and down till I reached the spirit body I had left lying on my couch, and for a brief moment as I re-entered it I lost consciousness; then I awoke to find myself in my own room, with those beautiful white angels hovering over me, symbols, as my father had said, of eternal protection and love.

CHAPTER XXXIV.--Conclusion.

My task is done, my story told, and it but remains for me to say to all who read it, that I trust they will believe it is as it professes to be, the true narrative of a repentant soul who has passed from darkness into light, and I would have them ask themselves if it might not be well to profit by the experiences of others and to weigh well the evidence for and against the possibility of the spirit's return. And you who would think the gospel of mercy after death too easy a one, too lenient to the sinners, do you know what it is to suffer all the pangs of an awakened conscience? Have you seen that path of bitter tears, of weary effort, which the soul must climb if it would return to God? Do you realize what it means to undo, step by step, through years of darkness and suffering and bitter anguish of soul, the sinful acts and words and thoughts of an earthly lifetime?--for even to the uttermost farthing must the debt be paid; each must drink to the last dregs the cup that he has filled. Can you imagine what it is to hover around the earth in helpless, hopeless impotence, beholding the bitter curse of your sins working their baneful effects upon the descendants you have left, with the taint of your past lurking in their blood and poisoning it? To know that each of these tainted lives--all these beings cursed with evil propensities ere they were born--have become a charge upon your conscience in so far as you have contributed to make them what they are, clogs which will continue to drag back your soul when it attempts to rise, until you shall have made due atonement to them, and helped to raise them from that slough into which your unbridled passions have contributed to sink them? Do you understand now how and why there may be spirits working still about the earth who died hundreds of years ago? Can you imagine how a spirit must feel who seeks from the grave to call aloud to others, and especially to those he has betrayed to their ruin as well as his own, and finds that all ears are deaf to his words, all hearts are closed to his cries of anguish and remorse? He cannot now undo one foolish or revengeful act. He cannot avert one single consequence of suffering which he has brought upon others or himself; an awful wall has risen, a great gulf opened between him and the world of living men on earth, and unless some kind hand will bridge it over for him and help him to return and speak with those whom he has wronged, even the confession of his sorrow--even such tardy reparation as he may still make is denied to him. And is there, then, no need that those who have passed beyond the tomb should return and warn their brethren, even as Dives sought to return and could not? Are men on earth so good that they require no voice to echo to them from beyond the gates of death a foreshadowing of the fate awaiting them? Far easier were it for man to repent now while still on earth than to wait till he goes to that land where he can deal with the things of earth no more, save through the organisms of others.

I met a spirit once who in the reign of Queene Anne had defrauded another of a property by means of forged title deeds, and who when I saw him was still earth-

189

bound to that house and land, utterly unable to break his chains until the help was given him of a medium through whom he confessed where he had hidden the true title deeds, and gave the names of those to whom of right the property should belong. This poor spirit was freed by his confession from his chain to that house, but not from his imprisonment to the earth plane. He had to work there till his efforts had raised up and helped onward those whom he had driven into the ways of sin and death by his crime. Not till he has done so can this spirit hope to leave the earth plane, and there he still works, striving to undo the effects of his past sin. Will anyone say his punishment was too light? Shall anyone judge his brother man and say at what point God's mercy shall stop and that sinner be doomed eternally? Ah, no! Few dare to face the true meaning of their creeds or to follow out even in thought the bitter and awful consequences of a belief in eternal punishment for any of the erring children of God.

I have in these pages sought to show what has been the true experience of one whom the churches might deem a lost soul, since I died without a belief in any church, any religion, and but a shadowy belief in a God. My own conscience ever whispered to me that there must be a Supreme, a Divine Being, but I stifled the thought and thrust it from me, cheating myself into a sense of security and indifference akin to that of the foolish ostrich which buries its head in the sand and fancies none can see it; and in all my wanderings, although I have indeed learned that there is a Divine Omnipotent Ruler of the Universe--its upholder and sustainer--I have not learned that he can be reduced to a personality, a definite shape in the likeness of man, a something whose attributes we finite creatures can argue about and settle. Neither have I seen anything which would incline me to believe in one form of religious belief rather than in another. What I have learned is to free the mind, if possible, from the boundaries of any and every creed.

The infancy of the race of planetary man, when his mental condition resembles that of a child, may be called the Age of Faith. The Mother Church supplies for him the comfort and hope of immortality and takes from his mind the burden of thinking out for himself a theory of First Cause, which will account to him for his own existence and that of his surroundings. Faith steps in as a maternal satisfier of the longings of his imperfectly developed soul and the man of a primitive race believes without questioning why he does so. Among the early tribes of savages the more spiritualized men become the mystery men, and then the priests, and as age succeeds to age the idea of an established church is formulated.

Next comes the Age of Reason, when the development of man's intellectual faculties causes him to be no longer satisfied with blind faith in the unknown, the mother's milk of the Churches no longer assuages his mental hunger, he requires stronger food, and if it be withheld, he breaks away from the fostering care of Mother Church which once sustained but which now only cramps and cripples the growing and expanding soul. Man's reason demands greater freedom and its due share of nourishment, and must find it somewhere, and in the struggle between the rebellious growing child and the Mother Church, who seeks to retain still the power she wielded over the infant, the Faith that once sufficed as food comes to be regarded as something nauseous and to be rejected at all cost, hence the Age of Reason becomes a time of uprootal of all the cherished beliefs of the past.

Then comes another stage, in which the child, now grown to be a youth who has seen and tasted for himself the joys and sorrows, the penalties, and pleasures and benefits of reason, and has thereby learned to put a juster value on the powers and limitations of his own reasoning faculties, looks back at the faith he once despised, and recognizes that it also has its beauties and its value. He sees that though faith alone cannot suffice for the nourishment of the soul beyond its infant stage, yet reason alone, devoid of faith, is but a cold hard fare upon which to sustain the soul now becoming conscious of the immeasurable and boundless universe by which it is surrounded, and of the many mysteries it contains--mysteries reason alone is not able to explain. Man turns back to faith once more and seeks to unite it with reason, that henceforth they may assist each other.

Now Faith and Reason are the central thought principles of two different spheres of thought in the spirit world. Faith is the vitalizing principle of religion or ecclesiasticism, as Reason is of philosophy. These two schools of thought which appear at first sight opposed to each other, are none the less capable of being blended in the mental development of the same personality, the properly balanced mind being that in which they are equally proportioned. Where one predominates over the other to a great degree, the individual--be he mortal or disembodied spirit--will be narrow-minded in one direction or the other and incapable of taking a just view of any mental problem. His mind will resemble a two wheeled gig which has a big and a little wheel attached to the same axle, and in consequence neither wheel can make due progress, the mental gig coming to a stop till the defect be remedied.

A man may be thoroughly conscientious in his desire for truth, but if his intellectual as well as his moral faculties have not been equally developed, his mind will be like a highway blocked by huge masses of error, so that the ethereal rays from the star of truth cannot penetrate it; they are broken and refracted by the obstructions, so that either they do not reach the man's soul at all or they are such distorted images of the truth that they are simply a source of prejudice and error. The intellect may be called the eye of the soul, and if the sight of that eye be imperfect the soul remains in mental darkness, however earnest may be its desire for light. The mental sight must be developed and used ere it can become clear and strong.

Blind ignorant faith is no safeguard against error. The history of religious persecutions in all ages is surely proof of that. The great minds of earth to whom great intellectual discoveries are due have been those in which the moral and intellectual powers are equally balanced, and the perfect man or angel will be the man in whom all the qualities of the soul have been developed to their highest point.

Every attribute of the soul, mental and moral, has its corresponding ray of color, and the blending of these forms the beautiful and varied tints of the rainbow, and like it they melt into one another to form the perfect whole.

In some souls the development of certain faculties will take place more rapidly than that of others; in some certain seed germs of intellect and morality will lie fallow and give no sign that they exist, but they are none the less there, and either on earth or in the great Hereafter they will begin to grow and to blossom into perfection.

Evil is caused by the lack of development of the moral attributes in certain souls and the over development of other qualities. The souls which are now inhabiting the lower spheres are simply passing through the process of eduction needful to awaken into active life and growth the dormant moral faculties, and terrible as are the evils and sufferings wrought in the process they are yet necessary and beneficent in their ultimate results.

In the sphere where I now dwell there is a magnificent and beautiful palace belonging to the Brotherhood of Hope. This palace is the meeting place for all members of our Brotherhood, and in it there is a fine hall built of what is the spiritual counterpart of white marble. This hall is called the "Hall of Lecture," and in it we assemble to listen to discourses delivered to us by advanced spirits from the higher sphere. At the upper end there is a magnificent picture called "The Perfect Man." That is to say it represents a man, or rather angel, who is relatively perfect. I say relatively perfect, because even the utmost perfection which can be imagined or attained, can only be relative to the still greater heights which must be eternally possible for the soul. Unlike Alexander who mourned that he had left no more worlds to conquer, the soul has no limits put to the possibilities of its intellectual and moral conquests. The universe of mind is as boundless as that of matter, and as eternal. Hence none can use the word perfect as implying a point beyond which progress is impossible.

In the picture this relatively perfect angel is represented as standing on the highest pinnacle of the celestial spheres. The earth and her attendant spheres lie far below him. His gaze is turned with an expression of wonder, delight, and awe to those far distant regions which lie beyond the power of mortal mind to grasp, regions which lie beyond our solar universe. They are become for the angel his new Land of Promise.

On his head the angel wears a golden helmet, symbolizing spiritual strength and conquest. On one arm he bears a silver shield typical of the Protection of Faith. His garments are of dazzling white showing the purity of his soul, and the wide outstretched wings symbolize the power of intellect to soar into the highest thought-regions of the universe. Behind the angel there is a white cloud spanned by a rainbow whose every tint and shade blended into perfect harmony shows that the angel has developed to the highest degree every intellectual and moral attribute of his soul.

The rich coloring of this picture, the purity of its dazzling white, the brilliancy of its glowing tints, no pen can describe, no earthly brush could ever paint, and yet I am told it falls far short of the beauty of the original picture, which is in the highest sphere of all, and which represents a former grand master of our order who has passed on to spheres beyond the limits of our solar system. Replicas of this picture are to be seen in the highest circle of each earth sphere in the buildings belonging to the Brotherhood of Hope, and they show the connecting links between our Brotherhood and the celestial spheres of the solar system, and also to what heights all may aspire in the ages of eternity before us. Yes, each one of us, the most degraded brother who labors in the lowest sphere of earth, and even the most degraded soul that struggles there in darkness and sin unspeakable, is not shut out, for all souls are equal before God and there is nothing which has been attained by one that may not be attained by all if they but strive earnestly for it.

Such, then, is the knowledge I have gained, such the beliefs I have arrived at since I passed from earth life, but I cannot say I have seen that any particular belief helps or retards the soul's progress, except in so far as this, that some creeds have a tendency to cramp the mind and obscure the clearness of its vision and distort its ideas of right and wrong, thereby preventing those who hold those beliefs from possessing the perfect freedom of thought and absence of prejudice which can alone fit the soul to rise to the highest spheres.

I have written this story of my wanderings in the hope that amongst those who read it may be found some who will think it worth while to inquire whether, after all, it may not be, as it professes to be, a true story. There may also be others who have lost those who were very dear to them, but whose lives were not such as gave hope that they could be numbered with those whom the churches call "The Blessed Dead who die in the Lord"--dear friends who have not died in the paths of goodness and truth--I would ask those mourners to take hope and to believe that their beloved but erring friends may not be wholly lost--not utterly beyond hope, yes, even though some may have perished by their own hands and under circumstances which would seem to preclude all hope. I would ask those on earth to think over all that I have said and to ask themselves whether even yet their prayers and their sympathy may not be able to help and comfort those who need all the help and comfort that can be given to them.

From my home in the Bright Land--so like the land of my birth--I go still to work upon the earth plane and among those who are unhappy. I also help to carry forward the great work of spirit communion between the living of earth and those whom they call dead.

I spend a portion of each day with my beloved, and I am able to help and protect her in many ways. I am also cheered in my home in the spirit land by the visits of many friends and companions of my wanderings, and in that bright land surrounded by so many memorials of love and friendship, I await with a grateful heart that happy time when my beloved one's earthly pilgrimage shall be finished, when her lamp of life shall have burned out and her star of earth has set, and she shall come to join me in an even brighter home, where for us both shall shine eternally the twin stars of Hope and Love.